Embracing Shiloh:
Daily Revelations of the Promised Messiah

Wayne Meads Jr.

Copyright © 2024 by The Salvation Army USA Southern Territory

The Salvation Army
1424 Northeast Expressway
Atlanta, GA 30329
Phone: 404-728-1300

Commissioner Kelly Igleheart, Territorial Commander
Lt. Colonel Carolee Israel, Literary Secretary
Jeremy Rowland, Director of Supplies and Purchasing

All Scripture quotations unless otherwise indicated are taken from the Holy Bible, New International Version, NIV® Copyright 1973, 1984, 2011 by Biblica, Inc.™ Used by permission of Zondervan. All rights reserved worldwide www.zondervan.com The "NIV" New International Version are trademarks registered in the United States Patent and Trademark Office by Biblica Inc.™

All rights reserved. No part of this publication may be reproduced, stored in a retrieval system, or transmitted in any form or by any means without prior written permission of the publisher. Exceptions are brief quotations in printed reviews.

Printed in the United States of America

Foreword

WHILE THE CHILDREN OF Israel were wandering in the Wilderness, God gave them the Tabernacle to not only be their center for worship, but as the assurance of His presence among them. Here they would come to offer sacrifices for their sins, to thank God for His provision and to seek His answers for their needs. When they were to encamp for a time, there was a cloud over the Tabernacle by day and flame over it by night until it was time to move on, when they were led to their next place on their journey.

When the Children of Israel was finished conquering the Promised Land, Joshua and the leaders of new nation needed a place to pitch the Tabernacle permanently. They chose Shiloh where it remained as the center of worship for Israel for centuries. Every Jewish person in every generation would trek to Shiloh during the feast days, for the dedication of babies, for the rites of cleansing and dedication. The judges of Israel had their government seat in Shiloh, and the prophets proclaimed their message from there. It only ended when David relocated the Tabernacle to Jerusalem in preparation for the Temple being built.

Captain Wayne Meads in this book invites you as the reader to make a similar daily spiritual trek just as the early Hebrew people did. As they sought the Lord at times of dedication, forgiveness, cleansing, for answers and for a word from the Lord, these devotions are written to help you hear from the Lord in whatever He has to say to you in a symbolic Shiloh. This might be in a favorite chair, at your desk, in a spot in a warehouse or at the side of your bed. The Holy Spirit can make any place sacred if your heart is open to Him and you are ready to hear.

May God bless you as you take your daily pilgrimage to Shiloh.

Commissioner Kelly Igleheart
Territorial Commander
USA Southern Territory

Acknowledgements

TO MY WIFE CLAUDIA, the love of my life, your unwavering support is the melody that keeps the symphony of our family in beautiful harmony.

To my precious children, Melody-Grace, Micah, and Lilah, each of you is a unique note in our family's song. You three are my greatest motivations and my truest teachers.

To my devoted parents, Wayne and Susan Meads, your examples of faith, love, and resilience have shaped me from my first steps to the ones that brought me through this journey.

And above all, to our Lord and Savior Jesus Christ, who is the cornerstone of my existence and the ultimate author of all hope and love, through which all things are possible.

Each one of you holds an irreplaceable space in my heart and within these pages – a testament of my love and appreciation that spans more than mere words.

With deepest affection and eternal gratitude,

Wayne Jr.

Introduction

IN A WORLD THAT often makes us feel overwhelmed and desperate to find something meaningful, a magnificent source of comfort and wisdom is found in the hands of our Savior, Jesus Christ. Real satisfaction and eternal happiness are found in a personal experience with our Maker. In the twin disciplines of prayer and meditation, we begin to discover His love and His mission for our lives.

Welcome to *Embracing Shiloh*.

Christ, the fulfillment of all prophecy, is the Shiloh spoken of in the title and text. In the Old Testament, Shiloh is mentioned in Genesis 49:10, where the Lord prophesied, "The scepter will not depart from Judah, nor the ruler's staff from between his feet until Shiloh comes; and to Him shall be the obedience of the peoples." Shiloh refers to the One who will hold the eternal dominion and accomplish the redemption of God.

This book is designed to stir and enlighten your spirit as we embark on an exploratory journey together. Whether you are a seasoned believer or just beginning to explore the Christian faith, this devotional will be a roadmap providing directions to a closer relationship with God and light the path to overflowing abundance.

The book's pages will discuss the Christian journey, its various aspects, and the joy of living a Christ-centered life. We shall explore themes like abandoning our worries to God, trusting in Him when we go through trials, learning to forgive like Him, and fulfilling our divine purpose. Each devotional includes biblical insights and practical application to be implemented in your life, contributing to your walk with God and enabling you to bear witness and become an embodiment of His love.

Finally but most importantly, the context of Christ as Shiloh refers to the Messiah whose mission is to bring peace and spiritual fulfillment to life's journey. Personified in Christ, peace is a way to become reconciled with oneself and others. Through Christ's teachings, one is directed toward inner peace and shown true hope, assurance, and deeper meaning of an existence that transcends worldly limitations. I pray that you keep sacred times each day as part of this pilgrimage.

Let us be "one" as we delve deep into the Bible, draw close to God's presence, and experience bliss as we walk side by side with our Lord. Remember, brothers and sisters, you are not the only one traveling the road we are on today. With God as our beacon, we can tackle life's hardships, reveling in Christ's joy with each stride.

Daily Revelations of the Promised Messiah

January 1: The Coming of Shiloh

Scripture for the Day
"The sceptre shall not depart from Judah, nor a lawgiver from between his feet, until Shiloh come; and unto him shall the gathering of the people be."

Genesis 49:10 (KJV)

The book of Genesis closes with a prophetic narrative that spans time to touch eternity. Jacob's words over Judah are more than a father's blessing; they are divine foretelling steeped in the covenant promises of God. The "sceptre" here is not just a staff but a symbol of leadership, authority, and continuity for the tribe of Judah—a forerunner of kings and, ultimately, the Messiah, referred to as Shiloh.

Theological insight unfolds as we recognize Shiloh as a title laden with meaning. It signals the coming of One who is to be the peace-bringer, in whom the nations will find their hope and unity. Scholars and theologians have long held that this reference points to Jesus Christ—the One who brings peace and to whom the sceptre truly belongs.

This anticipation of Shiloh reflects the heart of the gospel itself: unity in Christ, reconciliation with God, and the establishment of an everlasting kingdom. What we find in Genesis is not a conclusion but a promise that threads through the tapestry of Scripture, culminating in the life, death, and resurrection of Jesus.

As we ponder these divine assurances, our hearts are stirred by the knowledge that Shiloh has come, and His rule is one of peace and justice. In Him, the fragmented pieces of this world find coherence, the cacophony of discord finds harmony, and the hearts of the people find a gathering place. Hallelujah!

Prayer: Lord, the promise of Your Word from the days of old kindles a flame of hope in my heart. In the lineage of Judah, You painted the picture of Shiloh, the peace bringer—to whom belongs the sceptre and the obedience of nations. I stand amazed in Your presence, recognizing the authority that rests upon Your shoulders and the peace that comes from Your rule. Let my life be an offering, a gathering to the One who fulfills Your promises and joins the chorus of those who find their rest in Shiloh. In Jesus name, Amen.

January 2: Why So Sad

Scripture for the Day
"Clouds and thick darkness are all around him; righteousness and justice are the foundation of his throne."

Psalm 97:2 (ESV)

We seek rest from our heavenly Father who is the only unchangeable character in a world of doubt. The picture of clouds, dark and thick, is indicative of His transcendent nature since we have a mind that can put limits to His wisdom and ways. His thoughts and conduct are much deeper than ours.

But we still find solace in His righteousness and justice. The God we adore is not impulsive or unkind but lovingly just. He is the beautiful combination of mercy and truth, grace, and judgment.

In our journey of faith, there may be clouds and darkness covering the road. In such instances, we are required to believe in the constant character of God. His righteousness and justice are unchanging even in the face of confused circumstances. In His perfect wisdom, He leads us through the valleys and the mountaintops, going with us all the way.

Spend a moment to consider instances when you have seen the righteousness and justice of God in your life. Perhaps you have experienced the delight of mercy when you were released from painful loads of guilt by Him. Or maybe you have seen Him defend the oppressed and revive the dignity of those who have been humiliated.

May our God, who lives in the light give us His revelation and take away all clouds and darkness from our eyes. May we have hope in the knowledge that we are covered under the shadow of His throne and have everlasting peace.

Prayer: Heavenly Father, upon Your righteousness and justice, the foundation of Your throne, let my heart be unwavering and glad. May I close this reading of Psalm 97:2 with fear and respect, having in my thoughts that Your secrets are wrapped in mists and darkness everywhere I look, but Your light and truth lead me on my path. Amen

January 3: Embracing Grace for Transformation

Scripture for the Day
"For the grace of God has appeared that offers salvation to all people."
Titus 2:11

The Apostle Paul, in his instruction to Titus, reminds us of a gift that's both foundational and transformational: the grace of God.

The grace of God is an active force that has "appeared." It is not distant— it has stepped into the timeline of humanity, into the mess and the beauty of our lives. This grace personified in Christ Jesus offers salvation to "all people." This inclusivity breaks down barriers. Grace does not discriminate by race, status, or past transgressions.

Moreover, this grace of salvation isn't merely a ticket to eternity; it's the spark for change here and now. It educates us, as the passage continues in verses 12-14, instructing us to reject ungodliness and worldly passions to live self-controlled, upright, and godly lives. Grace is our teacher, and life is our classroom where we are daily students. The lessons of grace guide us to transformation, empowering us to embody the righteousness for which we were saved.

In times of spiritual fatigue, let us recall that grace isn't earned by tireless toil or perfect practice. It's given freely, a tender whisper reminding us that we are loved beyond measure, accepted beyond fault. The journey may be challenging, but grace assures us we are always loved.

Prayer: Heavenly Father, as I step into today, let me walk in the refreshing light of Your grace. Thank You for the gift of salvation which You have made available to all. Teach me to understand the depths of Your grace more fully, to reject what is ungodly, and to embrace the transformation You have for me. In Jesus' Name, Amen.

January 4: Flowing

Scripture for the Day
"Whoever believes in me, as Scripture has said, rivers of living water will flow from within them."

John 7:38

When Jesus uttered these words, He didn't mean a miserable splash of water. No, He talked about rivers, representing the endless source of life-giving sustenance. The images created bring a feeling of might, plenty, and continuous movement.

We are often thirsty, spiritually dehydrated, and out of gas in relation to our life. We try to get satisfaction from the things of this world, only to be left frustrated and tired. But Jesus gives us something else altogether. He assures that whoever believes in Him will be a channel of His life-giving Spirit. Not a still pool, but a powerful river of life.

How do we energize this overflow into our lives? It all depends on how strongly we believe in Jesus Christ. By having faith in Him, we let Him live in us, which makes Him the endless source of our strength and renewal. As we grow in intimacy with our Savior, our life becomes united with His divine nature, and His Spirit starts flowing through us.

Beloved, this is not a one-time experience but a daily journey of faith. It demands of us total submission to God, letting His love and grace renew and transform us each day. Remaining in Him through prayer, worship, and reading and studying His word, we release our spirit to be overfilled with His Spirit.

Meditate on the words of Jesus. Accept that He desires to employ you as His vessel of love and life. You should deliberately take steps every day to get to know Him better. In everything you do, seek His will, and be mindful of the need to submit your desires and plans to Him.

Prayer: Father, who is in heaven, we thank You for the promise of life – abundant and overflowing – that comes from believing in Jesus Christ. Please fill every chamber of my life with Your Spirit. Let my heart be a fountain of Your love, grace, and power. Teach me how to live in surrender daily, letting your living water flow through me and touch others. In Jesus' name, amen.

January 5: Committed

Scripture for the Day

"So, the three mighty men broke through the camp of the Philistines, drew water from the well of Bethlehem that was by the gate, and took it and brought it to David. Nevertheless, he would not drink it, but poured it out to the Lord."

2 Samuel 23:16

In 2 Samuel 23:16, we come across the brave deed of three great warriors who put their lives on the line for just one act of honor. Amid the battle, these three overcame all obstacles, breaching the enemy lines to get water from the well by the gate of Bethlehem. The act of water-fetching may appear insignificant, but the deed is an illustration of the unqualified loyalty and devotion to their leader, David.

By reflecting on this passage, we can learn lessons useful in our lives of faith. First, the dedication of these warriors to their leader. They courted an enormous risk to satisfy David's wish and bring him something to drink. Their faithfulness is a reminder of our calling to serve and support those in authority over us, be it our spiritual leaders, employers, or our family members.

Then, bringing water exemplifies going the extra mile in service. These men could have quit, whined or complained, given the odds that were against them. Instead, they showed up and sacrificially risked their lives for their king. It defines fully owning our obligations and not accepting a halfhearted approach in service to God and people.

Finally, the passage emphasizes the strength of unity and cooperation. These warriors didn't act alone. They operated as a single force, inspiring and supporting each other in their mission. They demonstrated true comradeship. We also are to be one in the body of Christ, lifting each other and pursuing common goals for the sake of God's kingdom.

May we take from these mighty warriors the spirit of sacrifice, dedication, and teamwork into our daily lives. May we do our very best to please our leaders, offer extra service, and love one another in the body of Christ. Be reminded that sometimes it is in the little acts of faithfulness that we have the greatest influence and bring glory to our heavenly King.

Prayer: Instill in me, O God, a heart that beats with courage and loyalty. Let me, too, be willing to go above and beyond for those You have placed in my life, to serve without seeking reward, and to love with the abandon of those who seek Your face above all earthly commands. Amen.

January 6: Intercession

Scripture for the Day

"Who is to condemn? Christ Jesus is the one who died—more than that, who was raised—who is at the right hand of God, who indeed is interceding for us."

Romans 8:34

Imagine this: You are in a heavenly court where the Accuser has prepared a long list of your offenses. The angels' jury is anxious, their pens ready to sign your guilty judgment. As you bear the gravity of the pending doom, sweat covers your forehead.

But wait! In dramatic fashion, there stepping up on the stage, is our lovely Savior, Jesus Christ, the greatest of all defense attorneys. You can hardly help but feel hope shine through as He steps forward. He approaches the Judge, who is also His Father and nods approvingly.

The Accuser character becomes the star of a brilliant scene, where he happily presents his case, citing every mistake, every defect, every weakness. The audience tenses, expecting the worst. There is no escaping from this mess.

However, with a glint in His eye, Jesus' throat clears, one eyebrow raised. "Father," He says, "do you remember that time when Peter denied me three times? Oh, and what about when Thomas doubted? Do not also fail to remember that Paul, or Saul, was as excited to persecute the early Christians as the Jews who killed Jesus."

The angels look at each other bewilderedly. "But those are sins!" The Accuser interrupts sputtering.

"Oh, indeed they are," Jesus grins. "But what you don't realize is that I died for those sins. I bore the punishment upon Myself so that whoever believes in Me shall be forgiven and receive eternal life."

Mic drop.

The angels burst into thunderous applause, drowning the high-pitched protests of the Accuser. The Judge, grinning, nods in assent. Your heart races with fresh wonder of what you have become.

Prayer: Lord, I am humbled by Your love, a love so deep that You would send Your only Son to bridge the gap between us, a love that continues to reach out through His perpetual intercession on my behalf. Lord, I am reassured that I have such an advocate with You, one who pleads for me and secures my redemption. Amen.

January 7: Divine Friendship

Scripture for the Day
"A friend loves at all times, and a brother is born for a time of adversity."

Proverbs 17:17

A good friend is not only for good times but also for hardships. Unfailingly, they stand in good and in bad, in successes and in problems. They love us when we're up and when we're down. A true friend is an example of God's constant and unconditional love.

Apart from friendship, the verse tells about brothers being created for times of trouble. Whether they are blood or spiritual brothers/sisters, they are there in each other's moments of difficulty. They give a helping hand, an ear to listen, and strength to overcome. That is a beautiful example of God's care in our lives.

Living in an era marked by temporary associations, we must be faithful friends and caring brothers and sisters. Can we love each other unconditionally as God does us? Let our friendship continue to be more than the pleasant times.

Today, reflect on your friendships and the sibling relationships in your life. Have you been a true friend, in even small things? Did you, being the older one, support your siblings, filling their void with the comfort and assistance that they needed the most?

Consider your relationships and your role. Seek opportunities to love, care, and be present for others, which becomes more important when the going gets rough. Love Jesus redemptively and reach out in friendship to the helpless.

Remember that real friends are a gift from God. It brings us happiness, power, and confidence. Therefore, let us esteem and foster these ties, pouring forth tenderness, kindness, and compassion on those who approach us according to how Christ has loved us.

Prayer: Let my heart be full of mercy, and only then shall I become a good friend and a loving brother or sister. May my deeds encourage others to experience the love of God in their relationships and all that they do. Amen.

January 8: Abundant Grace

Scripture for the Day
"Come, all you who are thirsty, come to the waters; and you who have no money, come, buy and eat! Come, buy wine and milk without money and without cost. Why spend money on what is not bread and your labor on what does not satisfy? Listen, listen to me, and eat what is good, and you will delight in the richest of fare."

Isaiah 55:1-2

In these powerful verses from Isaiah 55:1-2, we are invited to be partakers in God's abundant blessings. This is to all those who are thirsty and needy, whatever their economic state is. God calls us to come and receive freely what He can offer us; that is, to provide us with nourishment and sustenance.

In this world many things that offer satisfaction ultimately leave us with nothing. We may run after material things, success, or earthly pleasures, but we discover that they cannot quench the desire of the human heart. God tells us not to waste our time, energy, and other resources on anything that can never fulfill the deep-rooted desires of our hearts.

On the contrary, God creatively satisfies us with Himself, and does that completely. He calls upon us to listen carefully to His voice to obey His words. When we search for Him and shape our wishes to agree with Him, we discover He feeds us with heavenly food— an abundance of His love, peace, joy, and grace.

As we journey through each day, let us remember the invitation in Isaiah 55:1-2. Let us come to the waters, quench our spiritual thirst, and in His presence be refreshed. Let's invest in things that matter to us greatly from the soul care of the Lord. This is how we will find what we were looking for – the meaning of life. It is so much more than something passing during our fleeting days. It is what we are meant to live for.

Prayer: Father, develop in me a heart that unceasingly seeks You above everything else, knowing that You will answer every pressing need and fulfill the innermost desires of my being. Your victory flows through me like a rushing river. I glory in the fullness of Your love and truth. Amen.

January 9: Keep Knocking

Scripture for the Day

"Ask, and it will be given to you; seek, and you will find; knock, and it will be opened to you. For everyone who asks receives, and the one who seeks finds, and to the one who knocks it will be opened."

Matthew 7:7-8

The above words of Jesus tell us to approach the Father with boldness and persistence. He guarantees that when we seek His guidance, provision, and blessings with all our hearts, we will not lack. Our Heavenly Father wants to listen to our prayers, answer our petitions, and create doors of opportunity for us.

As believers we might sometimes feel reluctant and delay asking the Lord for what we want or desire. We may question whether our petitions are worthy and whether God really listens to us. But Jesus reminds us that God is a loving and generous Father eager to bless His children. He bids us to ask with boldness and without fear, knowing that our Father loves to give to those who seek Him.

In addition, Jesus instructs us to seek with all our hearts. Seeking is a deliberate action of pursuit. It is about searching for the will of God, His wisdom, and His righteousness in our lives. When we go after Him with all our hearts, we will have Him. God pledges to manifest Himself to seekers.

Prayer: Father, today I ask that Your will be done in every facet of my life and that I may be a living example to others so that they, too, may see that the heart's desires can be fulfilled through You. Amen.

January 10: Renewal

Scripture for the Day

"Therefore we do not lose heart. Though outwardly we are wasting away, yet inwardly we are being renewed day by day."

2 Corinthians 4:16

On our Christian journey, we are faced with suffering and tests of life that cause us to be tired, weary, and discouraged. We might wonder if our attempts to live for Christ are doing any good or if we can keep on enduring our difficulties. But in these moments, let us find comfort and inspiration in the powerful message of 2 Corinthians 4:16.

To the believers in Corinth, the apostle Paul writes words of encouragement and hope. He reminds them to keep their spirits high even when they start wearing out under the wear and tear of life's ill fortune and adversity. Any decay and decline that people may see on the outside point to a greater reality – an inward renewal that occurs daily.

Being Christ's followers, we are not what we see in the mirror or what we suffer in life. The eternal truth of our identity is centered on our relationship with God. Even though our bodies may worsen, and the world tries to rob us of hope, we can be assured that our inward being is being renewed day after day by the power of the Holy Spirit.

Adversity usually makes people concentrate more on their weaknesses and limitations. We may fixate on our shortcomings and fail to see the power that God has given us. Still, Paul points out that our power does not come from ourselves but from the unseen power of God. It is through our dependency on Him that we get the persistence and strength to face life's challenges.

Every day is an opportunity to evolve, change, and rejuvenate spiritually. Our faith is not a single event but a lifelong journey of being transformed into the image of Christ. In the same manner that a sculptor builds and shapes an statue, our Heavenly Father is always at work within us, making us vessels of His grace, love, and mercy.

Prayer: Give me, O Lord, the grace to not lose heart as I navigate the transient challenges of this world. May I always remember that these momentary troubles are achieving for me an eternal glory that far outweighs them all. Amen

January 11: Release The Past

Scripture for the Day

"Forget the former things; do not dwell on the past. See, I am doing a new thing! Now it springs up; do you not perceive it? I am making a way in the wilderness and streams in the wasteland."

Isaiah 43:18-19

In these verses, the prophet Isaiah proclaims to the Israelites a word of hope and restoration. God commands His people to free themselves from the hold of the past and look to the new things which He will soon do. He pronounces that a way will be made in the wilderness and rivers in the wasteland, symbolizing His incredible power to make life and change even in the most unlikely places.

These words were spoken by God to the Israelites thousands of years ago, and He speaks them to us today. God wants to cut off the chains of the past that hold us captive and block our progress. He desires to usher us into a season of freshness, restoration, and new opportunities. Nevertheless, to completely accept His new beginnings, we must be prepared to release the past and rely on His eternal love and direction.

The call of God says, "Remember not the former things, neither consider the things of old," is not an encouragement to erase our memories or discard the lessons we have learned. It is instead an offer to give our burdens and our former mistakes to Him, let Him heal our wounds, and make something beautiful out of our brokenness. It is an invitation to faith that God is making something new, even though the result is not yet visible.

We should realize that God is not imprisoned by our past or bound by our circumstances. He is a God of infinite possibilities who is particularly good at turning our deserts into oases, our brokenness into wholeness, and our trials into triumphs. In Him, we let go of our past and take up His new beginning, and we walk in confidence as He is always faithful in leading us ahead.

Prayer: Lord, enable me to release the old and embrace the fresh work You do in my life. Help me see the paths You are blazing in my deserts and the rivers You provide in my droughts. May my eyes be open to Your innovative Spirit, and may my heart be ready to walk in the new life You have promised. Amen.

January 12: No Fear

Scripture for the Day
"When I am afraid, I put my trust in you."

Psalm 56:3

Society offers us innumerable reasons to live in fear. We encounter trials, uncertainties, and difficulties that appear unmanageable, making us anxious and afraid. In these moments, Psalm 56:3 gives us a strong reminder in whom we should whose trust.

David, the author of this psalm, was in such a situation. He came to face foes that were out to hurt him, and he felt fear weighing heavily on his heart. However, even with his fears, David chose to trust in the unchanging faithfulness of God.

David's example gives us an understanding that when fear tries to capture our heart, our reaction should not be panic or hopelessness but a conscious act of putting trust in God. Rather than allowing fear to hold us captive, we are encouraged to give our fears to the One who is greater than any situation that comes our way.

Faith in God does not mean our fears will leave at once or our troubles will vanish. It is acknowledging that we serve a God who is all-powerful, a God who holds all our lives in His hands. Trusting in Him is our awareness that He understands the fears we have, the struggles we encounter, and that He faithfully accompanies us with every step we make.

Believing God in times of fear is a discipline and an act of focused choosing. Rather than concentrating on the present problems, we must meditate on His past faithfulness, His enduring love, and His constant companionship in our lives. Thus, we change our point of view from the momentary to the eternal, and we are consoled that God is in charge.

If fear knocks at your heart today, pause and acknowledge that you serve a God greater than any fear or challenges you to battle. Choose to trust Him, knowing He works everything for your good. By surrendering your fears to Him you will get His peace and strength that surpasses all understanding.

Prayer: Father, When uncertainty stirs within me, remind me of Your steadfast love that casts out every fear. May I draw comfort and courage from Your faithfulness, remembering that You are with me at every step, holding my life in Your gracious hands. Amen.

January 13: Participation

Scripture for the Day

"And let us consider how we may spur one another on toward love and good deeds, not giving up meeting together, as some are in the habit of doing, but encouraging one another—and all the more as you see the Day approaching."

Hebrews 10:24-25

We must live in a community as followers of Christ, supporting and encouraging one another as we journey in faith. In Hebrews 10:24-25, we are encouraged to cultivate relationships that promote love and spur us to acts of kindness, with an emphasis on assembling as believers.

Hebrews' author challenges us to think about how we can actively stir each other toward love and good deeds. This reflects that faith is not meant to be lived in isolation. We are created for community, living to share our lives, gifts, and resources with one another to reflect the love and character of Christ.

The call for deliberate community and affirmation is counter cultural in a world that often glorifies self-centeredness and discord. As we come together, we have the chance to encourage, stimulate, and cheer each other to lives that honor God and bring blessings to others.

Gathering together holds great importance in our spiritual development. It is during times like these that as the body of Christ we experience the power of unity, corporate worship, and the sharing of God's Word. Whether a person attends a church, joins a small group, or practices Christian fellowship, these purposeful get-togethers where we can build up each other in faith, own up to getting it wrong, and lend a hand to one another, are the ways in which Jesus' Church is built.

It is essential to note that our meeting should not be a mere duty or formality. We are called upon to be active participants, giving our love and encouragement and spiritual gifts to lift others. Given the fact that most of the world is full of negativity and discouragement, we as believers should be encouragers to each other and show mutual love and compassion.

Prayer: Father, Thank You for being my refuge, hope, and trust. In the face of fear, Your Word is the anchor for my soul, and in Your perfect love, I find the courage to face each moment. Thank You that I can meet with fellow believers in fellowship as part of Your body called the Church where You meet with us and where we meet with You. In the precious name of Jesus, I pray, Amen.

January 14: Free Indeed

Scripture for the Day
"So if the Son sets you free, you will be free indeed."

John 8:36

John 8 finds Jesus in an argument with the religious leaders of His time. Addressing those who believed in Him, He proclaims a truth that resonates through the ages: His freedom is of a different order. We are called as Christ's followers to live in the fullness of this freedom each day.

1. *The Source of Our Freedom*: Jesus pronounced that it is He, the Son, who can release us. This liberty is not just a temporary release from a physical or worldly confinement. It is deeper, down into the depth of our souls, and liberation from sins, guilt, and shame.

One must also realize that complete freedom cannot be attained by our own work or merits. Through the redemptive work of Jesus on the cross alone can we fully and eternally be free.

2. *Freedom from Sin*: One of the major parts of the freedom Jesus gives is freedom from sin. Sin is what divides us from God, enslaving us in guilt and condemnation. Yet by His surrender, Jesus paid the penalty for our sins, thus making a way for us to be united with the Father.

Believers are given the opportunity to resist sin and accept the righteousness that Christ graciously bestowed upon us. We, therefore, daily lay our cravings at the cross, believing the power of the Holy Spirit to overcome temptation and live a victorious life.

3. *Embracing True Freedom*: The liberty we have in Christ goes beyond forgiveness and redemption from sin. It also includes freedom from fear, anxiety, and the slavery of self-sufficiency. Having faith in Jesus, we gain confidence and assurance in His never-failing love.

Pause to consider the freedom in Christ that you have been given. Is there any place in your life that still feels trapped or heavy? Give these areas to Him today, and let His transforming power bring absolute freedom.

Prayer: Heavenly Father, As Your truth resounds in John 8:36, declaring, "So if the Son sets you free, you will be free indeed." My spirit rejoices in the liberty that comes through Christ Jesus. I am eternally grateful for the freedom that You have bestowed upon me—a freedom from the chains of sin and death, a freedom to live in the fullness of Your grace. Amen.

January 15: This Day

Scripture for the Day

"But if serving the Lord seems undesirable to you, then choose for yourselves this day whom you will serve, whether the gods your ancestors served beyond the Euphrates, or the gods of the Amorites, in whose land you are living. But as for me and my household, we will serve the Lord."

Joshua 24:15

In Joshua 24:15, we have a forceful declaration from Joshua, the leader of the Israelites, as he stands before the people. He presents them with a meaningful choice: Who will they serve? Will they opt for the traditions of their forefathers to worship the deities of the land inhabited now or choose to serve the one true God, the Lord?

This verse alerts us that life is a series of options and the most important choice we will ever make is who we serve. Joshua's ironclad devotion to serving the Lord is an example for all of us. He didn't allow an inch for compromise or doubt. Boldly, he declared, "But as for me and my household, we will serve the Lord."

As followers of Christ, we are confronted with the same decision every day. Will we succumb to the distractions and false gods of this world that sway our hearts, or will we, like Joshua, choose to serve the Lord with all our might? Today, let us renew ourselves in our commitment to work for God with all our hearts and be an unshakable example for our families and others around us. Like Joshua's choice caused blessings for the Israelites, our choice to serve the Lord will bring a life of purpose, meaning, and the endless love of our Heavenly Father.

Think of the impact your decision would have on your family and friends. In what way would you guide them into a life of serving the Lord? Request wisdom and grace to develop a spiritual atmosphere in which their faith would grow and become strong.

Prayer: Thank You, Lord, for giving me the choice so that I could break the bonds that held me, setting me free in the truest sense, and for granting me a life unshackled by the past. May I always walk in the triumphant victory of Jesus. In His mighty name, I pray, Amen.

January 16: All Eyes

Scripture for the Day
"Nothing in all creation is hidden from God's sight. Everything is uncovered and laid bare before the eyes of him to whom we must give account."

Hebrews 4:13

We suffer from doubts, indecisions, and at times pain in our journey of faith. Does God observe our suffering, our arguments, or our secret sins? We might doubt whether He even sees the pain in our hearts and the battles we lose within ourselves.

Today, let us take comfort in the truth revealed in Hebrews 4:13. The verse proclaims our God's all-powerful (omnipotent) and all-knowing (omniscient) character. No place, thought, and puzzle can avoid His divine omniscience.

The eyes of the all-knowing God keeps us before Him. His love is most profound. He is concerned about our happiness, sorrow, success, and failure. We should know that He is aware of our deepest fears, troubles, and wants. We can feel safe knowing we are traveling with God Himself watching over us.

The verse tells us that all is open and bare to the eyes of God. Everything is known to Him. He penetrates our mask and pretense. He knows our thoughts, wishes, and reasons. This should make us live a life of honesty, purity, and joy in being His.

That is why today we should seek comfort in the God who knows our secret sorrows and provides healing, direction, and forgiveness. We can fearlessly go to Him because He understands our human weakness and has mercy on our condition.

Prayer: Father, I pray that I will rejoice knowing that Your eyes are always upon me, directing me and illuminating my way. May my works, thoughts, and speech mirror the liberty of following Your will and the love which You have placed in my heart. Amen

January 17: We Pray

Scripture for the Day

"This, then, is how you should pray: "'Our Father in heaven, hallowed be your name, your kingdom come, your will be done, on earth as it is in heaven. Give us today our daily bread. And forgive us our debts, as we also have forgiven our debtors. And lead us not into temptation but deliver us from the evil one.' For if you forgive other people when they sin against you, your heavenly Father will also forgive you. But if you do not forgive others their sins, your Father will not forgive your sins."

Matthew 6:9-15

In Matthew 6:9-15, Jesus gave His disciples a great prayer which is commonly called the Lord's Prayer. It is an everlasting sign of our bond with our Father in heaven and forgiveness. A vital truth is hidden in these verses that can change our lives. Jesus instructs us about the value of forgiveness and how to seek it for ourselves and give it to others.

Forgiving is a godly action that reflects the love and mercy of God. Being imperfect, we require forgiveness on a regular basis as we often fail and make mistakes. Our Savior not only tells us to request forgiveness but also stresses the important action of forgiving our offenders. When we acknowledge our own need for forgiveness and offer it at the same time to others, we taste the freedom and the peace that forgiveness brings.

Prayer: Recite the classic version of the Lord's Prayer below:

Our Father who art in heaven,
Hallowed be Thy name.
Thy kingdom come.
Thy will be done
On earth as it is in heaven.
Give us this day our daily bread,
and forgive us our trespasses,
As we forgive those who trespass against us,
And lead us not into temptation,
But deliver us from evil.
For Thine is the kingdom and the power, and the glory,
forever and ever. Amen.

January 18: You Go, I Go

Scripture for the Day

"Then a teacher of the law came to him and said, 'Teacher, I will follow you wherever you go.' Jesus replied, 'Foxes have dens and birds have nests, but the Son of Man has no place to lay his head.'"

Matthew 8:19-20

The brief but significant meeting of Jesus with a lawyer gives us insight into what discipleship entails. He came to Jesus, bowed down, affirmed, and promised to follow Him wherever He went. It was an attitude of dedication and commitment but with Jesus's answer, the more hidden truth was brought to light, previously unnoticed.

Jesus responded with a statement that might seem puzzling: "Foxes have holes and birds have nests, but the Son of Man has nowhere to lay His head." Jesus lived a hard, nomadic lifestyle that He maintained during His earthly ministry. He didn't possess a living place or a fixed home. Instead, He was always wandering here and there while fully trusting in God's supply and guidance.

This answer shows the sacrificial and hard life of a disciple. Walking in the footsteps of Christ is a matter of total dedication and relinquishing things of this world, even the desire for assurance and comfort. It means us giving up everything – our intentions, ambitions, and even our creature comforts as we seek after the Kingdom of God.

Jesus's call is not to an uneventful, uncomplicated life. It is a summon to an arduous trip where the self will be surrendered, and its desires put to death. It demands abandoning worldly charm and embracing the life of God into our wishes. Rather than enjoying the continual pleasures of the world, we invest our time in God.

Prayer: Dear Lord, I am thankful for this reminder of what it means to be a Christian. Give me strength to hand over my desires for ease and safety to let Your will dominate my life. Lord, You are my strength. Let me follow You faithfully, even in such times when the path is unclear and seems a bit difficult. In Jesus' name, I pray, Amen.

January 19: God's Gift

Scripture for the Day

"May God give you heaven's dew and earth's richness—an abundance of grain and new wine."

Genesis 27:28

In each breath and step that we take, we are reminded of the overflow that God showers on His creation. The Scripture today tells us about the abundance and goodness that the Lord gives. The dew from heaven that enriches the earth every morning and the richness of fertile soil depict the divine provision accessible to every heart that seeks Him.

We recognize the provision of God. The blessing that Isaac bestows on Jacob is not just the hope of material wealth but also the acknowledgment of the presence of God in our lives and His generosity. Just as dew and fruit of the earth are gifts from God, His spiritual blessings – love, joy, peace, and hope – are also freely given.

In moments when we feel like a dry land looking for refreshment, God's promise of His blessing blooms in its own time to nurture our souls. It is beyond what we ourselves do because it a gracious act of divine favor, mirroring the character of our loving Creator.

May today find us coming to our tasks, relationships, and challenges with an expectant heart. Let us have faith in God's never-failing provision and endeavor to use the overflow of His plenty. May we be faithful in sowing seeds of kindness, love, and faithfulness. Look forward to a rich harvest that will feed us and enable us to be a blessing to others.

Prayer: Heavenly Father, You renew Your mercies every morning, and Your faithfulness is as vast as the sky. Just as the Earth yields its richness refreshed by the morning dew, I ask for Your refreshing presence to fill me today. Enable me, Lord, a heart that absorbs and acknowledges Your gifts, both physical and spiritual. Amen.

Embracing Shiloh:

January 20: The Hidden Word

Scripture for the Day
"I have hidden your word in my heart that I might not sin against you."

Psalms 119:11

Psalm 119 is a beautiful celebration of God's Word, highlighting its significance in our lives. In verse 11, the psalmist expresses a significant truth: hiding the Word of the Lord in our hearts helps us to avoid sin and continue to be faithful to our commitment to Him.

However, memorizing or reciting alone is insufficient to hide God's Word in our hearts. It means hiding His Word in the inward part of us, becoming a part of our thoughts, emotions, and ways. It includes a real longing to embody and practice the knowledge and truths distilled on the pages of the Word of God.

What is it important to store the Word of God in our hearts? First, it is a spiritual compass that directs our decisions and choices. Knowing Scripture teachings and principles intimately, will make us resistant to the pull of worldly temptations and sinful desires. The Word of God becomes the guardrail to hold our heart and mind to His truth.

Secondly, reflecting on His Word, we are conformed in our thinking and worldview, embracing the holiness of God and the redeeming power of His grace. In situations of temptation, the Holy Spirit can recall to our minds particular passages and teachings that keep us strong in submission.

Our hearts and minds get overwhelmed by the worldly influences in this fast-moving world. But when we are deliberately ourselves commit to hiding God's Word in our hearts, we set ourselves up to be transformed and guided as we experience spiritual growth.

Prayer: Thank You that we have Your Word, Father. Assist me to tuck Your truth in my heart so that I may follow Your will and withstand the trials of this world. Grant me the longing and strength to interact with Scripture daily so it can transform me by its power. In Jesus' name, Amen.

January 21: Hidden Treasure

Scripture for the day
"For the wages of sin is death, but the gift of God is eternal life in Christ Jesus our Lord."

Romans 6:23

Paul hits the profound truths of salvation, sin, the divine transforming power of God's grace in today's verse. He illustrates a comparison that captures the core of human nature and the greatness of God's redemptive purpose.

The first half of the verse states gravely, "For the wages of sin is death." This somber fact reveals the dark outcome of our sinful nature. Sin causes division between us and God such that our spirits die, and there is an eternal separation from God. Regardless of how we try to earn ourselves back to right standing, we cannot satisfy the debt sin requires.

But at this, the awe-inspiring beauty of God's plan is revealed. The verse goes on with the glorious claim, "But the gift of God is eternal life in Christ Jesus our Lord." Although sinful and powerless to save ourselves, God gives us eternal life through His Son, Jesus Christ.

Eternal life is not what we deserve for our works but what we get as a gracious gift from God. It is an unearned act of love and mercy given to all who profess their faith in Jesus as their Lord and Savior. By the sacrificial death and resurrection of Jesus, He made forgiveness, restoration, and everlasting communion with our Heavenly Father available to us.

In our everyday life, let us dwell in the freedom and joy of this gift. Let us obey, cling to the truth of God's Word, and grow in our relationship with Him. And being beneficiaries of God's marvelous grace, may we reflect His love and mercy to others, spreading the gospel of salvation through Jesus Christ.

Prayer: Heavenly Father, thank You for eternal life in Christ Jesus. Your unlimited grace and love make me humble. Assist me in valuing this gift and following a life that glorifies You. Enable me to reach the world with Your message so that others may also take part in the beautiful gift of eternal life. In Jesus' name, Amen.

January 22: Mature Effort

Scripture for the Day
"When I was a child, I talked like a child, I thought like a child, I reasoned like a child. When I became a man, I put the ways of childhood behind me."
1 Corinthians 13:11 (NIV)

Also known as the Love Chapter, in 1 Corinthians 13 the Apostle Paul wonderfully elaborates on the traits and significance of love. Verse 11 introduces a strong analogy in comparing the development and maturity of love to the natural development of a child to an adult.

During seasons of learning, discovery, and growth in childhood, we talk, think, and argue like children with limited knowledge and vision. Our motivations and desires are usually egocentric as we go through the world with childlike innocence.

However, as we increase in age and our faith journey, we ought to discard the ways of childhood. This does not imply that we outgrow childlike wonder, humility, and trust in God. Rather, it prompts us to grow in our comprehension, love and discipline.

Paul refers to the love in 1 Corinthians 13 as a selfless love, sacrificing, wanting the good of others before our own. It is a love that is patient, kind, and forgiving. It is a love that takes delight in truth and not possessive, jealous, prideful, and holding a grudge.

Growing in love is a process that demands deliberate action and yields to the work of the Holy Spirit who dwells in us. We must let God shape our attitudes, thoughts, and actions, conforming them to the example of love set by Jesus Christ.

Control in love involves the movement from self-centeredness to other centeredness. It includes learning to have a heart of compassion, grace, and forgiveness and aiming for reconciliation in relationships. It is the opposite of allowing bitterness or selfishness rule the heart and choosing to love even when it is hard.

Prayer: God our Father, I thank You for Your love that is beyond human comprehension. Teach me to mature and increase in love, letting me put off the ways of childhood. Change my heart into the image of the love demonstrated by Jesus. Enable me to love others unselfishly and sacrificially, demonstrating Your love in all parts of my life. In Jesus' name, Amen.

January 23: Spiritually Strong

Scripture for the Day

"Pray also for me, that whenever I speak, words may be given me so that I will fearlessly make known the mystery of the gospel, for which I am an ambassador in chains. Pray that I may declare it fearlessly, as I should."

Ephesians 6:19-20

Imagine sailing on an ancient ship, fighting against wild storms and pelting rain. A gale shrieks, threatening to rip the sails to shreds. However, in the middle of this uproar one passenger is not willing to give up and remains strong. He is called Paul, and he is on a mission to take the news of Christ to faraway places.

The Apostle Paul teaches believers about spiritual warfare and the need to wear the armor of God. In this passage, however, Paul humbly asks for prayer for himself. He seeks prayer, not that he would be removed from his circumstances, but that he would have courage and clarity in preaching the gospel.

This prayer request of Paul instructs us in a profound truth on the necessity and importance of spreading the Good News. Being followers of Christ, we are ambassadors of the gospel, representing our Father in heaven and His kingdom to the world. Like Paul was given the responsibility of being not afraid to proclaim the mystery of the gospel, we are also given with this task.

The prayer request of Paul reminds us of our need for divine enablement. All his knowledge and expertise notwithstanding, he understands his words and ability when sharing in the gospel are by God's grace and help. He humbly confesses his reliance on the Holy Spirit to speak through Him and set hearts aflame with the truth of the gospel message.

Today, let us pray for each other. Let us pray to God for the same courage and clarity that Paul desired. May He fill us to the brim with His Holy Spirit, to uses us as channels to share the truths of the gospel with wisdom, compassion, and unshaken faith.

Prayer: Dear Lord, our Father, I am kneeling before You to request boldness and clarity in preaching the gospel. Pour Your Holy Spirit into me so that I may articulate the truth about Your love and redemption. Enable me to live as a loyal gospel ambassador, showing Your grace and casting Your light upon the world. In Jesus' name, Amen.

January 24: His Alone

Scripture for the Day

"The earth is the Lord's, and everything in it, the world, and all who live in it; for he founded it on the seas and established it on the waters. Who may ascend the mountain of the Lord? Who may stand in his holy place? The one who has clean hands and a pure heart, who does not trust in an idol or swear by a false god."

Psalm 24:1-4

Picture splendid scenery, unfolding as far as the eye can see. The mountains tower in grandeur, the valleys sleep in quiet peace, and all of nature in its glory proclaims the name of its Maker. Admiring this masterpiece, you become aware that everything, every single living thing, belongs to God.

In Psalm 24:1-4, the psalmist tells us a great truth: the earth is the Lord's, and everything in it. This statement calls us to acknowledge God's ownership of all created things and points us toward the opportunity to approach Him with awe and devotion.

While we admire the harmony and unity of the natural world, we are willing, at the same time to view in amazement the sanctity and greatness of the Lord. He is the One who created the Earth and knitted all subtleties of it in a fascinating garb. All the world and all that is therein show His glory and declare His wisdom.

But the psalmist poses a question: "Who may ascend into the hill of the Lord? And who may stand in his holy place?" These questions compel us to look at ourselves and our hearts. We are called to a higher level of righteousness and purity to enter the presence of God.

To ascend the mountain of the Lord, we must have clean hands, symbolizing our acts and deeds. We should live a life characterized by ethical behavior and honesty and seek justice and righteousness in all we do. In addition, a pure heart is necessary, revealing inner attitudes, thoughts, and motives. It reflects an honest wish to glorify God and a genuine love for Him.

Prayer: Thank You, Lord, for the way nature proclaims Your glory. Thank You for breaking the bonds that held me, for setting me free in the truest sense, and for granting me a life unshackled by the past. May I always walk in the triumphant victory of Jesus. In His mighty name, I pray, Amen.

January 25: Trust and Obey

Scripture for the Day

"Teach me to do your will, for you are my God; may your good Spirit lead me on level ground."

Psalm 143:10

In the life of faith, we have moments when we are lost as to where and how to go about something. We are at a crossroads, yearning for heavenly guidance. In Psalm 143, David admits his reliance on the Lord's guidance and desires the Lord to teach him to do His will. David sees that real wisdom and guidance are from the Almighty, who knows our ways inside out.

Like David, who desired that the Spirit of God lead him, we should also ask the Holy Spirit to lead us daily. The Spirit of God gives us godly wisdom and the empowerment to walk in obedience. He makes us aware of the right way, prevents us from stumbling blocks, and allows us to make decisions consistent with God's purposes.

Do you stand today at the crossroads? Are you unsure which way to head? Pause and echo David's prayer. Humble yourself before God in submission to His majesty. Ask the Holy Spirit to be your teacher, guide, and lead you to level ground. Believe that He will guide your steps and will harmonize your choice with God's matchless scheme.

Prayer: My Father, who is in heaven, I come to You today humbly, declaring that You are my only God. I give up my desires and thoughts to You, requesting You to teach me to do Your will. Holy Spirit, I welcome You to take me to level ground, to lead me in every decision and every step I make. Endow me with discernment and wisdom to live in obedience and alignment with Your plans. Make my belief stronger as I depend on Your godly guidance. I pray in the name of Jesus, Amen.

January 26: Hearing

Scripture for the Day

"Do not merely listen to the word, and so deceive yourselves. Do what it says. Anyone who listens to the word but does not do what it says is like someone who looks at his face in a mirror and, after looking at himself, goes away and immediately forgets what he looks like."

James 1:22-24

As Christ's disciples, it is crucial that we not only listen to God's Word but also practice it. James impresses upon us the potential of deception when we hear the Word and do not live it. He compares this approach to a person who glimpses himself in a mirror and then forgets his reflection. Such forgetfulness prevents us from experiencing the truth of God and its effective work in our faith journey.

The Word of God is unrivaled in its ability to shed light on the darkness that is hidden within our hearts and to highlight the places in our lives where His intervention and transformation is required. It unmasks our weaknesses, sins, and insufficiencies. Nevertheless, if we only hear the Word without accepting its teachings, we rob ourselves of the chance to develop and become like Jesus.

Hearing the Word and acting upon it requires obedience and involvement in the will of God. It calls for us to make our thoughts, speech, and actions conform to the truth of the Bible. Living witnesses of God's grace, love, and righteousness are produced when we apply His Word in our lives.

Let's continue to reflect our lives in the looking glass of His Word. Let us not be hearers but doers, letting His truth overflow in us. Practicing our faith will manifest the transforming power of His Word, resulting in us living lives that glorify Him and bless others.

Prayer: Thank You for the gift of Your Word, gracious Father. Assist me to be both a hearer and a doer of Your Word. Let me not deceive myself when I only hear and do not obey in response. Open my eyes to see the parts of my life that Your changing will bring about. Grant me the boldness to be straight in my thoughts, speech, and actions with Your truth. May Your Word be my feet lamp, leading me all along. I pray in the name of Jesus, Amen.

January 27: Now Go

Scripture for the Day

"And the man got up and went home."

Matthew 9:7

Jesus recently worked a miraculous healing of a paralyzed man who is now totally recovered. The crowd was speechless, struck with awe and amazement at this tremendous miracle.

Being unable to move his limbs and carried on a mat, the man, at the mere word of Jesus, found himself not just healed but restored. In an instant, strength filled his body, allowing him to stand up and go home on his own. The happiness and joy of the paralytic as he felt the miraculous touch of Jesus can only be guessed at.

This story is testimony to wondrous might of the Son of man, Jesus Christ. We view Jesus not simply as a sage, seer, or physician but as the very Son of God, able to rejuvenate and transform lives instantly.

As Jesus physically restored the paralyzed man, He still restores and heals our brokenness today. It might not always be physical healing, but Jesus can heal our wounded hearts, reconcile broken relationships, and transform our lives.

What about the reaction of the paralytic man? He did not just get healed and continue his life as before. No. He rose up and went home, undoubtedly telling the incredible story of what Jesus did for him.

Similarly, when Jesus changes our lives, we are called to respond to Him with thanksgiving and an eagerness to share His supernatural work with others. Let us not hoard the good news, but share with anyone who might listen about the amazing powers of Jesus Christ, the Son of man.

Take a little time today to contemplate the deep authority and power of Jesus. Recall that no situation is too difficult or hopeless for Him. Genuinely give Him any places of brokenness or hurt in your life, trusting that He can repair, heal, and change all who come to Him.

Prayer: Jesus, Your power is awesome, and Your healing touch is greatly appreciated. Thank You for the ways You redeem and change lives. I lay before You the broken areas in my life, trusting You, Lord, to bring wholeness and healing. May I react to Your work in my life with thankfulness and readiness to share Your miraculous power to others. Amen.

Embracing Shiloh:

January 28: Seek and Ye Shall Find

Scripture for the Day
"Ask and it will be given to you; seek and you will find; knock and the door will be opened to you."

Matthew 7:7

Did you ever play one of those notorious claw machines, the ones that are supposed to entice you with the possibility of getting a good reward? It is as if these machines were created by an evil genius to try our patience. They usually make us angry as we grab at thin air. Just think what life would be like as a colossal claw machine.

Imagine yourself in front of this giant machine not filled with plush toys and glittering trinkets but with all the blessings, answers, and breakthroughs you want. The giant claw is hanging above, waiting for you to give an order. You decide to play and approach it with great expectation and a foolish grin. You carefully insert your coins, feeling simultaneously excited and expectant. In charge of the claw's movement, you can peek at the treasures of your future.

Feeling the thrill, you place the claw, ready to seize that one gift that has eluded you for so long. You hit the button as hard as possible, the claw descends, prepared to grasp what your heart truly yearns for. But the claw touches the prize looser than you wanted. It disappears, and you are just left moaning in disappointment.

Doesn't life sometimes feel like a massive claw machine? We are in an agonizing search for happiness, success, recovery, or meaning. We inquire, knock, and look, but end up frustrated and empty. But here's the thing: The Word's promises in Matthew 7:7 reveal a totally different thing.

Jesus here invites us to come to Him in boldness, not playing a cosmic claw machine but approaching Him as children who seek the heart of a loving Father. God is not like a claw machine operator who gets a kick out of watching us suffer. He is yearning for us to approach Him and rely on His faithfulness. Though it may seem like we have not won the jackpot just yet, each sincere cry of our hearts is heard and appreciated by Him.

Prayer: Teach me, O Lord, to ask with sincerity, seek with clarity, and knock with persistence, aligned with Your will and purpose for me. May my petitions reflect my desires and resonate with Your divine plan. Amen.

January 29: Be Certain

Scripture for the Day
 "So do not fear, for I am with you; do not be dismayed, for I am your God. I will strengthen you and help you; I will uphold you with my righteous right hand."
Isaiah 41:10

We are given a consoling and comforting word from God Himself. It is a sweet reminder that there is no need to fear or be discouraged because an Almighty God who is always by our side. During times of insecurity, challenges, or suffering, we find comfort and strength by knowing that He, our Heavenly Father, is holding us in His righteous right hand.

Fear consumes and incapacitates us, taking away joy, peace, and hope. But when we encounter fearful situations, God's Word remains unchanged: "Fear not." It is an order backed by a pledge of His continual presence and unvarying defense.

God promises us that He is with us. In all times, under all conditions, He is with us. He does not abandon us to face the challenges of life on our own, but He walks with us, leading and sustaining us. He keeps us with His righteous right hand that stands for His might, equity, and unfaltering love. In moments of weakness and distress, God's strength supports us. His help stands ready, and He kindly allows us to be strong in the face of whatever comes our way.

Today, whatever fears or worries weigh heavy on your heart, pause, and remember the words of Isaiah 41:10. Let them be planted in your spirit, generating peace for you. God is with you. He is your power, your rescue, and your lead. Believe in Him, for He is dependable in supporting and carrying you through any trial and difficulty.

As we walk through life held and strengthened by the hand of our Almighty God, timidness disappears from our lives. Each step becomes proof of God's faithfulness, and our hearts fill up with trust because we are not alone in this path.

Prayer: Father, thank You for being with me always and under Your constant attention. Remind me that with You, I should not fear or be discouraged. Lord, empower me to depend on You daily for direction and sustenance. Support me by Your right hand of righteousness. Strengthen my faith in You. May Your love and strength be in my heart as I meet what is ahead, knowing You are always beside me. In the name of Jesus, I pray, Amen.

Embracing Shiloh:

January 30: Is This Love

Scripture for the Day

"Love must be sincere. Hate what is evil; cling to what is good."

Romans 12:9

The biblical model of love is not a mere emotion or a temporary feeling but a conscious decision and an active behavior. It is the love that is selfless, sacrificial, and unconditional which goes beyond just superficial forms of showing love. Paul exhorts us to have our love honest, true, and pure.

Point 1: *The Love of Delusion*. This verse starts with Paul underscoring the virtue of charity. True love is not shallow or self-seeking but a selfless and deliberate practice of looking after others. As Christians, we are enjoined to love genuinely, out of our innermost selves. This love is not merely lip service or on the surface; it is the kind of love that needs proper care, understanding, empathy, and compassion. Let us ask God to lead us in the process of growing pure love in our relationships and interactions with others.

Point 2: *An Ignorant Worship of Beauty*. Paul tells us to hate what is evil. In this world, which is full of sin and with all its brokenness, it can be easy to become desensitized or tolerant towards evil. But as disciples, we must fight evil and corruption. This means fighting injustice, violence, dishonesty, and anything that is contrary to God's righteous standard. May we pray for the ability to pinpoint evil regardless of how it presents itself and, with God's power and His leading, oppose it boldly.

Point 3: *Holding on to the Good*. Apart from loathing evil, Paul also bids us to cleave to the good. Goodness is an attribute of the personality of God. It includes deeds of love, mercy, goodness, and virtue. As believers, we are called to seek and approve what is good. This involves deliberately looking for chances to help, doing good, sharing goodness with others, and ordering ourselves by God's Word and His precepts. We should endeavor to be living witnesses of the good in a world that is desperately in need of evidence of the transforming power of God's love. Let us abhor what is evil and boldly resist it.

Prayer: With a trusting heart, I ask for Your guidance and provision, seeking the path You have set for my life. In faith, I knock at the door of opportunity, knowing Your hand holds the key to my future. Amen.

January 31: Still The One

Scripture for the Day

"Do you not know? Have you not heard? The Lord is the everlasting God, the Creator of the ends of the earth. He will not grow tired or weary, and his understanding no one can fathom."

Isaiah 40:28

In this verse, we are refreshed thinking of the eternal character of our God, the One that designed the whole universe. It is a consoling and amazing statement of His might, strength, and perennial wisdom.

The verse begins with two questions: "Do you not know? Have you not heard?" suggesting that the truth about the nature and power of God is something that many people should know and accept. But in the face of trials or uncertainties, it is easy to forget His eternal nature and the amazing things He does.

Isaiah reminds us that the Lord is the everlasting God. He is timeless. We become tired, weak, and even falter in our understanding, but our God is always alert, never fatigued from caring for His creation. He is steadfast, faithful, and unchangeable in His love, wisdom, and mercy.

Contemplating this, we should be inspired to put confidence in the eternal God. In whatever uncertain or trying situation, we can be assured that our God is unchanging. His love never fails, and His will never give way. Through Him, every ordeal is a victory.

Prayer: I thank You for the assurance of Your listening ear and the unfailing love that attends to every prayer. In the transforming name of Jesus, I offer my deepest gratitude and place my trust. Amen.

Embracing Shiloh:

February 1: Seek And Wait

Scripture for the Day
"It is good to wait quietly for the salvation of the Lord."

Lamentations 3:26

We come across a lovely sign of the love and faithfulness of our God amid hopelessness in. These words by the prophet Jeremiah, bid us to a stance of patient waiting and confidence in the deliverance that comes from the Lord.

Patience is challenging in a world of quick outcomes and instant gratification. We become fidgety, anxious, or want to take things into our own hands. Nevertheless, Jeremiah calls us to wait silently rather than in passive resignation with a heart responsive to God's timing and sovereignty.

Waiting on the Lord is an expression of faith and submission. This is also the recognition that what His ways are much higher than our ways. His timing is impeccable. While waiting, we depend on His wisdom and have faith that He works everything for our good, even when we cannot see it.

We are brought into a much closer relationship with the Lord when we silently await His deliverance. We approach His heart, seeking His counsel meekly, giving up our desires and what we think should be the results. In this waiting, we discern God's peace, which passes all understanding and takes residence in His unchanging love.

In periods of waiting, it is most important to keep in mind that our God is the ultimate faithful one. He is not a god who is remote or indifferent but a caring Father who always wishes the best for His children. While we anticipate His salvation, we take comfort in His being actively involved in our situation, engineering every detail so that everything unfolds just right.

Prayer: Dear Lord, As I close this chapter of my day, I come before You in quiet reflection and heartfelt gratitude. Thank You for the blessings You have bestowed upon me, the love that surrounds me, and the peace that You promise. Amen.

February 2: Cross Walk

Scripture for the Day

"Blessed is the one who does not walk in step with the wicked or stand in the way that sinners take or sit in the company of mockers."

Psalm 1:1

The first verse of the book of Psalms reveals the idea of real blessedness – happiness, joy, and spiritual enrichment. The psalmist calls us to think about the way we walk and the friends we make. He draws a well-defined line between the blessed life and the ways of the world.

The psalm begins with a powerful declaration: Blessed is the one. Indeed, the blessed life is not measured by what we own, what we have accomplished, or how successful we are in the world. It is measured by our proximity to God and alignment with His ways. The psalmist also tells us that our blessedness results from our decisions and companions.

At first, we are advised not to walk in the counsel of the ungodly. We are called to repel the power and seductions of those who oppose God's will. We need to try to bring our thoughts, attitudes, and deeds into harmony with the truth and righteousness of His Word.

Then, we should avoid standing in the way that sinners take. This is a lesson for us to be aware of the winding roads in our lives. We are not to commit ourselves to the paths of sin that lead us to deviate from God's purpose. By looking away from sin, we allow God to transform us and enjoy the natural gifts He has prepared for us.

Finally, we are told not to sit in the seats of mockers. The people with whom we associate significantly impact our thoughts, values, and general way of life. We should select friends who support and inspire us along the way of God instead of those who mock or discourage us in our quest for goodness.

Prayer: In this moment of serenity, I ask for Your presence to continue guiding me, for Your wisdom to direct my decisions, and for Your love to inspire my actions. Instill in me a spirit of kindness and compassion towards everyone I encounter. Amen.

February 3: The Small Things

Scripture for the Day
"Whoever can be trusted with very little can also be trusted with much, and whoever is dishonest with very little will also be dishonest with much."

Luke 16:10

People tend to underestimate simple and minor duties. We tend to want monumental achievements or praise, desiring to create a significant impact without realizing that the faithfulness in the small things paves the way for bigger opportunities.

Point 1: *Small Habits of Trust*. This includes attention to little things is our personality and integrity. Jesus tells us that if we are faithful in little things, we will also be faithful in big things. Our time, resources, or relationships are all part of our lives, and all these and more can be opportunities to showcase faithfulness.

Point 2: *Steadiness and Perseverance*. Little loose truths often have big consequences. We are to be industrious and consistent in responding to tasks, however big or small they may be. The importance of a situation should not alter our faithfulness and integrity. Through developing an attitude of determination and persistence in all we do; we glorify God and lay groundwork for confidence in our lives.

Point 3: *Loyal in the Kingdom of God*. Foundational in the Kingdom of God are fidelity, stewardship, and confidence. By the way we are faithful in the small things we can prove we unite ourselves with God's intentions. Our faithful work will prompt Him to give us greater tasks. Faithfulness is not only a question of our human responsibilities but also a matter of our Kingdom's commitment. When we serve others, preach, or use our gifts, let us show faithfulness in all we do because we know that the favor of God comes to those who are faithful.

Prayer: Father, equip me to face the challenges ahead with courage and to spread kindness and compassion in a world in need of Your light. Help me to remember that in every thought and every action, I am to reflect the beauty of Your holiness. Amen.

February 4: Humility and Selflessness

Scripture for the Day

"Do nothing out of selfish ambition or vain conceit. Rather, in humility value others above yourselves"

Philippians 2:3

Our world is characterized competitiveness among individuals and groups who are often preoccupied personal success and fame. Contrasting this self-centeredness, the apostle Paul, in his letter to the Philippians, offers a radical view of Christlike humility.

Paul appeals to us to repel selfish ambitions and vain conceits, which can sabotage our relationships and separate us from the plan of God. Instead, he encourages us to practice the virtue of humility and to value and honor others' wellbeing over ours.

Humility is not weakness or self-abasement but a profound strength that rests on love and self-denial. It is about being willing to put aside our own interests, needs, and individualism to love and lift those who are in our lives. This kind of attitude breeds oneness, peace, and genuine fellowship in the body of Christ.

When we seek the Holy Spirit to shape our hearts, we experience our attitudes changing. We start feeling the happiness and satisfaction of serving and loving other people selflessly. We will no longer concentrate on self-promotion but make relevant friendships and build the wellbeing of others.

Today, let us meditate on the words of Paul in Philippians 2:3. Let us analyze our motives, deeds, and thoughts and surrender them to Jesus. May His Spirit enable us to live in humility and love, showing His character and honoring His name.

Prayer: Almighty Father, thank You for Your humble model of love. Aid me in getting rid of all selfish ambition or vain conceit from my mind. Let me be filled with grace to esteem others better than myself and indeed to love them. Change my thoughts and actions to live the life and be an image of Your Son, Jesus Christ. Amen.

Embracing Shiloh:

February 5: To Live is Christ

Scripture for the Day

"For me, to live is Christ and to die is gain."

Philippians 1:21

For many, life is filled with pursuing personal success, material wealth, and fleeting pleasures, the Apostle Paul's perspective in Philippians 1:21 makes us reconsider our preferences and find the real meaning of life.

Living for Christ means that Jesus is central and leading in everything we do. It is searching for His will above ours, fitting our wants to His wants, and leaving our schemes and ambitions at His feet. It involves Him forming our character, actions, and relationships to the nature of our Lord.

In addition, Paul says that "to die is gain." This phrase shows his resolute faith and confidence in the eternal promises of God. As Christians, we can derive comfort in realizing that death marks the beginning, not the end, of an eternal fellowship with our Savior.

Today, let us reflect on Paul's powerful words from Philippians 1:21. Let us assess what our lives are directed by. Are we living for Christ, or did the distractions and worldly ventures take over our devotion to our Lord Christ? May we reorient ourselves to the life in which Christ is the center and the goal.

Prayer: My Lord, I give myself to You anew this day. Enable me to live for Christ, searching for Your will above my own. May I only realize my identity, purpose, and fulfillment in You. Enable me to detach from earthly diversions and harmonize my heart with Your will. And living for You, let me have in the everlasting promises and coming gain that will never perish, hope. In the name of the Lord Jesus, I pray. Amen.

February 6: Extravagant Love

Scripture for the Day

"But God demonstrates his own love for us in this: While we were still sinners, Christ died for us."

Romans 5:8

Exhibiting a love that we cannot comprehend, God's love isn't based on who we are and what we have done. In fact, it is one of God's attributes.

The beauty of the gospel isn't just that Christ died, but He died at the time when humanity was at its lowest point, sin-laden, and furthest from being worthy of redemption. It is here in this "while we were still sinners" that we discover the wisdom of divine love. It was not a theoretical feeling; it was love in action, love demonstrated, love displayed.

The love of God was poured out at the cross, where Jesus took our iniquities upon Himself and offered us righteousness in exchange. It reveals that God's love for us is unwavering despite our defects. There is no sin that is too large, no chasm that is too wide for His mercy to fill.

Understanding this fact eliminates the myth that we should first sanitize ourselves and approach God. But rather, it's coming to Him that purifies us. We take our brokenness to the bottom of the cross, where mercy finds us, and love changes us.

This knowledge sets us free from the burden of justifying our worth and allows us to extend this love to others in the same way. We become channels of the same grace we did not deserve.

Prayer: Dear God, I cannot admire Your love towards me enough, a love so deep that You gave Your Son while I was steeped in sin. Thank You for showing us what love means. Assist me to live each day in the sunshine of goodness, scattering this unearned blessing to all who cross my path. Let my life be a living testimony of the love that has been so freely given to me. In Jesus' name, Amen.

February 7: Extended Love

Scripture for the Day
"For God so loved the world that he gave his one and only Son, that whoever believes in him shall not perish but have eternal life."

John 3:16

The phrase "For God so loved the world," presents us with a love that is both expansive and intimate. It cuts across all cultural, racial, and social barriers, reaching to the uttermost parts of the Earth. It is not a love by deeds or by our standards. It is a love that favors us despite our imperfections and failures.

Recognizing this divine love leads to a transformation that changes our whole being. In accepting that Jesus Christ came to the world not to judge but to save, we start to realize what was paid for our deliverance from sin and the gift of eternal life. His gift lights the way from darkness to His wondrous light, from death to life eternal.

The faith in Him and the reception of this promise is the essence of our faith. It breaks pride and introduces a humble grace, a blessing that is so valuable that one wants to give, share the good news, and live in the face of eternity.

As we consider this passage, may we reflect on the love that caused the Father to give His Son for us and be filled with unspeakable joy and peace.

Prayer: Loving Father, Your love for me is overwhelming. What You did by sending Jesus is the most gracious thing I could ever think of. Teach me to live each day in the knowledge, appreciating eternal life as given by Your Son. Reinforce my faith and enkindle my awareness of Your incomprehensible love. Let my life be a witness to Your grace and Your love. I pray in the name of Jesus. Amen.

February 8: Together For Good

Scripture for the Day

"And we know that in all things God works for the good of those who love him, who have been called according to his purpose."

Romans 8:28

Sometimes, life can have entirely unexpected changes. We confront trials, problems, and doubts that make us confused and disheartened. This verse is a reminder that in every situation, God is evident, and He works according to His perfect plan for those who love Him and are called according to His purpose.

Sometimes we struggle with how God can make all things work together for good when we suffer heartache, pain, or disappointment. However, this verse promises that there is nothing impossible for God. He can make beauty, healing, and restoration out of shattered pieces.

When we advance in love with God and synch our lives with His purpose, we can have confidence that He is working for us through us. Even if we do not comprehend His ways or timing, we can find peace in His faithfulness and unchangeable character. He is the conductor supreme who can turn the most discordant notes into a symphony of His grace.

Regardless of the doubts that we encounter, God's authority will be our trust. May this verse be a light of hope to all that His ways are higher than man's. Let us surrender our hearts and lives to His will, believing that He is making all things work together for all that is best for us, His glory, and His purpose.

Prayer: Father, As I close my eyes and bow my head, I feel calm as Your presence envelopes me. Thank You for the moments we have spent today in worship, reflection, and learning. I am grateful for the breath in my lungs and the love in my life, which are gifts from You. Amen

Embracing Shiloh:

February 9: Simply Trust

Scripture for the Day
"Trust in the Lord with all your heart and lean not on your own understanding; in all your ways submit to him, and he will make your paths straight."

Proverbs 3:5-6

Trusting God with all our hearts means entrusting with our whole existence—our aspirations, desires, fears, and doubts. It is a total submission that does not ration trust conveniently but presents it generously to our Lord. This trust brings divine peace, an unworldly calm that cannot be obtained by the world or taken away by it.

"And do not rely on your own understanding?" How many times do we get caught as victims of our own reasoning, attempting to decode life's tribulations and successes through the small scope of human perspective? Our perception may be wrong, influenced by prejudices, and molded by experience. Yet, God sees the whole fabric of our lives—past, present, and future—and leads us lovingly with complete knowledge and wisdom.

This verse does not tell us to throw reason out of the window but to recognize that our understanding should go side by side with great faith in God. He never fails to lead those who trust in Him and direct them this way and that with His Word and His Spirit of counsel.

God is not only able but is also willing to lead us through every step of our earthly sojourn. Confide in Him today's troubles and see how He orchestrates the good.

Prayer: Lord, here I stand before You with an open heart, wanting to believe in You. Enhance my faith to trust in You and not in my own ability. Grant my heart a place of rest in Your endless wisdom and Your leadership in every situation that I meet. You are my rock and my salvation; to You alone, I will cling. In Jesus' name, Amen.

February 10: First Focus

Scripture for the Day

"But seek first his kingdom and his righteousness, and all these things will be given to you as well."

Matthew 6:33

The environment around us tends to glorify a constant chase after material wealth, egoistic advantage, and instant gratification. But Christ directs us towards an elevated pursuit – a pursuit that changes what we value and what we want. To look for His Kingdom is to orientate our gaze toward the invisible but imperishable truths of God. It is to desire the things mentioned above—justice, love, peace, and the very presence of God Himself.

When we seek His righteousness, we not only seek to live our lives according to God's moral and ethical expectations. It is also to receive His righteousness, which is by faith in Christ, a righteousness that is not ours but one that covers us as a mantle given from a King.

Such pursuit promises provision. "Into you will be given also all such things," Jesus reassures. What consolation and assurance do we get from these words? Our needs, worries, and concerns are taken care of by the King Himself as long as we prioritize His Kingdom. We are not called to a life of anxiety but of faith and focused action.

This does not diminish the value of the work we do every day but puts it in terms of God's greater, overarching work. Every task, decision, and relationship are chances to glorify the Lord and see His Kingdom being made manifest on earth.

Prayer: Father in heaven, as I enter another day of Your creation, I seek the grace of finding You above all else. Let Your Kingdom be my highest ambition and Your righteousness my constant search. Lead my ways and meet my wants as I give You my will. Endow me with the knowledge to see Your hand in all things and the resolve to have faith in Your supply. I ask in Jesus' name. Amen.

February 11: Endless Strength

Scripture for the Day
"I can do all this through him who gives me strength."

Philippians 4:13

These are encounters we face as we in our when walk our faith is tried, and we feel inadequate or overwhelmed. Nevertheless, we have an unbelievable source of strength through Jesus Christ.

In Philippians 4:13, Paul says, "I can do all this through him who strengthens me." These words bear the powerful truth of hope, inspiration, and faith.

Paul is expressing contentment in all situations, either favorable or unfavorable. He admits that no matter the situation, his power lies in Jesus Christ. But instead of boasting about his abilities or self-sufficiency, Paul considers himself dependent on the Lord.

As we consider Paul's statement, we receive a principle for our lives. The strength of Christ is something that makes us able to tackle every situation, whether trials, temptations, or everyday tasks, with confidence and persistence. It is a reminder that we are not deserted in our trials, but we have at our disposal a supernatural force.

Today, take hold of this powerful truth from Philippians 4:13. Cover all your life with Christ's power. No matter what difficulties or challenges you are confronted with, He is the one who can empower you to win. Trust in His love that lasts and that is never shaken; His unrelenting promises; and His consistent presence.

Prayer: Father, I ask that what was sowed here will produce fruits in our lives so that we may develop in love, wisdom, and knowledge. It assists us in taking the thoughts and motivation of today into our lives in day-to-day interactions with other people. Amen

February 12: Finding Rest

Scripture for the Day

"The Lord is my shepherd, I lack nothing."

Psalm 23:1

Psalm 23:1 gives us a paradise of holy bliss. The imagery of the Lord as our Shepherd is deeply comforting, for it speaks to His close care, leading, and provision. The declaration "I need nothing" is an assertion of faith that goes beyond all earthly needs and conditions.

The function of the shepherd is to guide, feed, and guard. As a shepherd in heaven, our Lord does establish a connection with us. He knows what we require even before we seek it, and His provision is not only for our survival but for our thriving. David, the author of this psalm, knew this. Being a shepherd himself, he understood that sheep require care in all areas of their lives to enjoy health, and he saw this in God's providence over his life, too.

In the fold of God, we are called to lie down in green pastures and are led by still waters. He restores our souls and leads us in the paths of righteousness for His name's sake. A spiritual wealth of this kind is incomprehensible by the desert of fear and need. We are rich in the things that truly matter: love, peace, guidance, and eternal salvation.

To know God as your Shepherd is to know that you are not alone. You always having help. You are valued not by the success of the world but by the faithfulness of the Shepherd who died for His sheep. Therefore, to have nothing as far as the world is concerned is to have everything while we develop thankfulness for everything that we have in Him. In the valley of the shadow of death, evil, and sorrow, we are not afraid of evil, for He is with us.

Prayer: Faithful Shepherd, I accept Your lordship over my life and am glad about the wholeness I find in You. My needs, my ways, and my soul are known to You. In Your wisdom, guide me, and in Your strength, strengthen me. Make me find perfect satisfaction in Your presence, trust in Your care, and dwell in Your provision. Amen.

February 13: Joyful Anticipation

Scripture for the Day
"Be joyful in hope, patient in affliction, faithful in prayer."

Romans 12:12

We as Christians move through different seasons – happiness and unhappiness, success and failure. Amid the ever-changing circumstances of life, the words of Romans 12:12 show us how to live through them.

The verse opens with an instruction: "Be joyful in hope." As Christians, our hope is in Christ and His promises. This hope is not a passing feeling that changes with our circumstances but a steady belief in the goodness and dependability of God. It's a happy anticipation of what He plans and purposes for our lives.

To learn Christ is to realize that our happiness does not lie in temporary pleasures but in the never-ending life we possess in Him. It is a pleasure to make decisions, regardless of our state. It is built on the assurance that God arranges everything for our good.

The last part of the verse, "Be patient in affliction," instructs us. Life is bittersweet with various matters, trials, and tribulations. One can quickly get tired, lose hope, or question the goodness of God. However, as Christians, we are to persevere, remaining steadfast in the Christian Faith.

Accepting Jesus is finding comfort in Him in times of trouble, believing He will always be with us and never desert us. These trials purify our faith, strengthen our character, and strengthen us in God. Through patience in suffering, we show confidence in His omnipotence and faith that all things work together for our highest good.

Prayer: Father, this morning, as I stand at the door of this day, I want to say thank You for waking me up and for the new hope I found. Help me to walk in the light of Your love and to take the opportunities that You have set out for me. Amen.

February 14: His Renewal

Scripture for the Day

"Do not conform to the pattern of this world, but be transformed by the renewing of your mind. Then you will be able to test and approve what God's will is—his good, pleasing and perfect will."

Romans 12:2

When it comes to our faith journey, the world around us can easily influence and mold us. However, as Christians, we are held to a higher standard. Romans 12:2 reminds us of this, calling us not to conform to the world, but to be made new in our thoughts.

Life never stops force feeding us its ideologies, values, and priorities. Frequently, these messages oppose the teachings of Jesus and can cause us to move away from God's ideal for our lives. Yet, God gives us a call to deny conformity to the world's ways. Rather, we are to be transformed by renewing our minds with His truth.

The process of renewing our minds is giving up the ways of thinking that include world desires, selfish ambitions and thought patterns. It is while we surrender to God's transforming power that He changes our old thoughts to His truth, wisdom, and perspective. Our will grows to be like His will, and our deeds acquire His attributes.

Christ's transformation is a journey. It involves discipline, humility, and allowing God to work in us. We need to seek His presence, surrender ourselves to His guidance, and let Him in His mercy to continually renew our mind.

Today, let us meditate on our thoughts and let the Holy Spirit show us the areas where we might be following the world's ways. We need to renew our minds with the truth of God consciously, seeking His wisdom and discernment in everything we do. When we accept Christ's transformation, we will live in the peace, happiness, and satisfaction that is the result of living His good and perfect will.

Prayer: Lord, I ask You to renew my mind. Assist me in living in opposition to the patterns of this world and seek Your ways. Give me the knowledge and perception to know Your will and the power to do it in my life. Change my thoughts, wishes, and deeds in line with Your perfect will. In Jesus' name, Amen.

February 15: Embracing Presence

Scripture for the Day

"He says, 'Be still, and know that I am God; I will be exalted among the nations, I will be exalted in the earth.'"

Psalm 46:10

These words are not just an appeal to stillness but a heavenly command for awareness and understanding. The phrase, "to be still," involves an end of movement, a temporary break of the constant activity typical of our earthly life. It is a holy call to cease our labors, put off our loads, and meditate on the awe and rule of God.

In silence, we can breathe and move our attention from the busy urgency of our problems to the stability of the Almighty. This verse reminds us that God's wealth remains imperishable no matter what turbulence the world is experiencing or what personal battles we are fighting. This is a soothing assurance of His living and dominance and that God's purposes will succeed in the end.

"I am God," is not only knowledge in the mind but a heart and soul awareness of His nature and promises. This knowledge is liberating truth, setting us apart from the hold of fear and the pressure of self-reliance.

God's exaltation "among the nations" is proof of His majesty and the irresistible character of His Kingdom. In silence, we tune our hearts to this truth, nurturing a peace that surpasses comprehension and an unshakable trust in the face of change.

Prayer: Sovereign Lord, in the calm of this moment, I respond to Your invitation to "Be still and know that You are God." May this reality seep into my soul, quieting my fears and grounding my heart in Your unshakable rule. Show me how to find comfort and power in Your presence, to have faith in Your divine ordering of the world. Let my soul endure to praise You in every time of peace or strife. In Jesus' name, Amen.

February 16: By Grace Through Faith

Scripture for the Day
"For it is by grace you have been saved, through faith—and this is not from yourselves, it is the gift of God—not by works, so that no one can boast."

Ephesians 2:8-9

Most people want to win their salvation, thinking that by doing their good deeds and activities they deserve God's grace. Yet, the Word of God tells us something different. We can do nothing to rescue ourselves or gain God's love. Our salvation is absolutely a gift from God – a gift that we accept when we believe in Jesus Christ.

We do not understand the grace through which we are saved. It is grace, a gift from God due to His extreme love for us. We were sinners, separated from God by our transgression, but in His compassionate love, God sent His Son, Jesus Christ, to give Himself up to suffer and die for our sins. With His accomplished work on the cross, we have forgiveness, healing, and life forever.

Our works do not save us. Nevertheless, faith is crucial when it comes to obtaining God's gift of grace. Belief is how we trust in Jesus, recognizing Him as our Lord and Redeemer. Faith is not simply a matter of the mind. It is a belief that produces action. This trust entails offering our lives to Christ, submitting to His rule, and attempting to live in compliance with His teachings.

Knowing that our salvation is a gift makes us humble. We cannot glory in everything we have received and consider ourselves superior due to such gifts. We did not earn God's favor. The gift of salvation is freely available to all. We stand on equal ground before God, where through faith and God's grace all are admitted, irrespective of their place, achievements, or conduct.

Prayer: Father, protect me from harm and guide my steps in Your wisdom. May Your will be done in my life this day. Thank You for Your mercies that are new every morning. Great is Your faithfulness. Amen.

Embracing Shiloh:

February 17: Look Harder

Scripture for the Day
"You will seek me and find me when you seek me with all your heart."
Jeremiah 29:13 (ESV)

When thinking about this verse, the best adjective is "ardent." To seek God ardently is to pursue Him with fire-flaming passion, unrelenting devotion, and an insatiable craving for His presence. This means to seek Him with zeal, leaving nothing behind, giving up every part of our life to His divine will.

Consider the bliss that we find when we totally dedicate ourselves to genuinely searching for God in such a fashion. He assures us that we shall find Him! He is not an inaccessible deity but a kind Father who delights in revealing Himself to those who seek Him truly.

Let us be zealous as a God-seeker. May we have our hearts on fire with fervent love for Him as we seek His face continually. Let our worship be passion-driven, our prayers with intense hunger, and our life thirst only for His righteousness.

Ask: Am I seeking God with all my heart? In what areas am I holding back, or have I become complacent? Are there distractions or other priorities that have killed the fervor of my pursuit?

Prayer: Dear Father, I approach Your throne today, acknowledging that I should seek You with all my heart. Pardon me for the times I let distractions and laziness stand in my way to reach You. Set in my soul a fervent devotion that seeks a closer communion with You. Aid me in seeking Your face at the top of my list. In Jesus' name, Amen.

February 18: Big Plans

Scripture for the Day

"For I know the plans I have for you," declares the Lord, "plans to prosper you and not to harm you, plans to give you hope and a future."

Jeremiah 29:11

This promise was given to a people in exile, a reminder that even amid their struggles and the consequences of their disobedience, God had not abandoned them. His heart was, and always is, turned towards restoration and blessing.

God's declaration to "prosper" isn't a mere reference to material wealth but signifies a flourishing that permeates every aspect of our lives—spiritual, emotional, and physical. He aspires for us to thrive, to grow vigorously like a well-watered garden under His loving care.

And what of harm? The promise isn't immunity from trouble but a reassurance that the trials are not meant for our destruction. They are often the fertile ground where resilience is grown and character is forged, always within the bounds of His grace and mercy.

The Lord engineers a future infused with hope—a confident expectation that His Word will not return void but will accomplish what He desires. Hope in God transcends mere optimism. It is a steadfast anchor for the soul, mighty enough to withstand the storms of life.

This Scripture invites us to trust in the Architect of our destiny, to surrender our plans in exchange for His, which are immeasurably better. We walk by faith, not by sight, led by His promises, assured that our future is secure in His hands.

Prayer: Lord, You are the Author of all hope and the Architect of my future. Help me to trust in the plans You have for my life, plans designed for my good. In seasons of turmoil, be my peace. Shape my tomorrow with Your wisdom and fill my heart with the hope that only You can give. Amen.

February 19: COMMISSIONING

Scripture for the Day

"Go therefore and make disciples of all nations, baptizing them in the name of the Father and of the Son and of the Holy Spirit, teaching them to observe all that I have commanded you."

Matthew 28:19-20 ESV

This command of Christ is not a request to rest, but a sending. It is a commission that represents a journey, demanding both the making of disciples and the act of going. This requires patience, relationship building, and unwavering proclamation of the gospel through what we say and do.

This commission is between Heaven and Earth as we are called to conduct our mission in the trinitarian name of the Father, the Son, and the Holy Spirit. We are called to join the dance of heavenly salvation, bringing others into the household of God, joining them to the household of the redeemed.

To fulfill this command is to commit to a lifelong pursuit. We need to always look for where to spread the love of Christ, grow faith in others, and rejoice over the life-giving gift of salvation. Where we are is our mission field—our homes, workplaces, and communities—and to the ends of the earth.

The Great Commission unifies all of us, tied to the heart of Jesus, calling us to the transformers and messengers of the future and representatives of the never-fading Kingdom. In every act of discipleship, we repeat the obedience of Christ, echoing His self-sacrificial love and showing the way for others to walk.

Prayer: Father, if You say go, then without hesitation, I will go. Amen

February 20: Embracing Life

Scripture for the Day

"Turn from evil and do good; seek peace and pursue it."

Psalm 34:14

Psalm 34:14 actively commands an intentional pivot from the ways of evil—a deliberate journey toward goodness and peace. This Scripture calls us to a daily practice of renunciation and righteousness, a dual movement of turning away and walking toward.

The act of turning from evil signifies more than avoiding sin. It is aligning our hearts with the things of God, rejecting not just the deeds but the very root of wickedness that entangles the heart. In its place, we are to "do good," an action that requires effort, persistence, and the Holy Spirit's guidance within us. These good works are fruits of our faith, visible signs of an inward grace extended outward.

Yet this psalm beckons us further still—not only to be practitioners of peace but also active seekers of it. The peace of God is not simply the absence of conflict. It is the presence of divine wholeness and wellbeing. It is harmony that transcends understanding, a restfulness for the soul amid life's tempests. Our charge is to pursue this peace relentlessly, in our hearts, in our relationships, and across our communities.

This pursuit is part of our Christian witness, for in striving to emulate the Prince of Peace, we embody the very essence of the gospel. The world observes not only what we turn from but also what we are turned towards. When we embody the peace of Christ, we become living testaments of His transformative power.

Prayer: Heavenly Father, grant me the strength to turn from evil and the courage to do good. Instill in me an unquenchable desire for Your peace, that I may seek it fervently and share it generously. Amid a world of strife, may Your peace rule in my heart and guide my actions. Equip me to be a peacemaker for the sake of Your Kingdom and the display of Your glory. In Jesus' name, Amen.

February 21: Growth

Scripture for the Day

"When Jesus reached the spot, he looked up and said to him, 'Zacchaeus, come down immediately. I must stay at your house today.' So, he came down at once and welcomed him gladly."

Luke 19:5-6

Oh, the tale of Zacchaeus, a man with a height disadvantage but a heart full of curiosity and eagerness! Today, we look lightheartedly at this encounter between Jesus and our vertically challenged friend from Jericho. Fasten your seat belts as we journey through Luke 19:5-6!

Zacchaeus is perched atop a sycamore tree, eagerly trying to glimpse the famous Jesus passing by. Zacchaeus took tree-climbing to new heights, quite literally! In a world of social media, he'd probably be trending as the first "selfie-seeker" of his time.

Can you imagine the peculiar sight that day? A grown man, wrapped in garments more fitting for an executive boardroom, scrambling up a tree like an over-enthusiastic monkey.

Little did Zacchaeus know the surprise that awaited him. As Jesus passed by, He looked up, probably with a bemused smile, and called out to him, "Zacchaeus, come down immediately. I must stay at your house today." Talk about an unexpected plot twist! Zacchaeus must have swung down from that tree so fast that he left his sandals in the branches!

Imagine the reactions of the onlookers. "Did Jesus just invite Himself to Zacchaeus' house?" "Why would He choose the chief tax collector of all people?" "Is this some kind of divine prank?"

As Zacchaeus welcomed Jesus with great joy, it was clear that this encounter would forever change his life. Jesus saw beyond the quirky tree-climber exterior and straight into his heart. He knew that despite his profession and reputation, Zacchaeus was open to transformation.

Let Zacchaeus' story teach us. We may not have to risk our dignity climbing trees, but let's be open to encountering Jesus in unexpected ways. Remember, Jesus seeks us out, no matter our shortcomings or stature. He longs to transform our lives, to turn our quirks into shining testimonies. Who knows? Maybe one day, we'll all have our own "sycamore moments" that lead to divine encounters!

Prayer: Father, As the morning light spills into this new day, I pause to thank You for the gift of life and the fresh opportunity to live out Your purpose. With a heart full of hope, I seek Your guidance and wisdom as I prepare to step into the day's tasks and interactions. Amen.

February 22: Facing Fear

Scripture for the Day
"So do not be afraid of them, for there is nothing concealed that will not be disclosed, or hidden that will not be made known."

Matthew 10:26

The "them" in this verse can be the stifling voices of opposition or ignorance that stand before us when we proclaim the gospel. Jesus sends out His disciples, strengthening them with the words that courage should overcome their fears when they bring the news of the Kingdom. His words are a reminder that the truth of God's Word will triumph in the end.

When Jesus says that the hidden shall be known, the impotence of faith that is confined to safety and secrecy is exposed. We are lights in the dark, truth-tellers in a world fond of its secrets. To the follower, it is a consolation and a commission—a reassurance that although truth must endure the wrath of the day, a day of disclosure dawns when everything that is concealed is revealed.

This promise makes us bold, for we know that our labor in the Lord is not useless, and our proclamation is not empty. We are called to remain firm, to speak boldly, to live openly, and not to fear any reproach, for all will be revealed in the perfect timing of God.

Fear is unbecoming in the cause of the Kingdom. So, we are filled with the courage of God that enables us to talk instead of staying quiet, to do instead of doing nothing, to love instead of being indifferent.

Prayer: God, free me from the chains of fear that limit my testimony for You. Clothe me with holy boldness to announce Your truth to all, for I know that all hidden things will one day be revealed. May I continue with courage, unafraid of retribution, for I believe in Your rule and the triumph of Your righteousness. May my life stand for the courageous nature of Your Son, in whom I take my courage and determination. Amen.

February 23: Sabbath

Scripture for the Day
"For the Son of Man is Lord of the Sabbath."

Matthew 12:8

Rest is an elusive goal in a world running at a fast pace and that demands too much. The demands of work, obligations, and the pervasive noise of existence make us tire and feel overwhelmed. However, Jesus knows our humanity and offers a rest deeper, that goes beyond and fills our souls with peace.

In Matthew 12:8, Jesus claimed Himself to be the "Lord of the Sabbath." Indeed, the Sabbath was created by God as a day of rest and worship, a gift to His people. It was time to conclude work, meditate upon God's goodness, and feel His presence. On the other hand, the religious leaders of the time of Jesus had wrapped the Sabbath with numerous rules and regulations, making it a legalistic duty instead of a day for reviving and refreshing.

Jesus brought back the real meaning of the Sabbath. He showed that, as the Son of man, He is not only the Lord of the Sabbath but rest itself. He welcomes us into a rest that is above the day of the week and that permeates every part of our lives.

How does this concern us today? With Jesus, we can find peace while in turmoil and facing the challenges of daily routines. We are not slaves to our to-do lists or the incessant need to meet the expectations of everyone else. We can accept His provision of rest and let Him renew our weary spirits.

Genuine rest starts by recognizing Jesus as the Lord of our lives and casting our burdens and worries on Him. It is all about dedicating focused quality time to look for His presence, to learn His Word, and to praise Him. This way, we allow ourselves to feel His peace, joy, and restoration.

Prayer: Father, as the morning advances to the day, help me to stop and enjoy the easy blessings that I miss so often. Through both tests and victories, keep my spirit rooted in Your undying faithfulness. Amen.

February 24: Unfailing Salvation

Scripture for the Day

"Surely God is my salvation; I will trust and not be afraid. The Lord, the Lord himself, is my strength and my defense; he has become my salvation."

Isaiah 12:2

The prophet Isaiah clearly states that God is salvation Himself. We can trust that God's grace of salvation is certain and settled. Amid life's troubles and trials when we are afraid, we may ask, "Where is God?"

Believing in God's salvation means giving up our fears and doubts and to stop trusting in our own abilities. It is to rest all our hope in His infinite might, wisdom, and love. While we grow to release our anxieties into His trustworthy hands, we discover a deep feeling of tranquility and assurance that surpasses any human understanding.

In the world, trust is rare, and promises are often broken. In comparison, God is the one who is set apart, unchanging, and firm in His assurances. He is the one true enduring fact in our lives, always ready to stretch out His arm of salvation and rescue. His love for us is steadfast and unwavering, providing shelter in life's tempest.

In times when we are challenged by trials that seem to be overwhelming burdens, we need to realize that God is not only our Savior but our fortification and protection. He gives us the strength to endure obstacles, and His presence protects us from harm. God is with us, and we can confront each day boldly that His power is in us.

Prayer: Father, sanctify the work of my hands and the utterances of my mouth. May they mirror Your love and mercy. Lead my thoughts and actions to bring peace and happiness to all I meet. At the time of challenge, give me wisdom and light. Given me strength and endurance in crisis. Amen.

February 25: Sowing

Scripture for the Day

"The point is this: whoever sows sparingly will also reap sparingly, and whoever sows bountifully will also reap bountifully."

2 Corinthians 9:6

Within the fabric of the Kingdom of God, there is a principle sewn in it – the principle of sowing and reaping. This verse is not only a prescription of giving but also a lifestyle.

To sow sparingly is to live with a clenched fist. To sow freely is to live with an open hand. Generosity is not measured by the amount of what is given but by the nature of the giving heart. Sowing generously is an act of giving not only out of our plenty but out of our substance, willingly giving of our time, resources, and love.

This spirit is not an exchange formula but a transformative way of life that reveals our confidence in God's providence and goodness. It finds its source in God, who gave so abundantly and sacrificially in Jesus Christ. Abundant sowing is an application one of the tremendous lessons we have already had in the gospel – lessons of grace, mercy, and love.

Seeing this a promise of wealth is an error. The real harvest is mostly intangible – it could be happiness, spiritual development, or the fruits growing in the lives of others out of our generosity. The economy of God is also a different story. What we give is multiplied in ways that we might never know in this world.

Let us be sowers that sow seeds of mercy and gentleness profusely. Indeed, as we copy the generosity of our Creator, we can believe that our lives will harvest a crop of righteousness, peace, and the happiness that is borne from obeying God's word.

Prayer: Most kind Lord, who gives so abundantly to all, grant me a heart that sows bountifully. Let me copy Your generosity in every detail of my existence, relying on Your provision and on the rich harvest. Let my giving be a delightful worship offering, sown in faith and watered with Your grace. In the name of Jesus my greatest gift and my only treasure, I pray. Amen.

February 26: Discern for Yourself

Scripture for the Day

"Jesus replied, 'And why do you break the command of God for the sake of your tradition?'"

Matthew 15:3

The Pharisees were famous for their meticulous respect for tradition, but Jesus uncovers the peril of allowing human customs to eclipse divine law. Traditions are significant expressions of our faith, but if they start to replace or contradict the commandments of God, they tend to obstruct real worship and obedience.

Jesus invites us to discernment. At issue is determining whether our traditions are leading us to the presence of God or whether they have turned into stiff barriers that limit our perception of Him. Our deeds and convictions should not be judged by their historical duration and popularity but by their accord with the essence of God as exposed in the Bible.

He calls us to an uncluttered relationship with God, free from human rules and renewed by the living water of His Word. Our faith should be a living and lively communion with God, not a group of rites executed mechanically or out of duty.

This prompts us to return to the source of our faith: to love God with all our being, and love neighbors as Jesus has taught. In this way, we value the commandments of God over the tradition of man.

Prayer: Father, lead me to know Your will more than any other thing. Assist me to remain faithful to Your commandments and not be lured by human customs that might take me away from You. Let Your Spirit shine Your truth in my life that I may be Your servant with a whole heart. Teach me to live the purity and power of a genuine faith that worships You in spirit and truth. I pray in the name of Jesus. Amen.

February 27: His Promise

Scripture for the Day
"Therefore, say to the Israelites: 'I am the LORD, and I will bring you out from under the yoke of the Egyptians. I will free you from being slaves to them, and I will redeem you with an outstretched arm and with mighty acts of judgment."

Exodus 6:6

The ancient Israelites experienced a great tension. Enslaved in Egypt, crying out under the weight of oppression on one hand, yet, in Exodus 6:6, God declares with unshakable assurance: "I will bring you out... I will free you... I will redeem you."

God reveals Himself as "The Lord," the self-existent One who is utterly reliable and whose promises stand immovable. In an ever-changing world, the promises God made to Israel are a testament to His enduring faithfulness, and they echo still in the lives of believers today.

This Scripture is not just historical but also deeply personal. It reflects God's heart for each of us: He longs to lead us out from the yokes that bind us—whether they are sin, despair, addiction, or fear. He yearns to bring us into a place of freedom where we can serve Him joyfully without the chains of our past afflictions.

The image of God redeeming His people with an "outstretched arm" speaks to His might and readiness to act on our behalf. It is a display of power motivated by love, a definitive action that pledges liberation and new life. His "mighty acts of judgment" are assurances that no force, no matter how oppressive, can withstand His power.

As we reflect upon this powerful declaration, let us also remember our part in the narrative: to trust and wait upon the Lord, even when the night is at its darkest. His day of deliverance dawns brightly upon the horizon.

Prayer: Lord God, I trust in Your promise to bring me out from under the yokes of trial and affliction. I believe You are working even now to free me from bondage, to redeem my story with Your powerful love. Help me to hold onto Your promises with unwavering faith, looking expectantly for Your deliverance. Strengthen me in this season of waiting, and ready my heart for the freedom that is coming through Your mighty hand. Amen.

February 28: Waiting

Scripture for the Day

"Be patient, then, brothers and sisters, until the Lord's coming. See how the farmer waits for the land to yield its valuable crop, patiently waiting for the autumn and spring rains. You too, be patient and stand firm because the Lord's coming is near."

James 5:7-8

Patience is a virtue often praised, yet just as often, eludes our grasp. In a world marked by instant gratification, the call to patience is countercultural, running upstream against the torrents of haste and hurry. In the counsel of James 5:7, we find a metaphor that perfectly captures the necessity for patience — the farmer's watchful wait for the harvest.

Like a farmer who trusts in the unseen work below the soil, we too, are invited to trust in the unseen work of God in our lives and in the world. The farmer knows that the crop will need time, sun, and rain to grow. Similarly, spiritual growth and God's plans unfold in due time, often through seasons of silent and unseen nurturing.

This patience is not idle but active. It requires steadfastness of faith, an enduring trust that God is at work even when the earth seems barren. For the farmer, the valuable crop is worth the wait, and for us, the coming of the Lord, the ultimate fruition of our faith, is beyond worth — it is the climax of our hope.

In this Scripture, the mention of both "autumn and spring rains" signifies a period's beginning and concluding acts. Our lives are lived in the in-between, where the faith we espouse is refined, and our character is shaped in Christ's image.

Let patience, therefore, do its perfect work. Let us stand firm in hope, resisting the impulse to despair over what is not yet seen. Let us take joy in the process, knowing that the Master Gardener is indeed cultivating something beautiful.

Prayer: Merciful Father, instill in me the farmer's patience as I await Your promises and Your return. In seasons of quiet growth and periods of waiting, help me to trust in Your perfect timing. May I be steadfast and resilient, deeply rooted in the assurance that You are nurturing my spirit and preparing a harvest of righteousness in my life. Keep my eyes fixed on Jesus, the pioneer, and perfecter of my faith, until the day of glorious harvest. Amen.

February 29: Joyfully Hopeful

Scripture for the Day
"May your hope be joyful; patient in tribulation; faithful in prayer."

Romans 12:12

In the tension between joy and toil, Paul delivers a brief command that captures the Christian's call to endurance — to rejoice, be patient, and persist in prayer. Romans 12:12 gives us a formula of faith that lasts in all ages and situations, always relevant in our haste and restlessness.

Joy and hope are sisters in faith's household – where one is, the other is close by. Rejoicing in hope is a state of expectation for what God has promised despite the present reality or current sufferings. This hope is no empty optimism but is built on the reality of who God is and His history of being faithful.

Trials present a harsh contrast to hope, but they are the fertile ground in which patience ripens. As steel is made in the heat of a furnace, so our patience is tried and made stronger in times of trouble. It is not a sort of passive yielding but an active perseverance, a determination to stand firm when under pressure and to wait for God's salvation in the end.

To merge these qualities, Paul enjoins believers to pray. Prayer is the umbilical cord between us and the Father, the reservoir in which our patience is refilled, and our hope rekindled. It enables us to abide by God's grace and live our faith without hypocrisy.

In this Scripture, we find the rhythm of the Christian life: the joy dance, the patience march, and the constant talk with God through prayer. While we walk between the now and the not yet, may we hold this rhythm in our hearts.

Prayer: Almighty God, give me joy that springs up from hope based on Your promises. In times of tribulation, underpin my soul with patience that never fails. Let me be instant in prayer, to abide near You, finding solace and directions in Your perpetual company. Form my life into evidence of Your sustaining mercy. Make a faith that fills every breath I take. In the name of Jesus Christ, my Rock and Redeemer, I pray. Amen.

March 1: Unshakeable Presence

Scripture for the Day

"God is our refuge and strength, an ever-present help in trouble."

Psalm 46:1

Sometimes, life is strange and full of surprises. People look for shelter with all their might. But did you ever try to seek shelter in something you only partly trusted?

We all have moments when we turn to temporary fixes: gorging ourselves on our favorite comfort food, snuggling under a warm blanket, or even trying to get away from the world with an addictive television show. While these may bring about short-term relief, they cannot really provide any long-term satisfaction.

Envision God as the supreme sanctuary. He calls us to live with Him, to find peace and power in Him only. He is not a loose, temporary shelter but a solid fortress that is impregnable. In Him, the refuge is found as a sturdy anchor as life surges around us.

Think about God being our strength. Life is full of challenges. We quite often feel weak and overwhelmed. But here's the amusing part: We generally believe that we must draw strength from ourselves as if we can cope with all our problems alone. It is like trying to lift a heavy weight alone while there is a divine weightlifter beside us, willing to take the burden.

God gently reminds us that real power is in giving our burden to Him. Our might does not lie in our effort but in believing in His boundless force.

Finally, the verse tells us that God is an "ever-present help in trouble." Take a moment to enjoy the irony here. Need for help is usually felt at inappropriate moments. It is like God has a great sense of humor, coming exactly when we think it is all over.

Prayer: Father, as I journey on, bless my loved ones, friends, and all I shall meet. Help me to be an example of someone who has found his strength in You. Let me be a light of gladness, hope, and comfort to them as You are to me. Amen.

March 2: All You Can Eat

Scripture for the Day

"And he directed the people to sit down on the grass. Taking the five loaves and the two fish and looking up to heaven, he gave thanks and broke the loaves. Then he gave them to the disciples, and the disciples gave them to the people."

Matthew 14:19

Today, we find ourselves in the presence of a miracle that has delighted countless hearts throughout history. In Matthew 14:19, Jesus performs something truly extraordinary.

Imagine the scene: thousands of hungry people sitting on the grass, anxiously waiting for food. Then, with a surprisingly casual demeanor, Jesus peeks at the humble meal of five loaves and two fish in front of Him. Now, picture Jesus exclaiming, "Oh no! We forgot to RSVP! But don't worry, my friends. I've got this!"

Jesus looks up to heaven and offers thanks for the meal He's about to share. But hold on a second; did anyone notice how He broke the loaves? Picture Jesus gently tearing the bread apart, only to realize He's accidentally creating loaves for the unlimited breadsticks deal at a heavenly restaurant. His disciples must have had a difficult time not bursting into laughter as they received basket after basket of endless bread.

Let's not forget about those two little fish that came along for the ride. With Jesus, there's always a surprise waiting. Picture the disciples' expressions as Jesus multiplies the fish in such abundance that they start swimming in the overflowing baskets. "Hey, Peter, pass me that fishnet instead of a dinner plate, will ya?"

The beauty of this story lies not only in the miraculous multiplication of food but also in the lighthearted atmosphere Jesus brings. He knows how to make us laugh, even amid our hunger—both physical and spiritual.

Prayer: Father, as dawn breaks and I ready myself to step into the day, I pause to give You thanks. Your mercies are new each morning, and Your faithfulness is as sure as the sunrise. With a heart of gratitude, I celebrate the gift of this new day. Amen.

March 3: Reconciliation

Scripture for the Day

"So then, it was not you who sent me here, but God. He made me father to Pharaoh, lord of his entire household and ruler of all Egypt."

Genesis 45:8

Life's ups and downs make the hand of God hard to appreciate. His plans can be doubted, and abandonment is felt in adversity. However, the story of Joseph in Genesis teaches us that in the darkest moments, God is still in charge, orchestrating everything for good.

Genesis 45:8 is a turning point in Joseph's story. After being sold by his own brothers as a slave and living a life of misery, he is finally reunited with them. Joseph does not hold grudges or seek revenge. Instead, he opts for forgiveness and reconciliation. He lets his brothers know that he was in Egypt not because of their deeds but because of God's ultimate intentions.

The perspective of Joseph has a powerful message for us now. We tend to retain bitterness and resentment for betrayal, hurt, or injustice. But when we accept forgiveness, we become free from the power of anger and God works even in our pain.

As God did with Joseph's situation, He can also use our tests to reach His purpose. In adversity, we must remember that God is the supreme conductor of our lives. If we have faith in Him and give up the weight of being unforgiving, He will make something beautiful out of our suffering.

Accepting forgiveness is sometimes hard, but it is the price we pay for our spiritual and emotional health. Keeping grudges not only spoils our relationships but it also stunts our personal growth and keeps us away from God's blessings. We are in tune with God's heart of grace and mercy when we decide to forgive.

Prayer: Father, shield me from danger and lead my paths away from evil. Let Your presence be with me always, peace be my faithful protection, and the Spirit my permanent consultant. Amen.

March 4: Timely Healing

Scripture for the Day

"But when they arrest you, do not worry about what to say or how to say it. At that time, you will be given what to say."

Matthew 10:19

In our faith pilgrimage, we come to situations that may look like they are too challenging and overwhelming. They may even look threatening. These are the moments when we feel helpless and confused, afraid that we do not have the right words or means to triumph over the challenges ahead of us. However, Matthew 10:19 reminds us of one beautiful truth – when we rely on the guidance and power of God, He supplies us with all we need, even in the most difficult circumstances.

These words were spoken by Jesus to His disciples, who He was preparing for the persecutions they would experience as they spread the words of the Good News. He told them that when they are being persecuted and in times of trouble, they don't have to worry about what words they are going to say or how they will be said. Rather, they were told to rely entirely on God's supply, and He would give them the words and knowledge in every situation.

This passage addresses not only ancient disciples but us. We may not be led to imprisonment or persecution because of our faith, but certainly we face tests of faith, fortitude, and our ability to act. It might be a personal battle, a complicated relationship, or a situation that takes us by surprise. At such times, we can be strengthened in the knowledge that our Father above is with us and that He is coming to lead, supply, and empower us.

We can be assured that He would give us the words, wisdom, and courage to go through the most difficult situations.

Prayer: Father in Heaven, thank You for comforting me so that I do not think about what to say or how to say it in difficult instances. Assist me in giving to You my fears and worries, knowing that You are my fountain of wisdom, fortitude, and restoration. I pray in the name of Jesus. Amen.

March 5: Unwavering Faithfulness

Scripture for the Day
"Know therefore that the LORD your God is God; he is the faithful God, keeping his covenant of love to a thousand generations of those who love him and keep his commandments."

Deuteronomy 7:9

Where everything is changing, uncertainties abound, and promises are easily broken, it is comforting to know that our God is steadfast in His faithfulness.

We see relationships fail, trust violated, and commitments abandoned when we look around. However, the nature of God is entirely the opposite of the unreliability of human relations. He is faithful in His promises throughout generations.

The Bible gives us numerous stories in which God's faithfulness is shown. Starting with the deliverance of the Israelites from the Egyptians and through to Jesus's love on the cross are demonstrations of the faithfulness of God. This loyalty is based on His unchanging character. He is the same yesterday, today, and forever (Hebrews 13:8)

The beauty of God's faithfulness is that it is not confined to one generation. It covers a thousand generations, past and future. This guarantees us that the love and faithfulness of God is not seasonal. Today, as you read this do not doubt that God's faithfulness will last forever.

Whatever the conditions, God is faithful. During trials and challenges, we find solace in knowing that His love will never go away. His purposes for us give hope. He is with us always, our refuge in a storm and our heart's custodian.

Prayer: Lord, let me answer Your faithfulness by showing my love to You and obeying Your commandments. I will have more faith in You as I learn to trust You more and more. My life will demonstrate how transforming Your stubborn faithfulness is. Amen.

March 6: Entrusting to God

Scripture for the Day

"So neither the one who plants nor the one who waters is anything, but only God, who makes things grow."

1 Corinthians 3:7

First Corinthians 3:7 humbles the heart and realigns our sense of purpose. It reminds us that while our labor is central, the glory and the power of growth belong solely to God.

This Scripture is a gentle nudge to realign our self-perception – we are not the authors of life, merely instruments used by the Divine Craftsman. We are released from the burden of causing growth, allowing us to engage fully in our tasks without bearing the weight of the outcome. It is freeing to accept our limitations and His limitless power.

Acknowledging that it is "only God who makes things grow" changes our focus from the applause and accolades for ourselves to the One who calls us to participate in His grand design. We rejoice not in achievements credited to our names but in the miraculous, often unseen transformation commanded by His voice.

This truth isn't only for the ministry in the field but extends to the unseen landscapes of our lives, where we strive for personal growth and change. No amount of self-effort can ultimately change the heart or renew the mind; it is a work of God's Spirit and the growth that God gives.

Our task is faithful obedience — to plant and water with diligence, integrity, and love, leaving the results to God's capable hands. In this, we find joy as co-laborers with Christ partners in the sacred adventure of redemption and restoration.

Prayer: Heavenly Father, I am grateful for the role You have entrusted me within Your Kingdom. Help me to plant and water with faithfulness, always mindful that growth comes from You alone. May I not seek my glory but give all honor to You, the Giver of all life. In the tasks You set before me, grant me the grace to serve diligently and then, in humility, to step back and witness the wonder of Your Spirit, breathing life into all that has been sown. In the precious name of Jesus, I pray. Amen.

March 7: Infusion

Scripture for the Day

"Do not be anxious about anything, but in every situation, by prayer and petition, with thanksgiving, present your requests to God. And the peace of God, which transcends all understanding, will guard your hearts and your minds in Christ Jesus."

Philippians 4:6-7

In the hurried pace of life where worries are as many as the stars, the Apostle Paul's words to the Philippians stand out as divine comfort. "He is now of the opinion that you should not worry about anything," he advises, not as a suggestion but as an instruction of living in deep confidence in God.

Paul, writing from prison, familiar with suffering and fear, realized the human tendency to be anxious. Yet, he presents a spiritual formula that turns anxiety into peace, prayer, supplication, and thanksgiving. This way of communication with God is an act of faith, understanding that our circumstances are beyond our control but not beyond God's sovereign reach.

No matter how desperate the situation, we are given the invitation to come to the throne of grace with confidence. In prayer a miracle occurs when we make our requests known to God. A trade happens in the spiritual realm – our worries and burdens are sifted, and in the process, we get God's peace, which is indescribable, heavenly, and rises above this world's turmoil.

This peace is not conditional on us resolving our problems but rather a fort for our hearts and minds, divine protection against the onslaught of worry and despair, provided to us by our union with Christ Jesus. It is foundational to our faith—our life hidden with Christ in God, immovable in the chaos of a fallen world.

Prayer: Father in Heaven, in the quietness of this time, I let go of my worries and fears to You. I am thankful for the blessing of prayer and Your peace. Let gratitude fill my heart and keep my thoughts under the peaceful rule of Christ. I sleep in You, knowing that You make everything work for my benefit. In Jesus' Name, Amen.

March 8: Your Cross

Scripture for the Day
"Then Jesus said to his disciples, 'Whoever wants to be my disciple must deny themselves and take up their cross and follow me.'"

Matthew 16:24

At the core of the Gospel of Matthew is a call to a journey of genuine self-giving and sacrificial love. Self-denial is not only nullifying desires or practicing self-deprivation but rather putting the will of God above our own. It is acknowledging that our life is not something to be hoarded but a gift freely given in service to God and others. In His discussion of bearing the cross, Jesus does not make suffering seem romantic or endorse a stoic response to life's difficulties. Rather, He is calling us to accept the difficult assignment, realizing that it is the way to spiritual satisfaction and eternal life.

In the words of Jesus, the cross, a symbol of suffering and execution, turns into a paradoxical image of hope and salvation. Carrying our cross means following Christ, who did not reject His cross but received it as a means of overcoming sin and death. Every suffering and adversity of our pilgrimage representing a cross, when linked to Christ's sacrifice, has deep meaning, and does its share in the realization of God's salvation designs.

This verse is not a call to a comfortable way but rather to a life-giving one where through trial and sacrifice we find the real meaning of faith and the depths of God's love for us.

Prayer: Gracious Lord, Your Word in Matthew 16:24 calls me to live a life of more comprehensive discipleship. I ask for the power to renounce myself, to set aside my selfishness and arrogance, and to take up the cross that is mine to carry. Help me to completely take after You, to comprehend the self-sacrificing love that this passage wants me to embrace. Let my pilgrimage of faith be Your grace and Your Kingdom's service. I pray in the name of Christ. Amen.

March 9: Heart Healthy

Scripture for the Day

"My flesh and my heart may fail, but God is the strength of my heart and my portion forever."

Psalm 73:26

These words grip us to the core, revealing that human strength is limited and hearts do not hold. We suffer from physical diseases, emotional confusion, or spiritual fatigue, which torment us and drain our stamina. However, in weakness, the psalmist confesses that God is our unchanging power.

When we come to trials that seem too big, we are tempted to rely on ourselves, but our limitations defeat us. However, God calls us to shift our focus from our shortcomings to His absolute power. He guarantees us that He is our help, refuge, and fortress in the hour of trouble. When we confess that we depend on Him, He enables us to overcome even in tribulation.

Furthermore, the psalmist states that the Lord is the strength of our hearts and our portion forever. This statement strongly helps us sort out what is important where our wants are in relation to what God wants for us. God is our portion—our all-satisfying, fulfilling, and eternally joyous source.

Prayer: Father, You are my strength. As I move on, bestow Your blessings on my family, friends, and everyone I would meet. Let me bring them happiness, hope, and consolation as You do to me. Amen.

March 10: The Encounter

Scripture for the Day

"While he was still speaking, a bright cloud covered them, and a voice from the cloud said, 'This is my Son, whom I love; with him I am well pleased. Listen to him!'"

Matthew 17:5

In Matthew 17:5, a powerful moment takes place on the mountaintop – a snapshot of the glory and divinity of Jesus Christ. Such a scene discloses insights concerning our faith walk and what it takes to accept Christ as a whole way of life.

1. *The Revealing Presence*: As Peter, James, and John stood amazed, the presence of God surrounded Jesus in a bright cloud. This holy acknowledgment from the Father affirmed that Jesus is the Son of God – the One we should love and bow to. God's revelation forces us to open our hearts and minds to the fact that Jesus is not only a historical figure, nor just a wise teacher but the Messiah, Savior, and Lord of all the world.

2. *A Voice from Above*: A voice from the cloud said, "This is my Son, whom I love; with Him I am well pleased. Listen to Him!" This proclamation highlights the special bond that Jesus has with the Father. As Peter, James and John learned about Jesus by listening to God, our relationship with Him grows by listening to and living by the teachings of Jesus. When we prioritize paying attention to His voice through prayer, Scripture, and the promptings of the Holy Spirit, we become more like Christ.

3. *The Call to Listen*: The voice from Heaven tells the disciples to listen to Jesus. This underlines the value of submitting to Him and letting His words control our thinking, choices, and behavior. While we face difficulties, doubts, or even successes, let us stop and consciously turn to the advice of Jesus. His words are healing, wisdom, and light in our lives, making us go through each day with a purposeful and confident mind.

May the mountaintop experience help us realize how much Christ is willing to share with us. We should seek Him daily, listen closely to His voice, and surrender completely to His direction.

Prayer: Heavenly Father, As the dawn breaks and I ready myself to step into the day, I pause to give You thanks. Your mercies are new each morning, and Your faithfulness is as sure as the sunrise. With a heart of gratitude, I celebrate the gift of this new day. Amen.

March 11: Learn to Listen

Scripture for the Day

"The LORD came and stood there, calling as at the other times, 'Samuel! Samuel!' Then Samuel said, 'Speak, for your servant is listening.'"

1 Samuel 3:10

The storms of our whirlwind life sweep us into the state of wishing for guidance. Our mission is to discover our vocation and the unique way God has chosen for us. Samuel's story in the Bible is a good example that illustrates the necessity of hearing God's call and acting according to His words.

At that time, Samuel, a youth who served in the temple of the Lord, did not yet know the voice of God. However, God called his name because He wanted to talk to him. But Samuel, when he finally discerned that this was the voice of God, replied with openness, "Speak, for Your servant hears."

Just like Samuel, we may find ourselves in situations where we do not hear the voice of God amid all the noise and distractions around us. Nevertheless, God lovingly searches for us, calling our name and asking us to hear His will.

When we intentionally allow ourselves to hear God's call, we put ourselves in the proper position to get His wisdom, direction, and purpose. Listening does not only involve hearing the voice of God but also developing a spirit of openness, obedience, and submission.

God's voice is manifested in diverse ways: through the Bible, prayer, counsel of others, and urging within our hearts. We must possess a receptive spirit that is responsive to His voice and prepared to answer with an affirming "Yes, Lord."

Prayer: Father in Heaven, thank You for not giving up on looking for me and calling me by name. Assist me in having an open and ready listening spirit to hear Your voice. Empower me to react in submission and surrender. Lord, speak for Your servant is listening. In Jesus' name, Amen.

Embracing Shiloh:

March 12: No Other Name

Scripture for the Day

"Therefore God exalted him to the highest place and gave him the name that is above every name, that at the name of Jesus every knee should bow, in heaven and on earth and under the earth, and every tongue acknowledge that Jesus Christ is Lord, to the glory of God the Father."

Philippians 2:9-11

The path of our Savior, who though in the form of God, chose not to cling to His divine privileges but emptied Himself, taking the form of a servant, has defined for us the epitome of spiritual elevation. It is not through grandiose acts or loud proclamations that we reach closer to God but through a surrendered heart, through quiet steps of service and humility, that we ascend to the heights of heavenly wisdom.

When the clamor for attention and recognition often overwhelms the whispered calls to serve, let us be reminded that our Lord Jesus Christ, by His humility, was exalted far above all powers and dominions. This great truth beckons us to follow in His footsteps, assuring us that when we bow our knees in service and lift our hearts in love, we reflect the majesty of His name.

Carry this treasure within you. The Highest became the lowest and, by doing so, was raised to the pinnacle of glory. It is a reminder that true honor is not in the crowns we wear on our heads but in the washbasin and towel in our hands—the symbols of servitude.

Prayer: Heavenly Father, In reverence, I bow my knee and heart before You, acknowledging that Jesus Christ is Lord. Instill within me a spirit of humility that I may seek to serve rather than be served. As Christ was exalted through His humility, may my life give glory to Your name in every word and deed. May the reflection of Your Son's sacrificial love be evident in my actions, and may my tongue rejoice in the confession of His Lordship. Help me to live out this truth daily, honoring You in the heights and the depths, now and forevermore. Amen.

March 13: Gods Big Bang

Scripture for the Day

"In the beginning, God created the heavens and the earth."

Genesis 1:1

Consider the magnificence of God's power: all that we see, all that we are, started with His divine utterance. The heavens are woven with starlight, the Earth adorned with vegetation, crafted meticulously by our all-powerful Creator. This fills us with awe and tells us of God's nature and His sovereignty over the universe.

It is from nothing that God brought forth everything. By His spoken word, the void was turned into vibrancy, setting into motion the workings of life itself. This speaks volumes about the boundless possibilities that reside in the unlimited nature of God. If from mere emptiness, the world as we know and marvel at was formed, how much more can God weave together the unraveled threads of our lives into a beautiful tapestry?

Let us start this day by acknowledging God's creative mastery and rest in the assurance that the same power that commanded light to shine out of darkness is at work in us, molding us, shaping our days, and guiding our destinies. In our beginnings and endings, let us see the fingerprints of the Almighty, trusting that His ways are perfect and His plans for us are good.

Prayer: Heavenly Father, Author of Creation, I stand in awe of Your magnificent power, as declared in Genesis, "In the beginning, God created the heavens and the earth." I thank You for the beauty of Your work, which speaks of Your glory and majesty. Lead me in Your wisdom to walk this day deeply trusting Your plan. May I surrender myself to You, confident that You who started the story of life itself will lovingly pen each chapter of mine. Use me for Your creative purpose, and let my life sing praise to Your holy name from this day forth and forevermore. Amen.

Embracing Shiloh:

March 14: Crucified with Christ

Scripture for the Day

"I have been crucified with Christ and I no longer live, but Christ lives in me. The life I now live in the body, I live by faith in the Son of God, who loved me and gave himself for me."

Galatians 2:20

To be crucified with Christ signifies more than mere association; it speaks of an intimate union with Him in His death and resurrection. This represents our dying to the old self—the purging of our sinful nature—and rising to a new life, one that is governed and given vitality by the Spirit of Christ within us.

This new existence is not based on observance of the Old Testament ceremonial Law or human effort but is a life lived by faith. Faith in the Son of God, who loves us passionately, who sacrificed Himself on our behalf, has offered us the priceless gift of redemption and the promise of eternal life. Every break of dawn thus becomes a testament to this new life, a daily opportunity to demonstrate His love living through us, a chance to glorify Him in thought, word, and deed.

As we journey through this day, remember that we are not just living. We live through and for Christ. Our faith in Jesus is the lens through which we experience every facet of life and are empowered to overcome the world.

Prayer: Heavenly Father, who has given me new life in Your Son, My heart echoes the words of Paul, "I have been crucified with Christ, and I no longer live, but Christ lives in me." I am grateful for the sacrificial love of Jesus, who loved me and gave Himself for me. Help me to live this day and all days, fully immersed in the faith of the Son of God. May my actions, my words, and my thoughts reflect Your life within me. Empower me to carry this treasure, this precious life of faith, with humility and strength, that in all things, You may be glorified through Jesus Christ. Amen.

March 15: Have You Not Heard?

Scripture for the Day

"Have you not known? Have you not heard? The LORD is the everlasting God, the Creator of the ends of the earth. He does not faint or grow weary; his understanding is unsearchable."

Isaiah 40:28

To acknowledge that the Lord is everlasting is to find comfort in the truth that He transcends time; He exists without beginning or end. As our Creator, He holds all creation within His sovereign will, yet He is intimately involved in the intricacies of our lives. This brings us face to face with the boundlessness of God's power as it intersects with His personal care for us. We are not roaming through the cosmos unattended. We are under the vigilant gaze of the One who neither slumbers nor sleeps.

The message in Isaiah reminds us that our God does not waver because of our exhaustion or faltering strength. He does not grow weary. His understanding is unfathomable, carrying the depth of our struggles and the breadth of our hopes. It is this God, the inexhaustible One, who offers to renew our strength, to lift us on wings like eagles, so we can run without weariness, and walk without fainting.

As we go through our day, let us cling to this promise: our limitations are met by His limitlessness. His enduring strength becomes our support in times when our strength fails.

Prayer: Lord, the Everlasting God, Creator of all, I take refuge in Your unchanging nature and draw strength from Your inexhaustible power. I place my finite understanding into Your infinite wisdom, trusting that You will not grow tired or weary in Your watch over my life. Teach me to rely on You and not on my own strength, to wait upon You for the renewal of my spirit. May I soar on the wings of Your eternal love throughout this day, carrying within me the assurance that You, the Everlasting God, are with me always. In Your mighty and precious name, I pray. Amen.

March 16: Embracing Discipline

Scripture for the Day
"My son, do not despise the Lord's discipline or be weary of his reproof."

Proverbs 3:11 (ESV)

In Proverbs 3:11, we are told not to despise the Lord's correction or despise His reproof. These profound words show us the loving character of our Heavenly Father.

We tend to get discouraged in the face of challenges or difficulties. Most of the time, we wonder why we should suffer or go through testing. As God's children, we are not beyond correction. Like an earthly father lovingly disciplines his children, our Father in heaven does the same for us.

Discipline is not God venting His fury. It is His deep love, which is His desire for our growth and maturity. In the same way, a loving parent corrects a child to keep him on the right track, God corrects and guides us to be the best that we can be.

Rather than hating or being angry at His discipline, let us accept it with open minds and hearts. When God disciplines us, it is a chance for self-improvement, conversion, and the strengthening of our personality. By discipline, we learn to depend on the wisdom, guidance, and power of God rather than our own weak knowledge.

Today, when faced with correction, remember the words of Proverbs 3: Accept the discipline and reproof of God as they contain many great lessons, wisdom. Look to see His constant love for us. May we let His teachings fill our hearts as we strive to grow spiritually, believing that His ways are perfect, and His plans are for our ultimate good.

Prayer: Heavenly Father, I am thankful for Your loving discipline and correction in my life. Assist me to accept it with humility and gratitude, understanding that it is a process for my development and change. Endow me with the patience to make my vows come true and the knowledge to understand what ails me. Let Your loving hand draw me nearer to Your perfect will for my life. In Jesus' name, Amen.

March 17: Come Home

Scripture for the Day

"So he got up and went to his father. But while he was still a long way off, his father saw him and was filled with compassion for him; he ran to his son, threw his arms around him and kissed him."

Luke 15:20

The prodigal son's homecoming is a compelling story of penitence and forgiveness. "That he rose and went to his father." In these few words are the essence of the gospel. The repentant son resolves to leave his life of ruin, walking toward the father. It is a trip we are all welcome to take. When we are lost and spiritually hungry, our Father is waiting to embrace us and accept us with joy.

Notice the father's response. He does not passively wait. He hurries out, full of mercy, closing the gap quickly, re-forming the attachment even before a word of confession can be uttered. This is the picture of God's proactive love—grace that out-pursues our wickedness.

The hug closes the son's arrival. It represents the recovery of a sense of identity, ownership, and love. Our Father is not only forgiving. He restores. He exchanges rags for garments of righteousness, dishonor for honor, and isolation for intimacy.

We are beneficiaries of this unconditional love as Christ's followers. While we were yet sinners, Christ, out of this same love, laid down His life for our redemption. No matter how far away we wander, the grace of God is enough to gather us back into His loving embrace.

This day is for us to ponder the love of the Father and His efforts to return the lost children back to Him. Let us all recall that His mercy is wide enough to reach the farthest distance.

Prayer: Dear Father, I am grateful to You for Your never-ending love and mercy. I am grateful that You, as My Father, readily accept and forgive me. Assist me to welcome Your grace afresh this very day and to share that love and forgiveness with others. The warmth of Your loving hug is my joy; it is my sanctuary and brings me strength. In Jesus' Name, Amen.

March 18: Embracing Gods Unfailing Love

Scripture for the Day

"Give thanks to the Lord, for he is good; his love endures forever."

Psalm 118:29

During the month of March, we are to meditate on the constant love of our Heavenly Father. He loves us for eternity, which never fluctuates or diminishes. It is too hard for us to understand.

Consider for a while the infinity of God's love. It is a love that goes beyond our blemishes, wrongs, and mistakes. It is the love that enters the depths of our hearts and whispers, "You are forgiven. You are loved. You are saved."

In case of doubt or difficulty, God's love remains constant. It's a refuge, a force, and a light. It includes our past, our present, as well as our future, assuring us that we are never alone.

We can connect to God's love without any condition and live it in our relationships with people. May we do to others as we would like to be done unto us. May the world see in our actions a taste of His infinite love that is beyond words.

Prayer: Merciful Father, thank You for Your eternally unconditional love for me. Help me appreciate and portray the intensity of Your love and portray it in my dealings with others. May You render gratitude in my heart, and may Your love shine out to the world through me as the light. In Jesus' name, Amen.

March 19: Trusting God's Timing

Scripture for the Day

"But they who wait for the Lord shall renew their strength; they shall mount up with wings like eagles; they shall run and not be weary; they shall walk and not faint."

Isaiah 40:31

When we push quickly for instant results, we have little patience to wait and let the other person handle the situation. But God wants us to have faith in His timing and patiently wait for His will to be revealed.

To wait is difficult and stressful. It demands that we give up our wants and let go of power. Nevertheless, the beauty of waiting is found in the growth and renewal that happens when we submit ourselves to God.

Through waiting on the Lord, we renew our strength. We take a higher vantage point like birds that soar high and find the will to endure. We can run the race of life with patience and walk unshakeable in faith, knowing that His plans are worth the wait.

Even though waiting may appear as a time of postponement, it is a period of preparation. God uses this period to mold us, purify our nature, and direct our hearts to His perfect desire. He is continually working in the background, arranging things for our benefit in the end.

If you are currently in a waiting season, be encouraged. Believe in the perfect timing of God. Relinquish your plans to Him and let Him lead your way. While you wait, search for His presence, increase your faith, and relax in knowing that He is faithful to His word.

Prayer: Oh Lord, teach me to have faith in Your time. Assist me to give up my will and intentions, understanding that Your ways are far above mine. Revive my power as I look on You and help me to be made stronger in faith while I am waiting. In Jesus' name, Amen.

Embracing Shiloh:

March 20: Gratitude in Every Season

Scripture for the Day

"Give thanks in all circumstances; for this is the will of God in Christ Jesus for you."

1 Thessalonians 5:18

Gratitude is an attitude that can potentially change our lives. Despite the struggle when facing challenges, it allows us to keep looking not to what we are missing but to the abundance of riches we already have.

Gratitude is not related to our actual circumstances but our view of them. It is the intentional act of recognizing that God is still good to us, even in the hard times or the worst of situations – a marvelous reality. Practicing gratitude allows us to welcome God's happiness and peace.

In every season, there are remarkable things to be grateful for. Whether it's the sight of nature, the feeling of love towards our family and friends, or the grace we experience day by day, whatever it is, try to learn to be grateful to our Giver, the source of all good things.

When we have plenty and more than enough, thankfulness makes us realize all the blessings come from above. That generates a gracious attitude. In difficult moments, gratitude shows us the way by providing comfort through His faithfulness and clinging to a ray of hope even amid darkness.

Today, imagine you with God and tell Him what you are thankful for today. In every situation, let this be our way of showing Him thanksgiving as an expression of our faith in His divine purpose for us.

Prayer: Jesus, Thank You for sending me countless blessings. Enable me to always be thankful whatever season it is, whether I am in a time of joy or a sorrowful situation. Attune my heart to accept adversity as a directly from Your divine authority and strategy in that very moment. In Jesus name, Amen.

March 21: Embrace Possibility

Scripture for the Day
"For with God, nothing will be impossible."

Luke 1:37

Entering the new day, we should allow our hearts and minds to open to the vast potential before us. This world will give us obstacles, challenges, and limitations. However, there are no borders for God. He is the Lord of possibilities that are endless.

Believe in the impossible today. Those dreams, hopes, and visions may seem too gigantic but do not forget that you are not alone in this journey. The Lord is with you, and when you have faith in Him, He can convert impossible to possible.

Pray and let God handle your worries and doubts. Let Him fill your soul with hope, courage, and steadfast faith. Welcome the unpredictable, as miracles often occur in the throes of unpredictability.

Bear in mind that the plans God has for your life are much more than your mind can envision. Do not fear to dream bigger and pursue those dreams with unflinching faith. The sky is the limit when it comes to God.

Prayer: Father in Heaven, I give You thanks as You are the God Who makes all things possible. Today, I hand over my doubts and fears to You, knowing that all things are possible with You. Infuse me with Your hope, boldness, and steadfast trust. Grant me the courage to accept the unseen and believe in Your will for my life. In Jesus' name, Amen.

Embracing Shiloh:

March 22: Embracing God's Rest

Scripture for the Day
"Come to me, all you who are weary and burdened, and I will give you rest."

Matthew 11:28

The importance of rest can easily be ignored in life's busyness and projects. We always get stuck in the whirlwind of responsibilities, running after productivity and success. However, God, in wisdom so infinite, calls us to rest.

Today, respond to Jesus' invitation to come to Him and find rest. He understands the weariness of our tired souls, heavy loads, and the need for rest and restoration. With Him, we find rest that restores our physical bodies and peace to our hearts and minds.

Consider your priorities and timetable. Do you have space for rest and recovery in your schedule? Keep in mind that rest is not a privilege but rather a need for our welfare. Rest is the time when we can meet God and receive His messages for our lives.

Embracing the rest of God is not only a physical rest; it is a conscious choice to believe in God's provision and let go of our cares and concerns to Him. It is a recognition that God is sovereign, and we can rest in His presence.

During your journey through today's requirements, do not forget to leave some time for recharging. Take refuge in God and let Him refresh your soul. Receive the gift of rest and know His perfect peace.

Prayer: Oh Lord, I come to You, worn out and worried, and seek Your rest. Assist me in placing rest at the top of my priorities and taking pleasure in Your presence. I shoulder my frets and fears to You believing You are in charge. Refresh my soul and give me Your peace. In Jesus' name, Amen.

March 23: Embracing Wisdom's Call

Scripture for the Day

"Get wisdom; develop good judgment. Don't forget my words or turn away from them."

Proverbs 4:5

The journey for wisdom is sacred. It is not just knowledge that we accumulate but the deliberate practice of God's truth in our lives. An aware heart understands that the wisdom of righteous living stands by the holy Scriptures.

Each word from God is a gift, a teaching that forms my personality, shapes my choices, and determines my fate. To lose His words would mean aimlessly wandering in the wilderness away from the very essence of life.

In the Hebrew tradition, wisdom is not just the enriching depth of the intellectual but the wise life according to the will of God. It's a wisdom that cries out in the public square (Proverbs 1:20), begging all listeners to accept a life lived according to God's moral values. The wisdom found in Proverbs encourages us to embrace God's truth and His rule over all creation, prompting an awe that is the foundation of all wisdom (Proverbs 9:10).

Prayer: Lord, in this peaceful moment, I listen to Your call to seek the valuable treasure of wisdom. Enable me to value Your words and plant them in the depths of my soul. Give me the wisdom that I may not simply gather truths but incorporate them into the very substance of my life. Your wisdom will lead my footprints so that I follow the path of righteousness. In every choice, O Lord, let Your voice be the loudest, and Your divine wisdom be the guide upon my way. In the name of Jesus, Amen.

March 24: Cultivating Forgiveness

Scripture for the Day
"Be kind and compassionate to one another, forgiving each other, just as in Christ God forgave you."

Ephesians 4:32

Forgiveness is the commitment of the heart to lift the load of resentment, to make a peace bridge where the gap of a fight has been. It is the decision that reflects the core of the divine, the true nature of the love Christ showed on the cross. In the limitless mercy of God, I receive not only the pardon I seek but also the power to forgive others.

To be kind and compassionate is a radical act of faith, proof of the nature of God's love. It pushes every part of who I am to move beyond instinctive responses and conform to the greater attractiveness of reflecting God's character that calls into my life.

The theme of the Bible consistently includes God's mercy and the pardon for sins, carried out in the New Testament by the most important sacrifice of Jesus Christ. We who receive grace that surpasses our works are urged to give this same grace to other people. It is not a passive forgiveness but an active and intentional decision to create fellowship cleansed by grace.

Prayer: Father of all, in Your silence, I recall that Your mercy is absolute. You pardon in a way so profound that it even touches the hardest of hearts. Lord, form my soul with Your mercy that I may see them as You do. Grant me the grace to forgive as freely as You have forgiven me, to sow kindness where bitterness might want to grow. Let the love of Christ be my light, and the Spirit empowers me to practice Your forgiveness in all my interactions. In the healing name of Jesus, Amen.

March 25: Abiding in the Vine

Scripture for the Day
"I am the vine; you are the branches. If you remain in me and I in you, you will bear much fruit; apart from me, you can do nothing."

John 15:5

Today's verse calls us to live in close relationship with Jesus. Abiding in Him means tying our own existence to His activating life.

In a similar manner, the branches receive their nourishment and power from the vine, and we should borrow from the fountain of love and truth of Jesus to grow in our spiritual journey. Our Savior stresses the futility of independently trying to bear fruit, leading us back humbly to the one true Source.

Let us think of the fruit that Jesus talks about. It is not only the outward works but the inward change of characters – love, joy, peace, patience, kindness, goodness, faithfulness, gentleness, and self-control. Such fruit is proof of dwelling in Jesus, living according to His will and objectives.

Today, let us persevere rather than be discouraged by the obstacles that bar our way. In turn, we should choose to lean in closer to the presence of Jesus, aware that without Him all our attempts are futile. In Him, we still can demonstrate His love and grace to the world and thus shine the beauty of the divine Gardener's handiwork.

Prayer: Father in Heaven, I approach You with a heart eager to dwell in Your Son, Jesus. Like the branch itself does not bear fruits, it reminds me that without Jesus, I cannot do anything. Feed my soul with Your Word, and let Your love run through me that I may bear abundant fruit. I pray in the name of Jesus, Amen.

March 26: New Creation

Scripture for the Day

"Therefore, if anyone is in Christ, the new creation has come: The old has gone, the new is here!"

2 Corinthians 5:17

Being "in Christ" is not merely about affiliation. It is about being enveloped in the very essence of the Savior's life, death, and resurrection. When we put our faith in Christ, we are not just improved versions of our former selves. We are completely new creations. Our past, with its failures, sins, and the old way of life, is not just erased—it is replaced. This is the insight Paul offers us: our identity is redefined, not refurbished.

Think back to a time in your life before you encountered Christ. Remember the feelings of emptiness, the quest for meaning, and the desperate attempts to heal the brokenness within. Now, imagine that heavy, old garment being lifted off and replaced with a garment of praise, woven with the threads of divine purpose and righteousness.

Our lives in Christ are characterized by continual renewal. As we grow in our relationship with God, the "new creation" in us is nurtured and flourishes. This does not mean that life becomes free of challenges but that our way of facing them is radically altered. We confront the world with the courage and hope that comes from our identity in Christ—not in our own strength, but in the power of the One who makes all things new.

Let us walk boldly, in the confidence of our transformed identity, reflecting the glory of our Creator with every step we take on this earth.

Prayer: Father, thank You for the miracle of new life in Christ. I acknowledge that in Him, I am a new creation—old things have passed away, and behold, all things have become new. Help me to live out this truth every day, to shed the old habits and thoughts that no longer serve me. By Your Holy Spirit, teach me to embrace the new nature You have bestowed upon me, to radiate Your love, and to move forward in the purpose You have for my life. In Jesus name, I pray. Amen.

March 27: Give Thanks

Scripture for the Day

"Praise the Lord. Give thanks to the Lord, for He is good; His love endures forever."

Psalm 106:1

To thank the Lord means to see His hand in all the facets of our lives, from a massive mosaic of creation to every small detail of our personal stories. It assures us that even in our sufferings, His goodness endures. It is an invitation to believe in His consistency and His endless grace.

God's love is our buoy. In responding to uncertainty, we can cling to this pledge and be content to know that His love is an enduring covenant with His people. We were saved by this divine love yesterday. We are carried today and will be guided tomorrow.

Let this truth resonate in your heart today: He loves always. No matter the changes that come your way, no matter how the world around you shifts, His love remains a constant, shining light in the darkness. Enjoy, relax, and let it guide you to be the source of all that is His.

Prayer: Lord God of heaven, I thank You for Your steadfast love. Thank You for Your mercy that endures throughout every season of my life. May my life stand as a witness to the love that never fails, a love that lasts forever. Enable me to represent this truth in a world that so desperately needs hope. I thank You with gratitude and sing Your holy name. Amen.

March 28: God's Provision

Scripture for the Day

"Therefore do not worry, saying, 'What shall we eat?' or 'What shall we drink?' or 'What shall we wear?' For after all these things the Gentiles seek. For your heavenly Father knows that you need all these things."

Matthew 6:31-32 (NKJV)

The expression "do not worry," is not only a recommendation. It is an opportunity to feel the reality of God's sovereign care. Jesus calls us to go beyond our immediate problems to accept a wider view, one that recognizes God's divine supervision of both the minute and the monumental aspects of creation. The way of the air and the flowers of the field exist without human anxiety, beautifully and are wonderfully sustained by the hand of God.

In the same way, we keep in mind our worth to God. If He is so attentive towards nature, will He not more so towards us, His children, created in His image? It calls us to move from the poverty of worry to the generosity of worship.

It is freeing that when we first seek the Kingdom of God and His righteousness, our perception of needs and resources is altered. The limitation is found as we start to realize that our Provider is immeasurably more than our need.

Today, let us intentionally put aside the questions which disturb our peace. Instead of them, let us pursue the presence of God and His Kingdom. In the process of enjoining our hearts with His, our worries begin to disappear, replaced by His supply and blessing.

Prayer: Father in Heaven, I leave my fears and troubles to You, trusting that You hold my life in Your hands. Pardon me for the times when I have relied on myself rather than Your hand to protect me. Assist me to search for the priority of Your Kingdom, believing that as I do, You will provide for all my needs according to Your riches in glory. Thank You for the peace that goes beyond human understanding and for the joy of living without worrying under Your loving care. In Jesus name, Amen

March 29: Pure Joy

Scripture for the Day

"Consider it pure joy, my brothers and sisters, whenever you face trials of many kinds, because you know that the testing of your faith produces perseverance."

James 1:2-3

In today's verse, James's statement to "consider it pure joy," during suffering may appear as a paradox. But the more we get into this idea, the more we find a deep reality. The happiness to hold is not in the hardships, but in the transforming process they cause. It lies in a joy built upon the assurance that our faith, when tried, will produce patience.

Endurance is more than mere survival; it is the sustained belief that flourishes despite hardships. Through long suffering, our character is polished, and our confidence in the Lord is strengthened. Just as gold is tried by the fire, so our faith is made strong in the fiery furnace of trials.

These are God's tools used to form you into Christlikeness. Accept this process, for within God's grand design, every thread of challenge is embroidered together with His golden threads for you.

Approach the throne of grace with glad hearts that are ready to receive the joy and the knowledge that all your trials are nothing but the testimony of your steadfast belief.

Prayer: Merciful God, today I bow to You, recognizing that I am oppressed in many ways. Assist me in perceiving them as joy, for I believe You are causing them to generate perseverance in my faith. Bestow on me the patience to bear, the fortitude to remain steady, and the insight to recognize Your activity in every problem. I am glad, not in the trials purely, but in the strength they build in me, making me more like Your Son, our Lord, Jesus Christ. Blessed be His holy name. Amen.

Embracing Shiloh:

March 30: Wisdom From Above

Scripture for the Day

"If any of you lacks wisdom, let him ask of God, who gives to all liberally and without reproach, and it will be given to him."

James 1:5 (NKJV)

How comforting it is that God's wisdom is just a prayer away! This Scripture is more than merely an offer of divine revelation; it is a strong call to dialogue with the Creator who desires to lead us.

The word "ask" suggests humility and need. Seeking wisdom from God is an admission of our shortcomings and a declaration of our belief in Him. It is an acknowledgment that real wisdom is not just a result of human reason but a gift of God that forms and re-forms our thoughts, choices, and behavior.

The spiritual truth here is profound: The wisdom of God is not scarce or grudgingly given. He bestows generously on all, without reproach. This quality of mercy part of the nature of God signifying how unlimited God's grace is – in spite of our ignorance and failure, He is willing to enrich us with heavenly wisdom.

Let's boldly come to God and ask for the wisdom we need. "You will receive," is the promise' – not might, not maybe, but what we ask for in faith is guaranteed.

While we look for His direction, let us be responsive to the still, small voice of the Holy Spirit and the subtle molding of our perceptions. May His understanding guide us on the road of virtue, aid in our trials, and assist us in solving the riddles of life.

Prayer: Father, I come before You now, recognizing that I need Your heaven-sent wisdom. I pray that You assist me with Your guidance. Lead my mind, my actions, and my way. Thank You for the pledge that You will give without hesitation or a taunt whenever I ask in faith. May Your light guide my path so that I may glorify You in all I do. Amen.

March 31: True Power

Scripture for the Day

"Again, truly I tell you that if two of you on earth agree about anything they ask for, it will be done for them by my Father in heaven."

Matthew 18:19, NIV

This promise talks about the oneness, consent, and the communal aspect of our faith. In the unity of prayer, where hearts are aligned, and spirits accord, we access a spiritual law—the corporate might of faith-filled appeal.

This Scripture speaks of the relational nature of God and His purpose for His Church. We are not individual believers but rather a family, a community founded on the love and sacrifice of Christ. Our Savior, in these passages, is explicit in His assertion that when we come into prayer in complete unity of purpose and desire, the God takes note.

It is a reminder that we are to carry each other's burdens from the Lord, to pray for one another, and to blend our voices in seeking His will. This understanding is not only a set of phrases but a symphony of hearts, pulsating with the same heavenly rhythm as we bring our petitions to the Father.

As we think about this promise, may we be deliberate in cultivating relationships that promote this kind of spiritual unity. Look for a group of believers among whom you can agree in prayer and then make your supplication together before the throne of grace.

Prayer: Lord of Heaven, I come to You believing and grateful for my brothers and sisters in Christ. I treasure the covenant that when we agree in prayer, You hear us. I desire to join with others in my community and pray that we all will do Your will. Teach us to pray as one, and let our prayer become a sweet sound in Your ears. Amen.

April 1: True Help

Scripture for the Day
"In the same way, the Spirit helps us in our weakness. We do not know what we ought to pray for, but the Spirit himself intercedes for us through wordless groans."

Romans 8:26

How wonderful is it that we are not left to navigate our weaknesses alone! Our inability to express the depth of our needs or the complexity of our situations is met with divine empathy and assistance.

This verse touches the core of our relationship with the Holy Spirit. The Spirit dwelling within us acts as our Advocate, our Helper, who perfectly understands the groans too deep for words. God's Spirit intercedes on our behalf, aligning our inarticulate longings with the will of the Father.

This active presence of the Spirit in our prayers signifies that our spiritual communication is not one way. It is a sacred dialogue where even our sighs and silent aches are understood and elevated to God. The Spirit translates the language of our heart into the language of heaven.

In acknowledging this, let us find solace in the fact that the Spirit takes our fragmented prayers, our wordless petitions, and presents them to the Father with divine eloquence. What an incredible gift of grace, ensuring that our prayers are always heard and always perfect in the ears of God.

Prayer: Lord, I come before You in gratitude for the gift of Your Spirit, who intercedes for me in my weakness. I confess that there are times when I do not know what to pray for or how to articulate the groans of my heart. Thank You for Your Spirit that translates my innermost yearnings into prayers that reach Your throne of mercy. I rest in the assurance that, through the Spirit's intercession, my prayers are heard perfectly by You. In the name of Jesus, I pray, Amen.

April 2: The One True Priority

Scripture for the Day

"You shall have no other gods before me."

Exodus 20:3

This command encourages us to reflect on what we enthrone in our hearts. Have we allowed the world to erect idols that distract us from our true purpose? The idols of our time may not be golden calves, but they can be just as ensnaring, manifesting themselves as obsessions with wealth, power, or even the vain pursuit of perfection.

The spiritual truth that underpins this Scripture is simple yet profound: God is to be our ultimate focus, the only One in whom we find purpose and meaning. In the Bible's teaching, to place God first is more than priority; it's exclusivity. It's a call to worship the one true God in a world filled with many false ones, both externally and internally. We are to worship and adore the Lord with all our heart, soul, and strength.

Daily life rushes by, but this sacred reminder halts us, encouraging a shift in perspective. To follow this command is to release the idols we have held onto and allow God to reign exclusively. When God is first, everything aligns with His divine love and will.

Prayer: Dear Lord, on this day You've graced me with, I come before You in humble adoration. Forgive me for the times I have placed other "gods" before You, distractions that have clouded my vision and path. Help me to recognize and relinquish these idols, turning my heart wholly towards You. Steady my spirit so that in every breath and decision, I honor You as my one true God. Guide me throughout this day to live in the fullness of Your love and truth. In Your holy name, Amen.

Embracing Shiloh:

April 3: Reward of Sacrifice

Scripture for the Day

"And everyone who has left houses or brothers or sisters or father or mother or wife or children or fields for my sake will receive a hundred times as much and will inherit eternal life."

Matthew 19:29

Jesus speaks of a divine principle that transcends earthly reason: the principle of godly return. The world tells us that to give is to lose, but Christ tells us that to give up for His sake is to gain immeasurably more. This gain is not merely in quantity but of a quality that outshines the very essence of material loss. When we prioritize Him above all, we do not just receive a return on our investments, we inherit eternal life. This inheritance is vast, pure, and imperishable, kept in the heavens for us who believe and trust in Him.

Our God is not unrighteous to forget the labor of love and the sacrifices made in His name. Every tear shed, every moment of loneliness endured, and every step taken in faith is cherished and accounted for by our Heavenly Father. The hundredfold return is not just a future hope but a present reality, as we find richness in relationships, depth in our spiritual walk, and a peace that the world cannot give nor take away.

As you walk through this day, remember that the God you serve sees the deepest desires and the sacrifices you make. And in His divine economy, nothing is wasted—every act of obedience is an investment in the Kingdom that cannot be shaken.

Prayer: Heavenly Father, I thank You for Your promises that carry me through times of sacrifice and surrender. Help me to keep my eyes fixed on You, trusting in Your Word that assures me of a hundredfold blessing and eternal life. I lay down my desires, comforts, and securities to treasure You above all. Lead me, guide me, and use me for Your glory. In Jesus' Name, Amen.

April 4: Conquerors

Scripture for the Day

"Who shall separate us from the love of Christ? Shall trouble or hardship or persecution or famine or nakedness or danger or sword? As it is written: 'For your sake we face death all day long; we are considered as sheep to be slaughtered.' No, in all these things we are more than conquerors through him who loved us."

Romans 8:35-37

These verses pose more than a rhetorical question. It's a declaration of our certain union with the love of Christ. Trouble will befall us, hardship is limitless, persecution haunts, famine strikes, exposure threatens, danger lurks, and the sword is lifted against us. But none of them are powerful enough to sever the threads with which Christ has bound our hearts.

The spiritual insight here is important. The love of Christ is not dependent on the stuff we are going through. Our life in Christ is immortal, going beyond all human sorrows and staying with us in the darkest night. The love of God revealed in Jesus is not only a consolation but an almighty power that delivers triumph out of close calls.

We are more than conquerors when we trust Him, who loved us. God never promised us a stress-free life, but we are sure His love remains steadfast in the storm. The love that held Jesus on the cross can hold us in the hand of God if we are faithful to Him.

Prayer: Lord God, here I come before You now with a thankful heart for the infinite love that You always show to me. In daily change and chaos, Your love is my constant certainty. In moments of abandonment, give me words of comfort that confirm the bond between Your love and me in Christ. Let this assurance give me courage and hope, knowing that whatever happens to me, Your love is my shield and strength. Thank You for loving me with a love that never ends. In Jesus' name, Amen.

Embracing Shiloh:

April 5: The Leaven of the Kingdom

Scripture for the Day

"He told them still another parable: 'The kingdom of heaven is like yeast that a woman took and mixed into about sixty pounds of flour until it worked all through the dough.'"

Matthew 13:33

Heaven's Kingdom, as portrayed by Jesus, is dynamic. In the same way that a pinch of yeast affects the whole batch of dough, the Kingdom of God works quietly in all directions. As the children of God, we carry this robust yeast within us—the core of divine truth, grace, and love, which can influence the world around us in amazing ways.

When I think about this parable, it seems that the unnoticed acts of mercy, the peace wishes, the moments of pardon and justice are like yeast in the dough. These are not slight or trivial. They are the agents of change, development, and growth of God's reign in people's hearts and in the world.

We should not be tired of doing good, for our lives are baked with meaning and possibility. We are a divine blend, and we are to rise and change the environment we are put in. May the promise of God's coming Kingdom inspires us to live out this life in bold and faithful acts while we await the complete revelation of God's glory—glory is already at work in us.

Prayer: O God, I am overwhelmed by Your Kingdom's deep mystery in this world. Let me be the leaven of Your divine, helping spread love, truth, and justice. Assist me in trusting in Your silent but sure growth of Your Kingdom within me. May I be humble and persevering in fulfilling Your will, knowing that even the most modest deeds done in Your name carries the seed of eternity. I pray in the mighty name of Jesus, Amen.

April 6: Last and First

Scripture for the Day
"So the last will be first, and the first will be last."

Matthew 20:16

This transforming principle calls us to view life through the gospel lens. It mirrors the heart of God who does not see as the world sees, who blesses not according to man's standards but according to His grace and divine prerogative.

This biblical truth, reminds us of the great love of our Father in heaven, inviting all of us, no matter our status or past, to participate in His Kingdom work. The gospel is not the result of the initiative of the lucky or worthy but is a free gift to everyone, regardless of when they come to believe.

The final first is not just the exchange of positions but an appeal to humility and awareness that in the realm of God, the virtues of service, sacrifice, and love that do not seek recognition are supreme. It is reassuring to those who feel unnoticed or underappreciated in this world.

Let's be comforted by the truth that the grace of God is infinite and sometimes reaches the unworthy and the unexpected ones. This should instill in us an urge to share our lives not in endless rivalry but in merciful coexistence, helping each other, and rejoicing in the promotion of the lowest.

Prayer: God of grace, Your ways are beyond our ways, and Your thoughts are beyond our thoughts. I am grateful to You for the reminder that in Your Kingdom, the last is no less important than the first. Show me how to live this Kingdom principle in my everyday relationships. Assist me to have a heart that rejoices for others, serves without seeking to be acknowledged, and loves without seeking reward. May I never forget Your grace that grants dignity and reverence to all, regardless of their worldly rank. In obedience and belief, I take into my arms Your inside-out Kingdom, where the lowly are lifted by Your loving hand. In Jesus' name, Amen.

Embracing Shiloh:

April 7: Urgency of the Moment

Scripture for the Day

"Be on guard! Be alert! You do not know when that time will come."

Mark 13:33

As I read the words of Mark 13:3, I picture the intimate setting of trusted friends seeking answers from Jesus. They were eager to know when the prophecies would come to pass and what signs would precede these divine events. Their sense of anticipation is palpable, a feeling that often mirrors our own as we await the return of Christ and the fulfillment of His Kingdom on Earth.

In this Scripture, we are transported to the Mount of Olives, invited into this private conversation with Jesus. He speaks of watchfulness and awareness, urging His followers to be on guard and to discern the times. The message then is as crucial now: the call to vigilant faith is not one of fear but of preparedness – to live lives that resonate with the gospel, to embody His teachings as we anticipate the eventual fruition of God's promises.

This anticipation doesn't mean we become prophets of doom or get lost in chasing signs; rather, it's a spiritual posture of readiness—keeping our lamps lit, our hearts pure, and our hands at work in His service. This readiness propels us to live each day with purpose, love, and with a steadfast hope.

In prayerful reflection, feel the Holy Spirit encouraging you to stay awake in spirit, discern the times, and most importantly, stay anchored in the truth and love of Jesus, which sustains you through seasons of waiting.

Prayer: God, You are the keeper of time, the author of history, and the fulfiller of prophecies. Teach me, Lord, to live in watchful anticipation, not with an anxious heart, but with a spirit attuned to Your presence. Help me to stay rooted in Your Word and quick to love and serve. In Jesus' name, I pray, Amen.

April 8: Receive Him Now

Scripture for the Day

"He came to that which was his own, but his own did not receive him. Yet to all who did receive him, to those who believed in his name, he gave the right to become children of God."

John 1:11-12

This passage is a light of hope indicating that our relationship with God is the light that goes beyond manmade boundaries and human logic. To "receive" and "believe" means more than a casual recognition. They constitute an active, purposeful acceptance of the truth of Jesus Christ, a welcoming of the heart and mind to the transforming love of God.

In the spiritual sense, to receive is an act of hospitality that we bid Christ to come into our lives. Our believing in His name is not simply acknowledging an idea but placing of trust, hope, and life in Jesus, the Word incarnate.

In Christ, we are provided with an identity which survives failure or disappointment. It is cause for daily feasting, a source of unending joy as children of our Father. His love sought us in our hours of despair.

We should walk with dignity in the quiet assurance of those who have been snatched by grace, called by love, and honored with the title of being God's own.

Prayer: Heavenly Father, I am left so astonished at Your grace. You have called me out of the darkness and into Your amazing light, allowing me to be called Your child. Instill this identity in me so that I become living proof of Your love and a testimony of Your forgiveness. Assist me to become a complete recipient and holder of my position in Your family today and every day. In Jesus' name, Amen.

April 9: Assurance

Scripture for the Day
"Turn to me and be saved, all you ends of the earth; for I am God, and there is no other. By myself I have sworn, my mouth has uttered in all integrity a word that will not be revoked: Before me every knee will bow; by me every tongue will swear."

Isaiah 45:22-23

Isaiah extends a universal invitation. It is an invitation that goes beyond geography, culture, and time restrictions. It is a call to salvation that is as broad as the horizon itself, calling all within its reach. "Turn to me," says the Lord, not as a tyrant but as a loving creator.

This verse declares there is one true God: "for I am God, and there is no other." In other words, it is a testimony of the Lord's uniqueness, His sovereignty, and His role as the sole initiator of salvation. When we look to Him, we are not only changing the direction of our eyes but also reshaping our whole lives toward the only real source of hope and salvation.

Repent signifies to rely on Him and His saving power. We must recognize that our works are inadequate, and that real salvation comes from the One who created the stars and established the Earth.

This holy call is rich with the compassion of the One who understands our labor and fear. Here, rescue is not all God provides. He offers friendship. He calls us into a lifelong communion based on the stability of His unchangeable nature.

Despite uncertainties and moving shadows, we should hold firmly to the truth that our God reigns supreme, and His salvation is certain for anyone who turns to Him.

Prayer: O Lord most gracious! Your call for salvation is being heard around the world, like the sound of a trumpet. I come to You looking for shelter, advice, and redemption in Your loving embrace. May Your Spirit direct me so that I will always encounter Your holy face. I pray in Your holy name. Amen.

April 10: Heart of Commitment

Scripture for the Day

"'Hear, O Israel: The Lord our God, the Lord is one. Love the Lord your God with all your heart and with all your soul and with all your strength. These commandments that I give you today are to be on your hearts."

Deuteronomy 6:4-6

This the core of the Jewish Shema prayer. It is not an admonition but a command to align every part of our being with the heart of God.

As we meditate upon this passage of the Scriptures, we understand that love is not a sentiment. Rather, it is an act of our will —a declaration to give our allegiance to God, laying all else aside. It causes us to ask what we like and what idols are competing for our time, money, position, or relationships.

To love God with all our hearts means that we recognize Him with all our emotions, where our dreams, fears, and loves are found. To love with all our soul implies a total devotion at our core, our awareness, the part that looks for meaning and relationship. At last, to love with all our might means the desire to serve God in all our deeds, sharing our means, abilities, and time with Him.

This passage is called the Shema, the Hebrew word for "hear" or "listen." Israelites stated their loyalty to Yahweh in these words, identifying their monotheistic faith in a polytheistic time. Early Christians saw in Jesus the embodiment of Yahweh's character, and Jesus Himself quoted this verse, elevating it as the greatest commandment (Mark 12:29-30). It is a fundamental principle which focuses believers in every age as they seek to center their lives in love for God above all.

Prayer: My Lord, today I accept Your great commandment to me, and I will endeavor to open all the chambers of my heart to You. Let my soul vibrate in Your divine tunes, and energy flows through my body to do Your wish. Amen.

Embracing Shiloh:

April 11: The Measure of Grace

Scripture for the Day
"Do not judge, or you too will be judged. For in the same way you judge others, you will be judged, and with the measure you use, it will be measured to you."

Matthew 7:1-2

The heart's measure I extend to others becomes the measure that will be returned to me.

The King of Glory, who could judge us with righteousness and give us justice, chooses instead to offer us grace upon grace! Reflecting upon this, I cannot help but be humbled, knowing how I have often fallen short of His glory, and yet, His lovingkindness is abundant. This pierces the core of our daily interactions. We should mirror the grace of the Father, embodying the patience and love that He bestows upon us.

Throughout the day, I encounter souls, each navigating their own intricate paths laden with struggle and joy alike. It is a divine calling upon my life to embody His teachings by exercising forgiveness and withholding harsh judgment. When I measure others, not by their fractures but by their potential in God's image, I participate in the transformative works of the gospel.

Let us then be imitators of Christ, using grace when we interact with our neighbors, family, and even strangers. Because the same measure we use will be measured to us—compelling us to sow seeds of mercy and compassion, expecting a harvest of the same in our times of need.

Prayer: Heavenly Father, my Rock, and Redeemer, let Your Spirit guide me to judge not with the eyes of the flesh but with the heart of grace. Infuse my spirit with Your love, that my judgments may be overshadowed by compassion and understanding. In Jesus' name, Amen.

April 12: Renewal

Scripture for the Day

"The steadfast love of the Lord never ceases; his mercies never come to an end; they are new every morning; great is your faithfulness."

Lamentations 3:22-23 (ESV)

It is in our nature to falter, to wander, and to sometimes feel completely overwhelmed by our circumstances. Yet, the promise found in this Scripture is a powerful testament to God's unfathomable love for us. This love is not just a mere emotion but an active, powerful force that keeps us from being consumed by our failures or the darkness that sometimes seems so pervasive.

The constancy of God's compassion reveals His unchanging nature. The same God who was compassionate during the times of the prophet Jeremiah is compassionate towards us today. In a world that constantly changes, our souls can take refuge in the knowledge that God's love is steadfast.

Today, hold this truth close as you are greeted with fresh mercies every morning. Yesterday's shortcomings are behind you, and before you lies a new day filled with the potential for grace to unfold in every moment. With each sunrise, every breath we draw is a testament to His endless compassion and deep abiding love.

Prayer: Gracious and loving Father, in the freshness of this day, I stand in awe of Your faithful love. Your compassions truly never fail, and Your mercies are new every morning; great is Your faithfulness! May I walk in this truth, letting the knowledge of Your unfailing love sustain me through my day. Help me to extend this same compassion to others, acting as a vessel of Your grace. Thank You for Your promises that are as sure as the dawn. In Jesus' name, I pray, Amen.

Embracing Shiloh:

April 13: Each Other in Love

Scripture for the Day
"Bear with each other and forgive one another if any of you has a grievance against someone. Forgive as the Lord forgave you."

Colossians 3:13

The call of forgiveness is not only an exercise of will, but it is a mirror reflecting the nature of God Himself—a God who forgives us freely and completely.

Paul's words call me to a deep appreciation that forgiveness is part of the Kingdom of Christ. It is an act of release, not only for the person who is forgiven but for the person who forgives, too. The challenge is not to ignore the wrong but to opt for a way that reflects the redemptive mercy that God manifested to us through His Son.

This command represents the gospel. In the same way, Christ has forgiven us, we are therefore expected to also show the same grace to others. I do realize depth of this truth – that forgiveness is an outpouring of Christ's love through us, evidencing our nature as His followers.

As I journey through today, the words of Colossians 3:13 teach me to be patient and meek. Forgiving is not only an obligation but a gift that allows me to wear the garment of Christ's love. In every encounter, let me remember that since I was forgiven much, I should also forgive.

Prayer: God, let your compassion and humility be upon me this day. Teach me to suffer gladly and to forgive as freely as You have forgiven me. Grant me the peace of Christ, which dwells in my heart. May I share the mercy You have given me to my neighbors. Thank You for Your immaculate example of forgiveness. Through Jesus Christ, my Redeemer, Amen.

April 14: Trusting in God's Guidance

Scripture for the Day
"Do not be afraid or discouraged, for the Lord God, my God, is with you. He will not fail you or forsake you."

1 Chronicles 28:20

In 1 Chronicles 28:20, King David gives his son Solomon a vision as he nears the end of his earthly reign. He puts his faith in the Lord's words, spoken through the prophet Nathan, that God "will build a house for me" (1 Chronicles 17:11). Now, as David's kingdom is nearing its conclusion, he recognizes that it's time to step aside and let Solomon follow through on this divine promise.

David's words to his son speak of a surrendered spirit. He recognizes that his time as the leader is ending and that he must let go. He affirms that he has not wronged nor rebelled in all that the Lord commanded him concerning the commandments that the Lord made gave him (1 Chronicles 28:7). Solomon reverently acknowledges the Lord as the God who executed great kindness and truth with his father David (1 Chronicles 28:20).

As believers we also have divine promises in our lives. We must be willing to let go of present blessings and allow God's promises to unfold according to His timetable. There are seasons in our spiritual walk where we must give way to our successors and learn to trust the Lord's continued faithfulness. Trusting Him is believing He still keeps His promises to us, whether it's about finances, situations, or those in our spheres of influence. Let's follow David's lead and surrender our scepter of authority to the right person as directed by God (1 Chronicles 28:4), knowing that God is preparing the way.

Prayer: Dear Lord, As I close this day, I come before You in quiet reflection and heartfelt gratitude. Thank You for the blessings You have bestowed upon me, the love that surrounds me, and the peace You promise. Amen.

Embracing Shiloh:

April 15: Near to the Seeking Heart

Scripture for the Day
"The Lord is near to all who call on him, to all who call on him in truth."

Psalm 145:18

God's nearness isn't a variable. It's an unchangeable truth for those who seek Him with genuine hearts. The simple but most profound truth is that we gain access to the universe's Creator by only calling to Him is amazing.

The nearness of God is not determined by our perfection but by our willingness to search for Him. It is not our polished prayers that make God come close to us but our honesty and sincerity in expressing our need for Him. In joy and sorrow, confidence, and doubt, in each moment, God is as near as His name.

The closeness to God is not a spatial but spiritual one. The God, who is spirit, is here with us, is part of us, and gives us strength, peace, and comfort. To search for God in truth means to come to Him with a sincere, open heart, revealing our deepest thoughts and emotions.

During our life, do not forget that the Lord is close to the seeking heart. If you murmur your prayers in the silence or scream them among people, He is there. Today, being aware of the proximity of God, let this knowledge encourage you to touch Him.

What truth do you hold today? For what do you need to invoke him? Find peace in the knowledge that He listens to you and is at your side. Be joyful in His loving presence, and let it bring you peace in your heart the whole day.

Prayer: Heavenly Father, I thank You for Your promises that carry me through times of sacrifice and surrender. Help me to keep my eyes fixed on You, trusting in Your word that assures me of a hundredfold blessing and eternal life. I lay down my desires, comforts, and securities to treasure You above all. Lead me, guide me, and use me for Your glory. In Jesus' name, Amen.

April 16: The Divine Perspective of Time

Scripture for the Day
"But do not forget this one thing, dear friends: With the Lord a day is like a thousand years, and a thousand years are like a day."

2 Peter 3:8

The apostle Peter reminds us of the eternal nature of God – time does not rule Him like it rules us. One day or a thousand years is the same for the eternal Lord. The perspective of God on time is bigger than ours, inviting us to wait for His perfect timing. That's because His plans are beyond the days on a calendar or the hours of a day.

Think about the incredible patience of God. Just as the Lord does not hurry His work with impatience, He does not slow it down in keeping His promises as we understand slowness. Our impatience comes from not comprehending God's grand, infinite plan.

In this, we hope. God, who is not tied to time, does not forget our lives, dreams, and prayers but rather holds them safely in His hands. Delay is not denial from the Lord. Instead, it is the time He ensures that everything perfectly accords with His plan. Your waiting is not a waste. It is a frame for God's perfect work done in due season.

This should help you build a stronger faith in trusting the timing of the Lord and live in worship instead of worry.

Rather than watching time, trust His words. Instead of time, watch for His acts. For with the Lord, time is always now and His intentions for you are always of peace.

Prayer: Everlasting God, make me aware of Your divine view of time. Assist me to have faith in Your timing, to trust in Your promises, and patiently wait for Your excellent plans to come to fruition in my life. If I get nervous about the earthy clock, please tell me that with You, a day is equal to one thousand years, and one thousand years is equal to a day. In Jesus' name, Amen.

April 17: Anchored in Love

Scripture for the Day

"And we have known and believed the love that God hath to us. God is love; and he that dwelleth in love dwelleth in God, and God in him."

1 John 4:16 (KJV)

God's love is not an opinion but a living, walking truth that has the power to mold and recreate our lives. This truth invites us into reflection, allowing us to feel a deep and close relationship with the source of all affection. God's love is limitless, pure, and unconditional beyond what our mind can fathom.

In the sea of trials and tribulations of life, it is easy to become restless and to feel unanchored and floating. But there is a truth, a steadfast anchor for our hearts, that can hold us firm amid the storm: God's love for us. Today, we reflect deeply upon this divine affection through the words of the apostle John in his first epistle: "And we have known and believed the love that God hath to us. God is love; and he that dwelleth in love dwelleth in God, and God in him" (1 John 4:16, KJV).

We are called not only to know the love of God but to believe in it. To understand God's love, is to see that God will never change or fail. Belief in the love of God is a trust that we lean into with all our weight, knowing that it is strong enough to carry us, no matter the burden that we bear.

Prayer: Heavenly Father, I thank You for making me a new creation in Your boundless love. Help me to live this day fully aware of my renewed identity in Christ. Guide my steps, my thoughts, and my actions so that they may reflect the transformative work You have done in me. May my life be a testament to Your grace and power. May I be a bearer of Your love to everyone I encounter. In Jesus' name, Amen.

April 18: Be Strong and Courageous

Scripture for the Day
"Have I not commanded you? Be strong and courageous. Do not be afraid; do not be discouraged, for the Lord your God will be with you wherever you go."

Joshua 1:9

This mighty guarantee echoes through the ages, of the infinite help we receive from our Creator. It is a calling from God to be strong and courageous while we confront daily problems.

It does no promise that there will not be hardship but assures us that God is with us throughout the hardships. When fear beckons to us from the future, when decisions threaten to suffocate us, when we stand at the very edge of transformation, shaken and unsure—these words strength our hearts.

Today, accept that you are not alone. May the courage that comes from God's presence in you overflow into all your life. Tasks you are facing and actions you will take are covered by His guidance and cover. You are armed not by your power but by the assurance that you walk with the Lord.

In every word, in every action, and in every silent thought, comfort is found in the strong hand of God that leads you. Let your heart be troubled by neither fear nor despair. Be strong and be brave, God's love will endure.

Prayer: God, thank You for the Your presence in my life. You empower me to be strong and courageous. Today, I look to Your commands, gaining strength from a well larger than myself that never runs dry. Fear and discouragement should not find a place in my heart as I believe in You and Your constant backing. Amen.

Embracing Shiloh:

April 19: Hope and Perseverance

Scripture for the Day
"But if we hope for what we do not see, we wait for it with patience."

Romans 8:25 (ESV)

Paul, the apostle, and writer of much of the New Testament, grasped that hope has its source in what is not visible. Hope that is visible is no hope at all, for real hope extends into the unseen, believing for what is promised but not yet received. That is where the plant of patience grows – in the gap between a promise and fulfillment.

This patience is not passive acceptance but active patience. Christianity sees patience as steadiness, a virtue that Paul asks the believers to clothe themselves with as they await the glorious future of God.

This verse emphasizes a key element of Christian salvation – the "already but not yet" tension in which believers reside. We are already saved, but we expect the perfection of our salvation; we are already God's children, but we await the union with Him. This hope is what sustains our patience, as it finds its roots in the unchangeable promises of God, who cannot disappoint or fail.

Prayer: God Almighty, I appreciate You for the hope that stabilizes my soul in oceans of doubt. In moments of tiredness, let me remember that the object of my faith, even if not seen, is being woven into my story by Your faithful hands. Impart to me a heart of enduring patience in that I might abide with a spirit, not of sluggishness but of hope. Let my life mirror the patience of Christ, who did not even say a word when crucified for the sake of the joy that was set before Him. Let this day be proof of the faith I have in You and the patience You are growing in me. I trust in Your Word, and until the day they come true in totality, I patiently wait with a joyful heart. Amen.

April 20: Midst of Scarcity

Scripture for the Day
> "Though the fig tree does not bud and there are no grapes on the vines, though the olive crop fails and the fields produce no food, though there are no sheep in the pen and no cattle in the stalls, yet I will rejoice in the Lord, I will be joyful in God my Savior."
>
> Habakkuk 3:17-18

Habakkuk, faced with the destruction and desolation of his people, still makes a profound declaration of faith. This verse is a loud and clear voice of a religion that overcomes circumstances, of a joy that does not depend on the external but rather is rooted in the eternal.

Habakkuk could be glad, for he knew that joy was not with the current situation but with the presence of the Lord. This is the anchor for every believer: Our joy is based not on the shifting sands of this world but on the unchanging character of God. We are glad not because our lives are always comfortable but because our God is always true.

Joy is a form of defiance that helps to push away the despair easily found in our spirits. It is a spiritual discipline to find joy when the olive does not blossom, and there are no grapes on the vines. This type of joy declares faith in God's salvation and sovereignty. We proclaim that ours is a God who is worthy of praise even when the fig tree does not shall forth, nor fruit in the vines.

Prayer: Lord my God, in trials, I prefer to hold on to the joy that You give, never failing and not dependent on my situations. Through faith, I repeat the words of Habakkuk and confess that I will be glad in You. My soul shall rejoice in the God of my salvation. Empower me with Your happiness when the way is doubtful, and the crop is wasted. Your love is constant, and an undying love. Let my spirit fly to Your deliverance, and let my heart glorify Your name. May my life be the witness of the joy that You have prepared for me. I pray in the precious name of Jesus, the Lord, my Savior. Amen.

Embracing Shiloh:

April 21: Our Spirit

Scripture for the Day
"Blessed are the poor in spirit, for theirs is the kingdom of heaven."

Matthew 5:3

To be "poor in spirit does not describe the state of material impoverishment but rather a profound spiritual stance. It is a note of humility and an acceptance of our total reliance on God. It is an attitude of realizing that we are spiritually bankrupt and that our Heavenly Father is full of grace and mercy.

In a world that clamors for autonomy and respect, Jesus calls us to claim the contrary. He beckons us to approach Him in humility, recognizing our need for His forgiveness, direction, and renewal. Aware of our spiritual poverty, we become receptacles of the abundant blessings and inheritance of the Kingdom of heaven.

The status of being poor in spirit is the way to get rid of our pride and independence. It releases us attempts to succeed in God's eyes by our own actions and accomplishments. Rather, we submit our lives to God, in the understanding that it is His grace that allows us to exist, His love that changes us, and His Kingdom that satisfies the deepest cravings of our souls.

In addition, Jesus does not just bless the poor in spirit but calls them to the Kingdom of Heaven. By losing our pride and self-sufficiency, we are made heirs of a realm that is worth more than all earthly treasures. In the Kingdom of God, the last becomes first, the weak become strong, and the humble find exaltation.

Prayer: God, thank You for Your presence in my life. You empower me to be strong and courageous. Today, I admit my poverty and my need for You. I believe that only by doing so can I receive the Kingdom You promise for me. Amen.

April 22: Seek and Embrace

Scripture for the Day

"Wisdom is the principal thing; therefore get wisdom. And in all your getting, get understanding."

Proverbs 4:7

This compelling advice tells us of the foundational role of wisdom has in guiding us. Wisdom, according to the Bible, isn't mere knowledge or intellectual capacity. It's a practical understanding that aligns our lives with God's will and purpose. It is the principal thing, a treasure surpassing wealth, that guides us to live rightly, justly, and humbly before our Creator. The spiritual insight intertwined here is vital: to live wisely is to live in harmony with the divine order of things under the instruction of the Almighty.

We are urged to actively pursue wisdom — not passively wait for it to descend on us. Scripture underscores that obtaining wisdom comes at a cost. It may cost us our pride, our time, and our reliance on human understanding. But the return on this investment is life itself. To prize wisdom is to be molded to the image of Christ, the wisdom of God in the flesh (1 Corinthians 1:24).

Prayer: Most gracious Lord, Your Word teaches me that wisdom is the principal thing. With open hands and a willing heart, I come before You, seeking the treasure of Your wisdom. Though it may cost me all I have, empower me to understand Your truths and apply them to my life. For in gaining wisdom, I walk closer with You, my God, who is wisdom incarnate. May my actions reflect the discernment You bestow, and my decisions bring glory to Your name. In Jesus' name, Amen.

Embracing Shiloh:

April 23: Abundance Beyond Possessions

Scripture for the Day
"Then he said to them, "Watch out! Be on your guard against all kinds of greed; life does not consist in an abundance of possessions."

Luke 12:15

In the noise of our consumer world, we hear an invitation to a different way of life in the Gospel of Luke. This verse is an anti-materialism sentiment, telling us to desire not the growth of objects but the wealth of life in Christ.

God's wisdom blooms in the words of Christ, showing that our life's worth is not calculated by riches or prosperity. Jesus opposes the world's notion of abundance with the Kingdom reality of genuine abundance, resting in our relationship with God and others. We do not measure our value in physical assets but in spiritual wealth – love, joy, peace, and righteousness in the Holy Spirit.

In a society that is spellbound by the allure of more, Jesus's warning is as pertinent now as it was over two thousand years ago. Greed, the eternal hunger for more, can sneak into our hearts and take us away from the virtues of satisfaction. However, we as disciples of Christ, are to live lives of simplicity, generosity, and faith in God's care.

Prayer: Heavenly Father – the keeper of all wisdom, protect my heart from the dangers of greediness and the wrong security of possession. I desire to live the life that is truly life – a life of satisfaction, thankfulness, and reliance on You. Aid me in recollecting that my worth comes only from You and that real satisfaction is to be found not in the too much of things but in the plenty of Your face. Teach me to be truly alive, giving largely, and loving openly. Thank You for meeting all I need in line with Your riches in glory. Shall I lay up treasures in heaven, where they are safe and eternal? I pray in the name of Jesus. Amen.

April 24: Experiencing God's Compassion

Scripture for the Day
"Jesus had compassion on them and touched their eyes. Immediately they received their sight and followed him."

Matthew 20:34

In the rhythmic cadence of the Gospel of Matthew, we encounter a tender moment that captures the essence of Jesus' ministry. Within today's verse lies a profound narrative of healing and discipleship extending beyond physical sight to spiritual enlightenment.

The deeper insight here is the transformative power of Jesus' compassion. The Greek word used for "compassion" in the New Testament speaks of a deeply moved inward affection, a stirring of the soul that compels one to action. Jesus' compassion wasn't a mere feeling. It led Him to touch, to restore, to heal. His miracles were acts of love that brought wholeness not just to bodies but to lives.

Encountering Jesus and receiving His touch changed everything for these two blind men. They didn't just regain their physical vision. Their spiritual eyes were opened as they gained a new perspective and a purpose. They followed Him - a response of faith and discipleship.

This narrative invites us to reflect on how we, too, are recipients of Jesus' compassionate touch. Through His grace, we are called out of spiritual blindness to see life, ourselves, and others through the lens of His love and truth.

Prayer: Lord Jesus, Your compassion is a wellspring of healing and hope. As I meditate on the way You restored sight to the blind, I am reminded of Your tender mercies that are new every morning. Touch my heart, O Lord, that I may see Your grace at work in my life and be moved by compassion to serve others. Open my eyes to see the world as You see it, filled with people needing Your love and forgiveness. May Your love flow through me, bringing light to those who walk in darkness. In Your loving name, I pray. Amen.

April 25: Embracing the Light within Us

Scripture for the Day

"And this is the condemnation, that the light has come into the world, and men loved darkness rather than light, because their deeds were evil. For everyone practicing evil hates the light and does not come to the light, lest his deeds should be exposed."

John 3:19-20 (NKJV)

This verse reflects that human nature avoids light when not in it. The light is the symbol of the holy and just character of God that, through its purity, exposes the imperfections and sins in our lives. Sin hates exposure. Truth is a powerful antiseptic.

Jesus came as the light of the world. His presence demands a decision: Will we walk in the light and change, or will we slink into the darkness of denial and sin? By accepting God's light into our lives our sins are taken away by His mercy.

The beauty of the light of Christ is that it is not just exposure. It heals and reforms. When we decide to walk in His light, we are set apart for God, constantly polished and renewed.

Prayer: Heavenly Father, we are grateful to You for Your light shining upon us, pointing out the areas in our lives that need Your touch. Teach me to live a transparent life before You, Lord, not being afraid of the light, but rather finding it necessary as You transform me. Give me the courage to leave the darkness of sin and to walk in the light of Your holy Word. Let Your light cover my body, light my path, renew my mind, and bring me to wholeness and peace. I long to linger in Your light, enjoying the heat of Your love and the liberty of Your forgiveness. I pray in the mighty name of Jesus. Amen.

April 26: True Riches in Christ

Scripture for the Day
"Then he said to them, 'Watch out! Be on your guard against all kinds of greed; life does not consist in an abundance of possessions.'"

Luke 12:15

Jesus provided insightful teaching that cuts through materialism in the Gospel of Luke, opening a world that stretches beyond earthly possessions. Jesus alerts us that real life, fulfilled life, has nothing to do with the hoarding things of the world and all to do with the treasure within us.

We are to think deeply about our values. Jesus' rebuke against greed is simple yet radical. It goes to the heart of what society teaches us is crucial. In the Kingdom of God, plenty is not determined by things but in the riches of relationships, our link with God and people, as well as in the virtues we practice, such as love, kindness, and generosity.

Jesus is not warning us against wealth so much as showing us a richer wealth that cannot be affected by economic crunches or even taken away by thieves. It is the endless riches that are discovered in the process of seeking God's righteousness and serving our neighbors. When our hearts are set on these eternal investments, we find satisfaction that is beyond understanding.

Prayer: Father in heaven, I bow before You. Direct my heart towards the everlasting treasures that You prize—love, joy, peace, and righteousness in Your Holy Spirit. Aid me in avoiding the attraction of material things instead of locating my worth in my relationship with You and those You have entrusted me with. May my life be an example of real wealth coming from the heart at peace in You, a heart that gives love and good deeds abundantly. In the mighty name of Jesus, my real treasure, Amen.

Embracing Shiloh:

April 27: Persistent in Prayer

Scripture for the Day

"Then Jesus told his disciples a parable to show them that they should always pray and not give up."

Luke 18:1

Jesus is teaching us a crucial lesson concerning the nature of prayer and our relationship with God. He understands the trials we experience in our everyday existence—the irritations, the tedium, the silence that may return to mock us. Nevertheless, He advises us to keep the attitude of perpetual communication with the Father.

Prayer is not to be a routine religious practice. Rather, it is an act of faith that shows we trust God's timing and perfect will. It's coming to the foot of the throne of God, like the widow who persevered to that unjust judge until she received justice. If an unjust judge can grant what the widow asks, how much more will our just and merciful Father in heaven care for His children that cry out to Him day and night?

This a call not to be discouraged when delays are encountered. Our prayers are not just some words left in the air. They are a conversation with the living God who listens, who is concerned, and who moves. It becomes evident that God's timeline is different from ours. Prayer keeps our hearts aligned with His will, shapes our nature, and prepares us for the blessings yet to come.

Prayer: God, I stand before You with appreciation for the gift of prayer. Assist me to pray so that I will not only endure in prayer but also do so even when there seems to be delay or doubt. Grant me the power to rely upon Your perfect timing, knowing that Your will toward me is only good. When my spirit becomes tired, refresh me with Your Holy Spirit and remind me of Your promises. I ask this in the holy name of Jesus Christ, Amen.

April 28: He Is Strong

Scripture for the Day

"But he said to me, 'My grace is sufficient for you, for my power is made perfect in weakness.' Therefore I will boast all the more gladly about my weaknesses, so that Christ's power may rest on me."

2 Corinthians 12:9

Each sunrise reminds us of God's renewing mercies and His sustaining grace. It's in our nature to shy away from our weakness, to hide them from the world. But God invites us to an opposite approach. In 2 Corinthians 12:9, we find an intimate exchange between the apostle Paul and the Lord.

This Scripture pierces the facade of self-reliance that we often erect. Paul had pleaded for his thorn in the flesh to be removed, yet God's response was not liberation from the affliction but provision within it. God's grace doesn't always take away the challenges. Instead, it operates through them, transforming our insufficiencies into channels for His power.

God's power is completed and displayed gloriously in our weaknesses. When we are weak, when we come to the end of our resources, we find God waiting—ready to extend His strength. It is a divine paradox that in our inadequacy we become a showcase for His great power.

Instead of incessantly striving for self-improvement, we are to embrace our frailty, knowing that it leads us to depend more on God. This dependence isn't passive; it's an active, daily trust that God is enough for the day.

Prayer: Lord, I confess how often I've tried to mask my weakness, foolishly believing that I must be strong in myself. Thank You for the truth that Your grace is sufficient for me and that Your power is made perfect in my weakness. Help me to embrace my limitations and openly admit my need for You, knowing that it is in surrendering these to You that Your grace abounds. In the name of Jesus, who is my strength, Amen.

Embracing Shiloh:

April 29: Clothed in Christ's Compassion

Scripture for the Day
"Therefore, as God's chosen people, holy and dearly loved, clothe yourselves with compassion, kindness, humility, gentleness, and patience."

Colossians 3:12

This verse is not just instruction. It is a declaration of our new identity in Christ. As believers, we are called chosen, set apart for a divine purpose, and enveloped in God's enduring love. Embracing this identity means allowing these virtues to permeate our every action and reaction.

The richness of this text lies in the concept of sanctification. It suggests that after having been reconciled to God through Christ, there is a practical outworking of that reconciliation in our lives. We are to actively put on the character of Christ. The virtues, compassion, kindness, humility, gentleness, and patience are the garments befitting the redeemed, a wardrobe that announces our new allegiance and transformed nature.

This metaphorical clothing does more than cover; it reshapes who we are. To "clothe ourselves" with these qualities requires daily commitment, a purposeful decision to embody the life of Jesus in front of a watching world. The Spirit enables us as we choose to live this out.

In this world that often prizes power and self-promotion, these Christlike garments may seem out of fashion, yet they carry eternal value and are honored by our Father in heaven. Let us, therefore, dress ourselves intentionally with these, reflecting the beauty and grace of Him who called us out of darkness into His marvelous light.

Prayer: Gracious God, I am deeply grateful for being chosen, holy, and dearly loved by You. I ask You to guide me as I strive to clothe myself in compassion, kindness, humility, gentleness, and patience. May these virtues not only adorn me but also transform me into a clearer image of Your Son, Jesus Christ. As I interact with others today, let them see the beauty of Your grace reflected in my actions and words. Strengthen me by Your Spirit to make choices that honor You and display the work You are doing in my life. I pray this with a heart full of joy and thankfulness. In the name of Jesus, Amen.

April 30: Experience Christ's Peace

Scripture for the Day
"Peace I leave with you; my peace I give you. I do not give to you as the world gives. Do not let your hearts be troubled and do not be afraid."

John 14:27

In John 14:27, Jesus imparts a tranquil assurance to our restless hearts. This is not a peace that depends on circumstances or the transient offerings of the world. The peace that Christ gives can steady the heart even amid stormy trials. It is a peace that surpasses natural understanding—a deep, abiding sense that we are in the hands of the Almighty.

This peace that Jesus speaks of is a component of the Kingdom of God established within us. It is a fruit of the Holy Spirit, part of the new covenant blessings, and a testament to the living hope we have in Christ. As believers, we are not promised a life free of trouble, but we are granted a peace that can endure through every trouble.

Christ's words also carry an imperative: "Do not let your hearts be troubled, and do not be afraid." It is a call to faith, to trust in the care of God, to rest in the truth of His Word, and to let His peace rule in our hearts. When fear and anxiety knock, we need only remember His promise and the price He paid so that we might have peace—His very life.

Prayer: Lord Jesus, Your peace is a precious treasure, a calm amid life's storms. Thank You for giving me a peace that the world cannot provide. Let Your tranquil presence infiltrates my heart so that I may not be troubled or afraid. Help me to trust in You and to guard this divine peace as a sentinel, knowing that it is a gift from You—a testament to Your love and victory. Through Your Spirit, remind me continually that You are with me, and Your peace is mine to claim and share. In Your holy and comforting name, I pray, Amen.

Embracing Shiloh:

May 1: Unwavering Presence of God

Scripture for the Day

"Be strong and courageous. Do not be afraid or terrified because of them, for the LORD your God goes with you; He will never leave you nor forsake you."

Deuteronomy 31:6

In the unending pendulum swing of life, we look for a stronghold that can hold our faint heart. Deuteronomy 31:6 offers such a place. Moses addressed these words to Israel while they were on the verge of entering the Promised Land, a place of uncharted challenges and opportunities. In these sacred covenantal directions, we are called to remember that strength and courage are not our own, but flow from the presence and promises of God.

The insight here is powerful: our God is not far off. He is Emmanuel, God with us in every tribulation and victory. Strength and courage are not just the willingness to withstand outside adversity but also the ability to defeat the internal giants of fear and anxiety.

It is not the size of the wall that we see in front of us but the fact that our God is with us. This security releases us from fear and allows us to confront each day with assurance that we are not confident in ourselves but in God Himself, who never changes and His love which never fails.

Prayer: Lord God Almighty, I read Your words in Deuteronomy and put them in my heart. Give me the power and the courage which I get from knowing You are with me. Allow me not to be paralyzed by fear but carry on in faith, believing in Your presence, which abides with me, Your hand, which leads me, and Your love, which clutches me. Thank You for Your assurance of never leaving nor forsaking Your children. Even as I navigate the changes of life, may the staying power of Your steadfastness be my greatest source of comfort and hope. I pray in Jesus' mighty name. Amen.

May 2: Radiant Hope in Christ

Scripture for the Day

"I have told you these things, so that in me you may have peace. In this world you will have trouble. But take heart! I have overcome the world."

John 16:33

Jesus offers us a great promise in John 16:33, like a light at the end of the tunnel. The promise of Jesus is not a life without trouble. Rather, it is peace and victory amid tribulation. It is the foundation of the message – the peace of Christ is not the absence of troubles but the presence of Christ Himself.

Anchoring a mighty spiritual truth, this verse captures the message of triumph that Jesus has won. It is a triumph we cannot achieve ourselves but as part of Him. The world and its tribulations are not vanquished by our strength but by Christ's finished work at the cross. In Him, we have an unwavering peace that is never determined by earthly happenings but established on divine assurance.

To take heart is to have confidence, that is only achievable through our association with Christ. Adversities can be faced by believers with another spirit, a sacred assurance arising from the fact that we are the people of the One who has defeated sin and death.

While carrying out our everyday activities, we should adopt this peace that Christ gives. We should bear in mind that no matter what challenge we face, we do so with the great certainty that Christ has conquered, and in Him we have too.

Prayer: Lord Jesus, I cling to the promise You have given in John 16:33. You are my constant peace. Thank You for conquering the world and giving me the strength to live every day in hope. In Jesus's name, I pray, Amen.

Embracing Shiloh:

May 3: Aligning with God's Kingdom

Scripture for the Day
"Your kingdom come, your will be done, on earth as it is in heaven."

Matthew 6:10

To pray for God's Kingdom to come is to desire above all else that His righteous, perfect, and holy order as it is in heaven would visible here on earth. It is to prioritize His will over our plans, His majesty over our desires, and His authority over our autonomy.

This verse captures the essence of the Christian life. It is God-centered, not self-centered. The Kingdom of Heaven is marked by what God deems good, right, and true. We as His followers align ourselves with this divine reality. Jesus teaches us that to truly follow Him means to yearn for what He yearns for—to set our hearts on the advancement of His reign and rule in every corner of creation, especially our own hearts.

When we pray, "Your will be done," we are releasing control, acknowledging that God's wisdom surpasses our understanding. We are admitting that the Almighty God of the universe knows better than we do what needs to happen in our lives and our world.

As we recite these words Jesus taught us, let us recommit daily to being agents of His Kingdom, ambassadors of His will, and vessels for His purpose. May our lives resonate with the heartbeat of Heaven, eager for His plans to unfold.

Prayer: Heavenly Father, I humbly come before You today, echoing the words Your Son taught us to pray. Let Your Kingdom come, let Your will be done on Earth, in my life, as it is in Heaven. Align my desires with Yours, shape my actions to reflect Your righteousness, and use me as a conduit for Your divine purposes. Grant me the grace to trust in Your perfect will, knowing that it is good, pleasing, and complete. In the precious name of Jesus, I present this prayer. Amen.

May 4: A Christ-Centered Journey

Scripture for the Day
"Let all that you do be done in love."

1 Corinthians 16:14 (ESV)

In the hustle and bustle of our daily tasks, where actions often speak louder than words, we find a powerful directive in 1 Corinthians 16:14.

In this terse but powerful verse, the apostle Paul give direction to the Christian life in a simple injunction. It is an invitation to love in all our deeds, words, and thoughts. Love, God's definition of love, is not just a feeling but an act of will, a life decision to care for others, representing the selfless love of Christ.

In the New Testament, love is a distinguishing feature of a made-over life in Christ. It is the first fruit of the Spirit, the new commandment of Jesus, and the perfect fulfillment of the law. Paul exalts love as the king of virtues, without which all our pursuits, no matter how noble and well-intentioned, are turned into nothing.

Doing all things with love means that our everyday encounters are permeated with the grace and mercy of Jesus. Our service is not driven by the desire for accolades or payment but by sincerity for the well-being of others. It is the response to every act, big or small. Love is the power that compels and steers us.

As we continue with our daily activities, let's cling to this call. May love be the filter through which we see every situation and the gauge by which we measure our reactions. By embracing this love-oriented approach, we resemble the One who is love made flesh and who extends His hand to a world that is in dire need of His touch.

Prayer: Heavenly Father, I am grateful to You for Your love that I cannot measure and that You showed us in Your Son, Jesus. Lead me with the will and power to do all in love today. May Your Spirit lead my deeds, my words, and my thoughts so they may be a picture of Your love. In the name of Jesus, Your ultimate love, Amen.

May 5: Shining Light in the World

Scripture for the Day

"Let your light shine before others, that they may see your good deeds and glorify your Father in heaven."

Matthew 5:16

Jesus here calls us to be lights in a world that often dwells in shades of grey. The light He speaks of is not our own; it is the radiance of the Spirit within us, the unquenchable kindling of divine grace and love.

To "let your light shine before others" is an active statement. It's an encouragement with a responsibility. We're to live out our faith visibly, not as a loud proclamation meant to draw attention to our piety, but as a soft, steady brightness that guides others towards the heart of the Father. Our deeds become the beams that break through the darkness. Each act of kindness, each word of truth, each decision made in love should reflect the light of Christ.

This verse is central to the Christian witness. It's a reflection of missional theology that asserts believers are called to not just partake in salvation but to partake in the mission of God. Our good works are not the grounds of our salvation but the fruit of it. By participating in God's redemptive plan for the world through our actions, we mirror His character, leading others to experience His love and grace.

Prayer: Heavenly Father, ignite within me the holy flame that burns away pretense and sets my soul ablaze with Your pure light. Help me to embody the teachings of Your Son so that my life may be a testament to Your unfailing love. I pray that through my actions, people may glimpse Your glory and be drawn to You. Thank You for entrusting me with the mission to shine brightly in a world that needs Your light. Amen.

May 6: Children of God

Scripture for the Day

"See what great love the Father has lavished on us, that we should be called children of God! And that is what we are!"

1 John 3:1

Pause for a moment and ponder the vastness of God's love. It is not a love that can be measured but one that is poured out lavishly upon us. This profound love is freely given, transcending our understanding, so much so that we are graced with the most endearing term of relation: children of God.

Being called children of God signifies an intimate and personal relationship with the Creator of the universe. It's an assurance that goes beyond mere titles; it's an identity woven into our very existence. As His children, we're endowed with an inheritance, a promise of eternal life, and the promise of a perpetual place in God's loving presence.

The apostle John is emphasizing the radical nature of God's love. In ancient times, the notion of God as a "Father" marked a revolutionary shift from the more distant deities of surrounding cultures. Moreover, the concept of humans as "children" of God implies that the connection between God and believers is inherently relational. It underscores the grace that is integral to Christian belief. As God's children, we are called not only to receive this love but to embody it, to extend this same lavish grace to others.

Prayer: Abba, Father, my heart swells with gratitude for the immeasurable love You have bestowed upon me. You have called me Your child, and in that calling, You have given me value and worth that surpasses all understanding. Help me to live confidently as a reflection of Your love, to walk in the righteousness that befits Your heir, and to extend Your grace to those whose lives intertwine with mine. In Jesus' name, Amen.

May 7: Hosanna to the Son of David

Scripture for the Day
"The crowds that went ahead of him and those that followed shouted, 'Hosanna to the Son of David!' 'Blessed is he who comes in the name of the Lord!' 'Hosanna in the highest heaven!'"

Matthew 21:9

The triumphal entry of Jesus into Jerusalem stands out as a moment of jubilant prophecy fulfilled and the foretaste of a victory that would forever alter the spiritual landscape.

The word "Hosanna," was originally a plea for salvation, meaning "save, please." Yet, in the mouths of the expectant crowd, it became a shout of unbridled praise for the arrival of the long-awaited Messiah. The people recognized Jesus as the Son of David, the rightful heir to the throne, and the one who came bearing the name and authority of the Lord.

As the palms were strewn and cloaks laid down before Him, a king was welcomed, not with the clanging of swords and the pomp of a conqueror, but with the humble cries of hope from a people yearning for deliverance.

Matthew 21:9 encapsulates the messianic expectation of the Jewish people and the fulfillment of Old Testament prophecies. It also predicts the ultimate purpose of Jesus' mission—to bring salvation, not through political or military might, but through the sacrificial love on the cross. "Hosanna in the highest heaven" transcends a cry for earthly deliverance, pointing towards the celestial victory over sin and death.

Prayer: Lord of salvation, my heart joins the ancient chorus, singing "Hosanna!" to You. Blessed are You who comes in the name of the Lord, bringing peace where there is turmoil and offering restoration where brokenness has taken root. Let my spirit be stirred by the same anticipation that filled the hearts of those who paved Your way with palms, and may my life reflect the profound gratitude for the salvation You've provided. In Jesus' name, I pray. Amen.

May 8: United in Christ's Kingdom

Scripture for the day

"If a house is divided against itself, that house cannot stand."

Mark 3:25

These words are a foundation for understanding stability in society and relations as well as a compelling call to unity within the body of Christ.

Jesus spoke this in response to accusations casting doubt on the source of His miraculous power. The spiritual insight extends beyond the defense of His miracles; it applies to all levels of human relationships, from our inner lives to the global Church.

Christ's metaphor of a divided house speaks powerfully into ecclesiology, the study of the church and its functions. As Christians, we comprise the spiritual house of God, and it is our unity that reflects the nature of the triune God we serve, Father, Son, and Holy Spirit, who is three in one. When we allow division in the church, we not only weaken our witness to the world but also deny the very nature of God who is perfect unity.

Prayer: Heavenly Father, Your Word reminds me that a house divided cannot stand. I pray for Your Spirit of unity to permeate Your church. Bind us together with cords of love that cannot be broken and fortify our hearts against the temptations of division and strife. Help us to remember that we are one body, unified by one Spirit, and called to one hope. May our collective witness be as a city on a hill, undivided and shining brightly for Your glory. In the name of Jesus, I pray. Amen.

Embracing Shiloh:

May 9: Faith That Heals

Scripture for the Day

"Jesus turned and saw her. 'Take heart, daughter,' he said, 'your faith has healed you.' And the woman was healed at that moment."

Matthew 9:22

Within the bustling crowds that often surrounded Jesus, we observe a solitary figure—a woman whose suffering had distanced her from the vibrancy of community life. Her ailment was not simply physical; it carried a weight of isolation that pressed into her very soul. Yet, in her desperation, she pushed through the crowd, believing that if she could just touch the hem of Christ's garment, she would be healed.

When she reached out, her touch was so light it could have gone unnoticed among the jostling bodies. But it didn't go unnoticed. Jesus felt power leave Him. He turned, not in irritation but with compassion, and honored her: "Your faith has healed you." Here, the spiritual insight unfolds—faith in Jesus' power to heal and restore is itself a conduit for His healing grace.

Jesus' response reveals the intimate connection between faith and the power of God. This is not just a testament to the woman's faith but also serves as an illustration of the salvation Jesus offers. The woman's faith was an acknowledgment of her need and of Christ's sufficiency. Healing came when, in faith, she reached out to the only One who could make her whole. Similarly, our own approach to Jesus, wrought with the brokenness of sin, should be marked by humble faith that reaches for the Savior.

Prayer: Lord Jesus, just as You turned to acknowledge the woman who reached for You in faith, I pray that You see me as I extend my heart towards Your mercy and grace. Let me be emboldened by Your love and seek Your healing touch in every area of my life. I ask for the faith that acknowledges my utter dependence on You, faith that believes in Your power to save and restore. In Your holy and compassionate name, I pray. Amen.

May 10: The Compassion of Christ

Scripture for the Day

"Saying, 'If you, even you, had only known on this day what would bring you peace—but now it is hidden from your eyes.'"

Luke 19:42

Picture the King of kings, the Prince of Peace, with tears flowing down His face, staring at Jerusalem, the center of the Jewish faith. It was so blind that it couldn't see the time of God coming in the name of Jesus. His heart was not only hurting because of what they did to Him, but what they were doing to themselves.

This Scripture calls us to ponder the very things that are really peace—identifying Christ, obeying His commandments, and accepting Him as Lord over our hearts. It is a peace that is beyond human comprehension; it is the *shalom* of God—perfection, wholeness, wellness, and unity.

Luke 19:42 provides us a window into the fact that God loves His people very much and wants reconciliation and peace. Jesus' lament over Jerusalem is a moving declaration of the consequences of refusing Christ's peace, that is, that spiritual blindness leads to ruin. He prophesizes the city's future destruction in 70 AD as well as the spiritual desolation which will accompany a life without God.

Prayer: Lord Jesus, as You wept over Jerusalem, give me a heart that weeps over my own indifference and the brokenness around me. Grant me the insight to understand what qualifies as peace and the bravery to seek after it. Let me see the ways of peace You have revealed, the route of love, justice, and humility, to not be led by pride or tradition but be always conscious of Your peace and Your presence. Assist me to be a tool of Your peace, spreading to the world which is fervently in need of love and reconciliation that In Your name, I do pray. Amen.

Embracing Shiloh:

May 11: The Way, the Truth, and the Life

Scripture for the Day
"And I will ask the Father, and he will give you another advocate to help you and be with you forever."

John 14:16

Today's verse reflects the intensity of God's love for us – a loyalty so strong that in a bodily absence, God sustains our spiritual company and help. We are always accompanied. The prospect of the indwelling presence of the Holy Spirit is not only a hope for the future but a reality of the present. With every difficulty, every laugh, and every normal daily happening, the Spirit is right there with us, providing companionship and guidance.

In theological interpretation, we see the mystery of the Trinity. The Father sends the Son, the Son requests the Father, and the Son sends in the name of the Spirit. This divine interrelation mirrors the deep interconnectedness we are called to. Being indwelt by the Holy Spirit, we participate in the Trinity's divine dance of love, and we can even see and feel God.

Within life's chaos, when we are confused or scared, the Comforter turns our hearts to the teachings of Christ and empowers us to live them. The Spirit gives peace to our hearts and is an instrument of transformation, molding us into the image of Jesus every day.

Prayer: O Father, I thank You for the Spirit of truth whom You have promised to be with me forever. In each lonely or doubtful moment, let me know the comfort of Your touch and the counsel of Your wisdom. May Your Spirit develop my soul, instructing and recalling Your truths. Guide me through each day with the certainty of Your love and the strength to go wherever You lead me. I pray in the name of Jesus. Amen.

May 12: Commissioned with Purpose

Scripture for the Day
"Therefore go and make disciples of all nations, baptizing them in the name of the Father and of the Son and of the Holy Spirit."

Matthew 28:19

Matthew 28:19 serves as a herald call for every believer. This command, known as the Great Commission, captures the Christian mission. Christ does not send us out alone or unequipped. He sends us with the authority and presence of the Triune God.

We are entrusted with a divine directive that stretches beyond borders and ethnic lines. It is a missionary call to action that includes us in God's redeeming work for the entire world. The Trinitarian formula signifies the transformational work of God in three persons, each playing a distinct and harmonious role in our salvation and in the sanctification of new believers.

The Father creates and sustains, the Son redeems and reconciles, and the Holy Spirit comforts and sanctifies invites us into divine relationship. As we carry out our commission, we do so in the name of a God who is relationship itself, implying that our mission is deeply relational. It's not just about spreading doctrine or increasing numbers but about welcoming people into an eternal, loving relationship with the Godhead.

When we advance in this mission, we are living testimonies to the unity and love that flows from the Father, through the Son, and in the Holy Spirit. Our evangelistic efforts echo the relational heart of God, desiring that all might come to know Him and be immersed in His transformative love.

Prayer: Blessed Trinity, I stand in awe of the grandeur of Your mission and the privilege to partake in it. Grant me the courage and strength to step out in faith, make disciples, and extend Your Kingdom across the earth. May Your love be the force that drives me, and Your wisdom be the light that guides me in the mighty name of Jesus. Amen.

Embracing Shiloh:

May 13: Empowered Witnesses

Scripture for the Day

"But you will receive power when the Holy Spirit comes on you; and you will be my witnesses in Jerusalem, and in all Judea and Samaria, and to the ends of the earth."

Acts 1:8

Amid the stress of life, we may quickly feel incompetent in response to our spiritual calling. Yet, Acts 1:8 gives an empowering and direct commission from Christ Himself. This Scripture not only speaks of the indwelling of the Holy Spirit but also identifies our role and mission as the presenters of His word.

This verse tells of the Spirit's enablement in the life of a Christian. It is the sign of the change from Jesus' earthly ministry to the age of the Church— an age of the presence of the Spirit among the followers of the Way. We are not just mere onlookers but witnesses who are called to testify about the gospel's truth with our words and actions.

Our testimony originates from the operation of the Spirit within us who strengthens us and endows us with various gifts and boldness needed to testify about the gospel. A pattern of evangelization which starts locally, then transcends cultural and geographical divisions, going to the ends of the Earth, is outlined. It mirrors an ever-widening circle of power, based in local ministry but reaching to world mission.

We are part of this ongoing narrative, summoned to testify about Jesus within our communities and beyond, impelled by the same Spirit that enlivened the early Church. The very power that brought Christ from the dead helps us to conquer obstacles and deal with opposition, thus assuring believers that their endeavors are supported by divine power.

Prayer: Sovereign Lord, filled with a vision of the might of the Holy Spirit, I receive my mission to be Your grace's witness. Let my life unveil Your love, and let my words resonate with the hope in Your gospel. I want to expand my vision to look beyond my capabilities and welfare and reach out to the ends of the Earth. I pray in the mighty name of Jesus, Amen.

May 14: Inspired and Equipped

Scripture for the Day

"All Scripture is inspired by God and is useful to teach us what is true and to make us realize what is wrong in our lives. It corrects us when we are wrong and teaches us to do what is right."

2 Timothy 3:16 (NLT)

With the breaking dawn of a fresh day, the divine breath of God sweeps over the scenery of our lives. The Scripture today reminds us that every word in the Bible is not only a text but the divine breath of our Creator that is intended to direct, form, and prepare us for every good work. Let us inhale that breath deep into our lives with the life-giving power of God's Word.

The Bible is not merely a historical document or ethical guidebook but the living and active voice of God (Hebrews 4:12). In this God-inspired Scripture, we know it is the heart of our Father and His will and realize His intention for our lives. It serves fourfold: teaching us the gospel truth, correcting our errors, rebuking sin, and training us in the way of righteousness, much like a loving parent does to a child.

God's Word is also a kind of custom-made course that molds our character and makes us whole, both for our way of life on Earth and for the spiritual mission we are to fulfill. Its pages tell us the tale of redemption, the instruction for the wise, the teachings of Jesus, and the righteous calls to action from those who have gone before us in faith.

Today, reflect on how God's Word has been a lantern to your feet and a light onto your path (Psalm 119:105). Let it penetrate your spirit and be edified and thoroughly deployed to accomplish all God has called you to do.

Prayer: O God, Almighty and Everlasting, breathe Your Holy Spirit in me as I ponder Your Word. I shall allow it to be rooted deeply in my heart and become productive in my life. Correct my fault, chasten my sin, and teach me in the right. May Your Scriptures become my road for life as I walk through the labyrinth. In Jesus' name, Amen.

Embracing Shiloh:

May 15: Confessing Faith for Salvation

Scripture for the Day

"If you confess with your mouth that Jesus is Lord and believe in your heart that God raised him from the dead, you will be saved."

Romans 10:9

Romans 10:9 is a call for personal confession of our salvation and a sincere conviction. Our salvation is not only saying words as such but in the reality of believing in the Lordship of Jesus Christ and the resurrection itself.

The theology of salvation is an intricate and profound discipline that makes us aware of the fact that it is not a word; it is the condition of a person who became different. "To confess, Jesus is Lord" is to offer our lives, to accept His rule over us, and to conform our will to the divine. It recognizes His final sacrifice on the cross and His victory over the grave, which destroyed the chains of sin and death for man.

As we eat this Scripture, let it also dwell in our spirit. Love in the heart is the rich soil where faith grows, and the declaration of our lips is the fruit it bears. This believing is not an idle faith; it involves the whole person requiring us to do, to live, to love differently. For in the beating chambers of our heart, we accept grace's presence. With our mouth, we voice the joy of salvation.

Today, let us guard our faith with the truth of this Scripture. Take a minute to declare Jesus as Lord not only in your mind but also in your everyday life. Allow it to reflect your deeds, direct your choices, and serve as the lighthouse of hope that brightens your way.

Prayer: Dear God, in the newness of this day, I confess with my mouth, "Jesus Christ is Lord." I have unshakable faith that You have raised Him from the dead, and by this faith, I am saved. May my heart be always set in Your truth, and may my life be a mirror of the glorious truth of Your resurrection power. In Jesus's precious name, I pray, Amen.

May 16: We are all Qualified

Scripture for the Day

"Even on my servants, both men and women, I will pour out my Spirit in those days, and they will prophesy."

Acts 2:18

Reflecting on the stirring event of Pentecost as described in Acts, we are reminded that the Holy Spirit's outpouring transcends all barriers. It is a gift bestowed upon both men and women, servants, and masters alike. This inclusivity highlights a fundamental truth—God's Kingdom embraces all without prejudice.

In those days, prophesying was understood as both a declaration of God's divine will and a revelation of understanding brought forth under the Holy Spirit's inspiration. Today, the same Spirit that was granted to the early believers is given to us, empowering our words and actions as we become the messengers of God's redemptive story.

This is your heritage as a disciple of Christ: to be a proclaimer of truth, a beacon of God's love. You are not isolated in this endeavor; you are a part of a great tapestry of witnesses, woven together by the Spirit's unifying work. Embrace this promise and carry it with you, dear friend, as you walk in the Spirit's unity and prophesy with a heart of compassion and wisdom.

Prayer: Lord, I am reminded of Your promise in Acts—that Your Spirit is poured out upon all flesh, without distinction. I ask for the courage to live a prophetic life, to boldly speak and live out Your truth in my words, my deeds, and my relationships. May the love of Jesus be manifested in me and through me to all those I encounter. Pour out Your Spirit afresh on me this day, that I may be an agent of Your grace and hope. In the name of Jesus Christ, I pray, Amen.

Embracing Shiloh:

May 17: Strength in Waiting

Scripture for the Day
"Wait for the Lord; be strong and take heart and wait for the Lord."

Psalm 27:14

Waiting for the Lord is a movement of faith. It is a statement that our faith is not locked in time but in the eternal. When all troubles flow incessantly around you, let the stability of the Word of God serve as a rudder. Strength does not mean you will not feel the heavy weight of your burdens. Rather, it means you can endure, depending on the strength God gives.

Courage for this support is not found in us standing alone. It includes our strengthening each other in times of weakness. We are not meant to be alone. We bear each other's waiting, as you carry one another in prayer and communion, for the same reason that Christ carries us in His gracious love. The waiting, remember, is not a wasted time, for in it we are changed and made ready for the purposes God has set for us.

Embrace the wait today. Be mighty, not in the flesh but in the Holy Spirit. Take comfort in knowing that God is with you, doing all things for your good and His glory.

Prayer: Heavenly Father, I come to You in silence, desiring to have You near me and to experience Your tranquility. Lord, let me trust in Your timing with faith and strength. Let me have the energy to go through the day. Not my energy but Yours. May my heart rejoice in Your Word and abide in Your love. Amen.

May 18: Ears to Hear

Scripture for the Day
"Then Jesus said, 'Whoever has ears to hear, let them hear.'"

Mark 4:9

Today's call is to an invitation into a deeper communion with the divine, beckoning us to incline our spiritual ears to the whispered truths of God's Kingdom.

This charge from Christ after delivering the Parable of the Sower is a pivotal moment of both invitation and challenge. It challenges us to examine the state of our heart: Are we receptive soil, ready to nurture the seeds of salvation that God scatters upon us? Jesus is revealing a universal spiritual principle: to truly hear is to actively listen, to understand, to let the Word of God take root in our lives so that it may yield a harvest of righteousness.

In a world clamoring with distraction, the simple act of hearing becomes an act of devotion. It requires us to clear our agendas, to still our inner noise, and to tune in to the frequency of the Spirit. For those willing to listen, the voice of God is never silent. Through Scripture, prayer, and the world around us, He speaks.

Today, let us be those with ears to hear—open and responsive. Let us listen not just for affirmation of what we already believe but for the growth-inducing truths that sometimes sting before they heal. In a posture of humility, let us welcome the Word that confronts, corrects, and inspires.

Prayer: Lord God, I come before You with ears open, ready to receive Your holy Word. Help me to hear the message You have for me this day with clarity. Remove the distractions that cloud my hearing and the stubbornness that resists Your guidance. Plant Your Word deep within me that it may bear abundant fruit in my actions and attitudes. Make me sensitive to Your voice above all others and obedient to Your will so that I might grow in wisdom and grace. Amen.

Embracing Shiloh:

May 19: Infused with His Spirit

Scripture for the Day
"I have filled him with the Spirit of God, with wisdom, with understanding, with knowledge and with all kinds of skills."

Exodus 31:3

In this chapter, we see God's empowering presence in the life of Bezalel, whom He filled with His Spirit to do great works. The skills, wisdom, understanding, and knowledge are endowments of God Himself—gifts not bestowed carelessly but with divine purpose.

This passage is more than a historical narrative. It defines a larger truth about God's involvement with gifts and talents He gives us. It points out that God is closely related to the whole creative process. He is the first artist and worker, and when God asks a man to do something, He also gives him the necessary tools.

As you dwell on this Scripture today, know that the God who equipped Bezalel also has equipped you. The abilities that you have – the wisdom, talents, or gifts – are not only things of personal attainment but the work of the Spirit in you. The infinite Artist has, by His wisdom, decided to work through you to manifest His glory and beauty to the world.

Take heart that you are not alone in your efforts. In the grandest or the supposedly small tasks, you are anointed with the Holy Spirit to do works that echo into the eternal. Through every act that is performed in His name, you partake in the holy activity of bringing the Kingdom of God to earth.

Prayer: God, I thank You for raining Your Spirit on me and favoring me with wisdom, understanding, knowledge, and talents. Teach me to identify and utilize the gifts You have endowed me with for Your honor so that I might be aware of Your presence and will in all I undertake, with You as the fountain of all creativity and competence. Amen.

May 20: Child of God

Scripture for the Day
"So in Christ Jesus you are all children of God through faith, for all of you who were baptized into Christ have clothed yourselves with Christ."

Galatians 3:26-27

In these verses, the apostle Paul provides us with a powerful image of our identity in Christ. He speaks of a spiritual reality that is as real as the garments we wear. We are children of God have been clothed with Christ Himself.

Our faith in Jesus grafts us into God's family, making us heirs to His promises. Clothed with Christ, we wear His righteousness, character, and virtues—as if His life becomes our spiritual attire.

This metaphor speaks to the intimacy we share with Christ, indicating that our relationship with Him is not distant or abstract but as close as our very skin. To be clothed in Christ means we no longer present ourselves to the world in our flawed condition but are covered, protected, and beautified by Jesus' purity and love.

As we go about our day, let this be at the forefront of our minds: our identity does not come from worldly accolades or material possessions but from the fact that we are children of God, robed in Christ's righteousness.

Prayer: Heavenly Father, I am in awe that You call me Your child through faith in Your Son, Jesus. Today, let me walk with the conscious awareness that I am clothed in Christ. May His life and love be evident in my every word and deed. Amen.

Embracing Shiloh:

May 21: Seeking God

Scripture for the Day

"You will seek me and find me when you seek me with all your heart."

Jeremiah 29:13

This Scripture opens windows, revealing a God who doesn't hide from us but who desires to be found. This seeking is a pursuit of loving engagement with the One who is ever near, who responds readily to the sincerest yearning of the human heart.

Our God is not an impersonal force operating from afar; He is intimate, responsive, and present. He reveals this about Himself through Jeremiah: His accessibility is linked to the posture of our hearts.

Seeking God with our entire being involves all aspects of our person—our emotions, intellect, will, and spirit. It is an active longing that surpasses casual interest or routine devotion. To seek God wholeheartedly is to place Him as the ultimate pursuit above all other desires, the One treasure outvaluing the rest.

As we step into our day, let us do so with hearts ablaze, earnestly searching for the presence of God in every moment and every interaction. Let the fullness of our hearts be the compass that directs us to His love and truth.

Prayer: God, Your Word stands as a beacon, calling me to seek You with all my heart. I desire to enter this day with a spirit of wholehearted pursuit of You. Strip away the distractions that pull my focus from You. Open my eyes to see You, my ears to hear You, and my heart to receive You. And in finding You, may I know the joy and peace of Your eternal presence. You are my greatest quest, and in You, my heart finds its rest. In Jesus' name, Amen.

May 22: Walking as He Walked

Scripture for the Day
"Whoever says he abides in him ought to walk in the same way in which he walked."

1 John 2:6

To dwell in Him is to walk in the path of Jesus, to live His lifestyle – the things, the works, and His love for others.

Herein lies a compelling truth: Christianity is more than mental assent to a body of dogma or observance of a moral code. It is a living imitation into Christ's life. Since those who declare to dwell in Jesus should emulate His behavior, this verse calls for a thoughtful break to evaluate the structure of our daily living.

To walk as He walked is the picture of a living faith. He walked this world in humility, served with kindness, and loved without limit. He lived a prayerful life, obeyed the Father, and met human needs. Therefore, to walk in His ways is to live a life in rhythm with God's love and grace.

This journey is not of perfection but of seeking the Perfect One. We are not called to repeat Christ's miracles as followers but to imitate His characteristics: love, patience, kindness, and forgiveness. We might lack pace in our walk, but within us, His Spirit is leading and strengthening us for the journey.

When you end today, think about how your life can be more like the life of the One who makes you His. The question in every decision and every interaction is, "What would Jesus do?"

Prayer: Lord, assist me to move in the direction of You – living Your love, Your truth, and Your mercy. Guide my way, instruct my decisions, and shape my actions so that they show a heart changed by You. Enable me to live out being owned by Jesus and be a genuine image of You in this world. By Your grace and for Your glory, I want to live like this. In Jesus' name, Amen.

Embracing Shiloh:

May 23: Rest in the Rhythm of God's Grace

Scripture for the Day
"You shall work six days, but on the seventh day you shall rest; even during plowing time and harvest you shall rest."

Exodus 34:21

Exodus 34:21 calls us to a rhythm of rest woven by God Himself into the fabric of time. This divine pattern established for ancient Israel beckons us still with the wisdom of heaven, to recognize sacred tempo in our own lives.

This Scripture speaks not only of physical rest from labor but of a principle of the need for spiritual rejuvenation and a deliberate remembrance of our dependence on God's provision and rule. In a world that celebrates ceaseless activity, keeping the Sabbath is a countercultural act that recenters our focus on the eternal rather than the temporal.

As we engage in our work throughout the week, may we do so with diligence and integrity, mindful of the fact that our labor is ultimately unto the Lord. Yet, when we reach the designated time for rest, let us lay down our tools, silence our devices, and rest in obedience to God's commandment. The Sabbath rest is a gift, an oasis in time that allows us to reorient our being towards God and to engage in restorative practices that nourish our body, soul, and spirit.

As you embrace this day, let it also be a reminder that our ultimate rest is found not in a day but in a Person—Jesus Christ, our Lord, who invites all who are weary and burdened to find rest in Him.

Prayer: Gracious Lord, I thank You for the gift of work and the satisfaction it brings. Yet, I am also deeply grateful for Your command to rest, which reveals Your care for my well-being. Instruct me, O God, to honor the Sabbath rest, to pause from my labor, and to reflect on Your goodness and provision. May this pattern of rest teach me to trust in You, to release the grip on my tasks, and to find my peace in the rhythm You have set. Amen.

May 24: Shining Bright

Scripture for the Day
"You are the light of the world. A town built on a hill cannot be hidden"

Matthew 5:14.

As we journey through life, we find ourselves walking in shadows. Some of these are cast by challenges and pains that we face; others are the very real darkness of the world around us that can sometimes seem overwhelming. Yet, into this darkness, the words of our Savior Jesus Christ shine like a beacon of unquenchable hope in today's verse.

What a tremendous calling! You are not merely moving through the dark. You are called to be a source of light in it. Light in the Bible often symbolizes purity, truth, and the divine presence of God. As bearers of His light, we are called to reflect His character – His purity, truth, and love. Jesus doesn't simply suggest that we might occasionally flicker like a small candle. He declares that we are like a city on a hill, bold, visible, unashamed of the gospel, and radiating the glory of God.

What does this mean for us daily? It means that our faith is not a private affair but a public testament. It's not hidden but visible in our actions, words, and the very way we conduct our lives. This is an empowering reminder that each act of kindness, every word of truth, and all our endeavors of love contribute to a greater testimony of God's transforming power in the world.

Prayer: Heavenly Father, thank You for calling me to be a light in this world. Help me to fully embrace this honor, displaying Your love like a torch that gleams in the darkest of nights. Please guide my steps so that I might walk boldly in the path of righteousness, casting a warm and guiding glow for all those wandering in darkness. May my life reflect Your beauty and point others to Your eternal light. In Jesus' mighty name, Amen

Embracing Shiloh:

May 25: Unshakable Hope

Scripture for the Day

"For I know that my Redeemer lives, and that at the last he will stand upon the earth; and after my skin has been thus destroyed, then in my flesh I shall see God,"

Job 19:25-26

Today, let us look at the words of Job, a man who was well acquainted with suffering but never wavered in his belief. Emerging from the dust of despair, his voice declared God's glory.

Job's unshakable spirit is a proof of the faith that is formed in the crucible of affliction. He lays bare a foundational Christian belief: the guarantee of a mighty Savior, a renewing Advocate who finally resurrects and justifies. This Redeemer is no one else but Jesus Christ, whose resurrection is the assurance of our resurrection.

In the resurrection, we see the core of our hope: The certainty that in this life, nothing is permanent, not even death. This hope makes us patient and immovable in faith, no matter what storms of life.

So, with hope immortal, let us face this day not as the victims of our circumstances but as the victors through Him who loves us. May the enlightenment of our Savior's vitality foster consolation for the worn-out souls and kindle in us an inextinguishable light.

Prayer: God, during my trials, Your Word is my lamp. I dwell in Your Word that my Redeemer lives. Let me be steadfast in faith, Lord, and Your nearness, always. Can I trust my spirit will reside in Your grace forever, even if my physical strength fails? For I know that my Redeemer lives, and at last He shall stand upon the earth. Amen.

May 26: The Way, the Truth, and the Life

Scripture for the Day

"Jesus answered, 'I am the way and the truth and the life. No one comes to the Father except through me.'"

John 14:6

Nestled in the heart of the Gospel of John, we find a profound declaration by Jesus that serves as an anchor for our souls.

This powerful verse declares Jesus' unique place in our spiritual life. In calling Himself the "way," Jesus indicates that He is our path to divine relationship, not merely a guide pointing us toward God but the actual road we travel. Jesus, as the "truth," acknowledges that the fullness of God's reality is expressed in Him. He is the genuine revelation of God, in whom we can trust entirely. And as the "life," Jesus becomes the source of eternal life, sustaining and endowing us with spiritual vitality that transcends earthly existence.

This verse reveals that all pursuits of spirituality, enlightenment, or salvation outside of Christ are fruitless. He asserts that the connection to the Father is made possible solely through a relationship with Him. Jesus' exclusivity as the way to God may confound the world's wisdom, which boasts many ways, but in this divine assertion, there is simplicity and profound peace. It spares us the confusion of many paths and guides us on the singular journey that leads to eternal fellowship with our Creator.

Prayer: Heavenly Father, thank You for providing me with the ultimate compass in Jesus. Amid life's complex decisions and diverse directions, guide me through Your Son, who is the way, the truth, and the life. Strengthen my faith to trust in Him as the only pathway to You. Clear my heart of any deceit or distraction that pulls me from the truth Jesus embodies. And invigorate my spirit with the life He promises that I may live fully in Your purpose. In Jesus' name, I pray. Amen.

Embracing Shiloh:

May 27: Made in the Image of God

Scripture for the Day
"Then God said, 'Let us make mankind in our image, in our likeness.'"

Genesis 1:26

In the genesis of time, when the world was just a new canvas, the Divine Painter decided to create His masterpiece—a creation that would represent His very form.

We are created in the very likeness of our Maker. This great fact reveals a deep sense of who we are and our purpose. To be in the image of God is to be dignified and valuable and to have a duty to reflect His character to the world. Our calling is to be stewards, to protect the creation as our Creator did while forming the world with such care and love.

This being in the image of God makes humans the vessels to receive God's grace and dwell with Him in the sacred place. The image of God is engraved in every human face. We see the shadow of His likeness in every act of goodness, justice, and compassion.

Our common heritage unites us, making us see each other not in terms of differences but in a shared ancestry of divine image-bearers. We base communities that glorify God on this by acknowledging His image in every person we meet.

Prayer: God, Assist me to welcome the deep grace You have given me and to fulfill my calling with honor. May Your love guide me as I manage Your creation and respect the image of You in my brothers and sisters. Lead me to act justly, love mercy, and walk humbly in Your likeness. Amen.

May 28: Path of Transformation

Scripture for the Day

"But if a wicked person turns away from all the sins they have committed and keeps all my decrees and does what is just and right, that person will surely live; they will not die. None of the offenses they have committed will be remembered against them. Because of the righteous things they have done, they will live."

Ezekiel 18:21-22

This passage helps us understand redemption. If we go astray and get tangled in our sins, the Lord assures us that transformation and renewal are never too far away. The promise is clear and unwavering: repentance brings life. This is not only a matter of survival but of a life that is bright, and perpetual based on an unalterable love of a merciful God.

This verse cancels out any idea that we are chained to our past. The justice of the Creator is not exclusively punishing. It is creation-oriented to life and growth. It challenges the deterministic idea that could enslave us with hopelessness and invites us to a new story where grace conquers all and our sins do not have to have the final say.

We are the ones who have the power to choose, stressing personal responsibility in our spiritual journey. The decrees of God are not random regulations but ways to decency and tranquility. Doing what is just and right means we are acting in accordance with divine will, and we are partaking in the sacred endeavor of healing our world and our souls.

Prayer: Father, I stand before You with a repentant heart. Though You know my weaknesses and shortcomings, You embrace my coming back to You. God teach me how to not return to my evil ways so that I may keep Your statutes and do justice and righteousness. Lead me with Your compassionate love, and let my life be a testimony of the mercy of renewal. Amen.

Embracing Shiloh:

May 29: Abundantly Rewarded in Faithfulness

Scripture for the Day

"God is not unjust; he will not forget your work and the love you have shown him as you have helped his people and continue to help them."

Hebrews 6:10

The world may not always recognize our labors of love, but today's Scripture is a tender assurance that the Almighty sees every act of kindness and every step taken in faith. Hebrews 6:10 is a soothing balm for the weary soul, reminding us that the God we serve is just. He never forgets the work we do in His name.

How comforting it is to know that the love we exhibit towards others, especially to those in the family of faith, reflects our love for God and becomes a testament to our faith. We are not simply toiling in vain but rather sowing seeds that will one day blossom into a harvest of righteousness. When we serve, support, and nurture one another, we become God's hands and feet on earth, living out a vivid expression of His boundless love.

When moments of doubt arise, when you feel your efforts are insignificant or overshadowed by greater challenges, remember that God's accounting is perfect. He sees the full extent of your faithfulness and the genuine love you've poured out. Reward from God is not always in material gain or immediate recognition but found in the peace and joy that comes from serving Him with an unyielded heart.

Prayer: Gracious Lord, I thank You for the promise that You see and value every effort I make in Your name. Instill in me a spirit that does not grow weary in doing good. Give me strength to continue aiding my brothers and sisters, reflecting Your grace and compassion. And when the day ends, let me rest in the assurance that in Your divine registry, nothing I do for You is ever forgotten. In Jesus' name, Amen.

May 30: Pressing Toward the Goal

Scripture for the Day

"Brothers and sisters, I do not consider myself yet to have taken hold of it. But one thing I do: Forgetting what is behind and straining toward what is ahead, I press on toward the goal to win the prize for which God has called me heavenward in Christ Jesus."

Philippians 3:13-14

With life's demands and the noise of its distractions, it is easy to become entangled in earthly concerns. Yet, the apostle Paul, in his letter to the Philippians, invites us into a higher understanding of the Christian journey.

Paul's words resonate with a relentless determination, painting a vivid image of an athlete fixed on the finish line, straining forward, leaving everything on the track. The goal exists not within the tangible rewards of this world but in the eternal embrace of God's kingdom. Paul encourages us to pursue spiritual maturity and the eventual perfection that comes when we shall see Christ as He is.

The prize we seek is sublime – it is the "upward call of God in Christ Jesus." It is not a call to a place but a call to a relationship, an invitation to know Christ and be found in Him. To press on speaks of a daily commitment to grow closer to Jesus, to allow our values, actions, and our very lives to be transformed by His love and grace.

Life's journey is strewn with trials and tribulations. Paul was no stranger to suffering. Yet, he counts all things as loss for the surpassing value of knowing Christ Jesus. It is this knowledge that fuels our endurance, propelling us forward, eyes not on the past but on the glory that lies ahead.

Prayer: Heavenly Father, I come before You today with a heart inclined toward Your heavenly call. In this moment of reflection, I thank You for the grace that covers my past and the hope that illuminates my future. Lord, help me to fix my eyes on Jesus, to lay aside every weight, and to run with perseverance the race marked out for me. Amen.

Embracing Shiloh:

May 31: Faith Comes by Hearing

Scripture for the Day
"Consequently, faith comes from hearing the message, and the message is heard through the word about Christ."

Romans 10:17

The road to faith usually starts with a single humble listening act. Within the sacred text of Romans, we find a great truth that contains an important truth about our spiritual journey.

This verse calls us to a spiritual practice nearly as old as the religion itself: the practice of listening. With a lot of noises in our daily routine, getting our ears to listen to the voice of the divine can be a challenge. However, the apostle Paul emphasizes that it is in this careful hearing of the Word of God that our faith is nurtured and grows.

Faith in its true sense is not only a belief but a living trust in the Creator. God wrote this narrative and calls us to a journey of redemption, hope, and love.

The Word of God is not just the text to be read – it is a voice to be heard. It sounds in our hearts and reverberates in our deeds. When we open our hearts to hear the whispered truths of God, His wisdom starts to soak all our daily decisions and relationships. Our faith is not made stronger by seeing but by hearing—by accepting the words of God spoken into our lives.

Considering the significance of hearing the Word of God, let us approach communion with Him to hear not only but also comprehend and live the Word of God.

Prayer: Heavenly Father, attune my ears to the melody of Your voice and open my heart to the harmony of Your truth. May Your Word ring clear amid life's noise, guiding me, transforming me, and building a faith within me that stands firm against the tempests of this world. In Your holy name, I pray. Amen.

June 1: Embarking on a Journey

Scripture for the Day
"And this gospel of the kingdom will be preached in the whole world as a testimony to all nations, and then the end will come."

Matthew 24:14

Today, we turn our hearts to what Jesus said in Matthew 24:14, reminding us of the pivotal role the spread of the gospel plays in God's sovereign timeline. As disciples of Christ, we are entrusted with the divine responsibility to share the good news of salvation contained in the gospel message of the transforming power of God's love and grace.

The Scripture speaks of "the gospel of the kingdom." This isn't merely a message of personal salvation. It's the proclamation of God's ruling authority, superior to the flawed realms of human governance and broken systems. It is comprehensive, offering hope, restoration, and peace to a fractured world. Despite the tumult that surrounds us, and the spiritual battles waged, this mission remains as vital now as ever.

Jesus is not just predicting the future. He is commissioning His followers into a global movement that proclaims the fulfillment of His Kingdom's arrival. There is a divine interplay between our evangelistic efforts and the events that will herald the end of the age. Every act of witness, therefore, participates in moving history toward its climactic fruition.

This verse isn't merely informational; it's motivational. It calls us to action, to be ambassadors of hope, and practitioners of the Kingdom ethos in our daily walk. Let's carry the Kingdom's message beyond our comfort zones, trusting that it's not by our might but by the Spirit's power that hearts are turned to God.

Prayer: Heavenly Father, King eternal, Your Word is a lamp unto my feet. Empower me today to be a faithful bearer of the gospel of Your Kingdom. Open doors for Your message to echo through my words and deeds, and let my life serve as a living testimony to Your grace. May Your Kingdom come, Your will be done, on earth as it is in Heaven. Amen.

Embracing Shiloh:

June 2: Be Confidant

Scripture for the Day
"Now faith is confidence in what we hope for and assurance about what we do not see."
Hebrews 11:1

The book of Hebrews speaks to the sojourners of faith, to those who are called to trust not in the uncertain and fleeting shadows of the world but in the unchangeable character of God. Hebrews 11:1 doesn't merely define faith. It presents faith as the very substance of our spiritual existence – the assurance of things hoped for, and the conviction of realities not perceived by the human eye.

Faith, according to this Scripture, is not a passive wistfulness but an active, daring confidence in God. It is placing our full trust in His promises, His timing, and His perfect will, even when the evidence before us suggests otherwise. The depth of faith lies in its ability to anchor us, not to the shallow sands of visible circumstances, but to the bedrock of divine truth. As we walk in faith, we align ourselves with the patriarchs and matriarchs before us who "by faith" stepped into God's unfolding story.

The call to faith challenges us to move beyond the limits of our senses and to rely on the God who spoke the universe into existence. To have faith is to join in the chorus of the redeemed, testifying to the reality of God's Kingdom at work both in us and through us. It endorses the truth that while we may not see the full picture, we trust God's redemptive plan – a narrative far greater than our individual stories.

As you go out today, let your steps be guided by faith. Embrace the blessed assurance that God is at work, forging the unseen by His faithfulness.

Prayer: Lord of all Hope, I come before You humbly, my heart brimming with hope anchored in faith. Through the unseen, amidst my uncertainties, grant me the grace to see with eyes of faith. May the assurance of what I hope for in Christ and the conviction of what I cannot see with mortal eyes embolden my spirit. In Jesus' mighty name, I pray. Amen.

June 3: Embracing Unity in Christ

Scripture for the Day

"...so that there should be no division in the body, but that its parts should have equal concern for each other. If one part suffers, every part suffers with it; if one part is honored, every part rejoices with it. Now you are the body of Christ, and each one of you is a part of it."

1 Corinthians 12:25-27

The apostle Paul calls us to a vision that recognizes our integral part in something far greater than ourselves. It is an important reminder that we are not isolated believers but collectively the body of Christ, each with unique functions yet united in purpose.

This biblical insight pierces the heart, revealing a truth beyond a surface-level understanding of community. Our individual identities do not fade away. They are fulfilled when connected to the body of Christ. Within this divine organism, our gifts are not for self-promotion but for the common good. The hand cannot function without the arm; the eye cannot see without the brain. In the same way, we cannot fulfill our calling in isolation.

The beauty of this teaching lies in its depiction of Jesus as the head of this body, orchestrating its activities in perfect harmony. It is by His life that every part is sustained, and through His love, diversity melds into unity. This is not only a call to recognize our place in the body but an invitation to rejoice in the beauty of every other member's role.

As today unfolds, let your gaze fall onto others within the church with a new appreciation. Recognize in them the craftsmanship of God, made to fit alongside you, to work with you and at times to support you. We must cherish diversity, hold each other up in difficulties, and celebrate victories together.

Prayer: Gracious God, thank You for calling me into the magnificent body of Christ. Help me to appreciate my role and to honor the roles of others. Teach me to collaborate, not compete, to contribute, not compare. In Jesus name, I pray. Amen.

June 4: Preparedness in Faith

Scripture for the Day
"Therefore keep watch, because you do not know the day or the hour."

Matthew 25:13

The uncertain hour of the Lord's return is a repeated theme throughout the gospels, and here in this passage, there is a call to maintain readiness. The parable of the ten virgins, which culminates in this verse, separates the prudent from the ill-prepared, providing a timeless lesson that calls for preparedness of heart and spirit.

This teaching deeply roots us in the concept of the already and the not yet. We live in the tension of the Kingdom of God that is here now, established by Christ, and yet not fully realized until His return. The command to keep watching is not only a caution against complacency but an invitation to live in a state of hopeful expectation and active engagement in the mission entrusted to us.

This alertness is not about predicting times and dates but embodying the values and ethics of the Kingdom. Each day offers a new canvas on which our faith is painted through loving service, fervent prayer, and unwavering proclamation of the gospel's hope. To "keep watch" is to live consciously, intentionally embracing every opportunity to reflect the love and light of Christ.

Let us step into this day with a renewed commitment to be vigilant and wise stewards of the time God has given us. May we invest our talents, serve with our gifts, and spread His love, knowing that in this spiritual wakefulness, we mirror the expectant bridal community, ready for the coming Bridegroom.

Prayer: Lord Jesus, instill in me a spirit of alertness and preparation. May my lamp be filled with the oil of Your Spirit, my light shining brightly in a world that thirsts for Your truth. Teach me to number my days in wisdom, seize the sacred moments to serve, love, and await Your coming with joyful anticipation. I ask this in the precious name of Jesus, Amen.

June 5: Shelter of the Most High

Scripture for the Day

"Whoever dwells in the shelter of the Most High will rest in the shadow of the Almighty. I will say of the LORD, 'He is my refuge and my fortress, my God, in whom I trust.'"

Psalm 91:1-2

Today's reading is a personal declaration, a standing point, and a faith resolution. One person's faith opens to us all the areas of security unparalleled in the Lord. It bids us to declare, with the psalmist, that God is our refuge and fortress.

In a world teeming with uncertainty, where threats to our peace and stability loom large, these words provide immense comfort and strength. God is not merely a provisional sanctuary or a transitory refuge. He is a fortress—untouchable, indestructible, and immortal. To call Him our refuge means that in Him we find shelter from the dangers and tempests of life.

It is what our faith is all about – confidence in the ever-present and protective God. To understand that our safety comes not from the lack of danger but being in the company of our Lord. With Him, fear loses power, and anxiety is disarmed. Belief in God as our stronghold and shelter is dynamic. It reassures our faith every day, knowing that our security is not determined by our circumstances but by the Lord.

May this truth add courage to your heart. With every trial that emerges, answer with the affirmation, "He is my refuge and my fortress." Let this statement change how you are living your day, how you are facing challenges, how you are dealing with other people, and in the first place, how you rest your soul in His care.

Prayer: My God, my strength and my refuge, my heart trusts in You. Amid today's noise and clamor, I find comfort in Your undying strength and protection. When fears surround me and shadows loom over my way, remind me that You are stronger than my fear, more real than my doubt. In the name of Jesus. Amen.

Embracing Shiloh:

June 6: The Strength of My Heart

Scripture for the Day

"I love you, Lord, my strength."

Psalm 18:1

Our relationship with God is based on knowing Him as the origin. In Him we are grounded, which is why we endure. The recognition of God as our strength is an act of faith and adoration, meaning we admit that all our talents and perseverance are from Him. We are love Him in a spirit of thankfulness and a sense of our neediness.

What do we mean when we say God is our strength? It expresses that God is all-powerful, and in Him alone can we find the nourishment for our souls and the might for our feet as we travel the Earth. It highlights the close association of God's provision between our human weakness and divine power.

By saying that our love for the Lord is our strength, we do not just seek refuge from the storm; we build all our lives in the safety of His unshakable qualities. The storm may not cease, but our hearts can continue, strengthened by the faith in the One who holds all power and authority.

As we walk through trials and triumphs, let us echo this psalmist's testimony, a song of victorious overcoming, acknowledging that all that we are and all that we have come is from our great God who deserves all our love and praise.

Prayer: Sovereign Lord, I declare my love to You, for You are my fortitude. In weakness, Your strength is my stay; in uncertainty, Your truth is my promise. Assist me in never forgetting that You are the unshakeable pedestal on which I stand. Embed in me a heart that searches for You first, a character that is blessed by Your company, and an existence that represents Your unshakeable might. I ask it in Jesus' mighty name, Amen.

June 7: Compassion That Transcends

Scripture for the Day
"Who is a God like you, who pardons sin and forgives the transgression of the remnant of his inheritance? You do not stay angry forever but delight to show mercy."

Micah 7:18

In times of uncertainty and spiritual drought, this verse is like a refreshing spring, revealing that the Almighty, who, despite our failings, chooses to offer pardon and steadfast love.

Who is like our God? His character is unparalleled, and His mercy is unconditional. Micah, an Old Testament prophet, knew all too well the shortcomings of Israel and the righteous judgment they deserved. Yet he exclaims the nature of God, which stands contrary to human vindictiveness. While we often hold grudges, but God releases His righteous anger in favor of compassion. This reveals that at the very core of God's being is an unwavering commitment to restore His people.

The Lord's forgiveness is active and transformative. He casts our sins into the depths of the sea, as Micah assures us later. This vivid imagery teaches us that our transgressions are not just hidden but are made irretrievable, lost in the fathomless mercy of God.

In response to such immense grace, our souls are called to humility and gratitude. We find peace in His promises, and those once weighed down by guilt can now dance in the freedom of His forgiveness. God's tender mercy invites us to come to Him, to shed the burdens of our trespasses, and to embrace the joy of a clean slate.

Prayer: Gracious and merciful Father, how astounding is Your love that washes away every stain of my sin. In Your presence, I stand in awe, for there is none like You, O God. Your compassion never fails, and Your mercies are new every morning. Thank You for delighting in mercy over judgment. I ask for a heart receptive to Your grace and quick to forgive others as You have forgiven me. Amen.

June 8: Embracing the Mystery of God's Timing

Scripture for the Day

"But about that day or hour no one knows, not even the angels in heaven, nor the Son, but only the Father."

Matthew 24:36

Christ speaks of His coming again, longed for by believers with hope through history. God has hidden from mankind the exact date when He will call up the living and the dead alike to face the original Judge someday. This secret is the greatest of mysteries reserved to the Father alone.

This verse is divine direction for the believer to entrust his life into the able hands and the perfect planning of God. It teaches an attitude of being always ready, distinct from being enslaved by excessive worry. This is active responsibility and vigilance instead of acute phobia guided by irrational counting.

"Day or hour" secrecy conveys the problem of our focused intentions about tomorrow's goal and teaches us to make every day special because we do not know if the next one could come. It calls us towards a life of Spirit-driven ambitions, on acquiring spiritual values, service to others and love. God's organizing of events is mysterious to us. But in this uncertainty lies we trust God.

This Scripture should be a reminder that we should not deviate into date-setting but rather be strengthened in our disciple lifestyle.

Prayer: Heavenly Father, You are the keeper of time, and in Your hands, all things unfold according to Your perfect plan. Help me to trust in Your timing and to relinquish the need to know all the answers. Strengthen my faith to be steadfast and alert, serving You wholeheartedly as I await the coming of Your Son. Grant me the wisdom to use my time wisely, to love generously, and to live expectantly, cherishing every day as a gift from You. Amen.

June 9: Embraced by His Spirit

Scripture for the Day

"For those who are led by the Spirit of God are the children of God. The Spirit you received does not make you slaves, so that you live in fear again; rather, the Spirit you received brought about your adoption to sonship. And by him we cry, 'Abba, Father.' The Spirit himself testifies with our spirit that we are God's children."

Romans 8:14-16

According to the Scriptures, God recognizes those who receive Christ as Savior are His children, who inherit nothing less than the Kingdom of God. It is not that we have earned it by our merit but that the only One who makes it possible is Jesus Christ, who extends grace to us. The Spirit calls us to follow, surrendering, our place, laying down before Him so that we can live the Father's desire. He guides our choices and actions; our mind is built on righteousness, peace, and joy of the Spirit who lives in us.

Moreover, being led by the Spirit reflects our identity: not only does God regenerate us, but He also speaks to us. We have the Spirit alerting us during those moments when that tiny voice helps us realize where we belong. So, our spiritual walk concludes with this incredible realization: that the results of a surrendered life will unfold as a blessing — love, joy, peace, patience, kindness, goodness, faithfulness, gentleness, and self-control.

Prayer: Abba Father, thank You for the treasure of being called Your child. I am humbled and grateful for the assurance that Your Spirit leads me. Teach me to recognize Your voice more daily and follow in unwavering faith. May Your Spirit shape my desires to align with Your will, guiding my steps toward acts of love, kindness, and righteousness. Amen.

June 10: Life in Abundance

Scripture for the Day

"The thief comes only to steal and kill and destroy; I have come that they may have life and have it to the full."

John 10:10

Here the contrast couldn't be starker: the thief who ravages and the Good Shepherd who gives abundantly. The thief is a symbol of loss and desolation, but Jesus comes as the bringer of life. Life brimming with divine purpose, joy, and fulfillment is characterized by the fullness of communion with God.

Fullness of life is the heart of the gospel. Jesus does not offer a life that skims the surface of spiritual depth. He offers a vibrant life, saturated with meaning and radiant with the glory of God. It is a life that transcends our limitations and circumstances, touching eternity with every breath we take. To have life to the full is to be filled with the peace that surpasses understanding, hope that does not disappoint, and love that knows no bounds.

Jesus, as the Good Shepherd, lays down His life for His sheep. He does this not out of obligation but out of love, enabling us to live lives that are truly free and rich with purpose. The life Jesus provides counteracts the damage the thief seeks to inflict. It is a restoration, reclaiming what was lost in Eden—intimacy with God, eternal purpose, and relentless joy.

As we embrace this verse today, may our hearts be encouraged. Let us walk boldly in the fullness of life granted to us through Christ's sacrifice and love.

Prayer: Lord Jesus, You are the giver of life, the One who restores my soul. Help me to embrace the entire life You came to give, to recognize the lies of the thief, and to dwell in the abundance of Your love and grace. May my heart be ever grateful for Your sacrifice and my life reflect the fullness found only in You. In Your precious name, I pray, Amen.

June 11: Patience in the Promise

Scripture for the Day

"The Lord is not slow in keeping his promise, as some understand slowness. Instead, he is patient with you, not wanting anyone to perish, but everyone to come to repentance."

2 Peter 3:9

Take a deep breath and let the weight of the day slip from your shoulders. As you settle into this moment, consider the vastness of God's patience. In a world when waiting even a few seconds for a computer to load can cause frustration, our Lord waits for generations with a heart full of love.

The Scripture today, 2 Peter 3:9, touches on a wonderful truth about the nature of God. He is not governed by our ticking clocks or bound by the impatience that so often drives our actions. God's timing is not a sign of reluctance or forgetfulness but of His merciful patience.

When it feels like things are moving at a maddening pace, and you're caught in the whirlwind of life's demands, God is invites you to acknowledge His gentle rhythm. His promises are like the dawn; they do not hurry, yet they never fail to arrive.

God's delay in fulfilling His promise of Christ's return reflects His desire for all to find salvation. He is compassionate, giving each one of us the opportunity to turn toward Him. You are a living testament to His patience, for His love has sustained you until this very moment, and it is His love that beckons your heart to seek Him every day.

Carry with you the peace that comes from knowing that God's timing is perfect, His presence is constant, and His love is unwavering. He is not slow but is giving us time to grow, to know Him more, and to reach others with His message of redemption. What a comforting thought that we are held within the patient, loving plan of the Almighty.

Prayer: Dear Lord, in the quiet of this moment, I come before You with a heart that is both grateful and at peace, knowing that You are so patient with us. Your promises are as steadfast as the sunrise and as sure as the tides. I thank You for not being slow to act but rather for waiting with a heart full of love, desiring none to perish. Amen.

Embracing Shiloh:

June 12: The Pursuit of the Shepherd

Scripture for the Day

"What do you think? If a man owns a hundred sheep, and one of them wanders away, will he not leave the ninety-nine on the hills and go to look for the one that wandered off?"

Matthew 18:12

This question posed in Matthew 18:12 invites us into a moment of reflection on the value of each soul to the Shepherd. Jesus is not teaching a lesson in animal husbandry but is revealing the depths of divine love and the lengths to which it will go to reclaim even one lost soul.

The parable of the lost sheep is a compelling portrayal of God's relentless pursuit of us as individuals. It disrupts the worldly economy of worth, where majority and quantity often overshadow the one, the singular, the seemingly insignificant.

This single sheep represents any one of us when we stray—caught in brambles of doubt, wandering in valleys of despair, or standing precariously on ledges of fear. The Shepherd's response? He actively seeks out the one. The ninety-nine are secure, but His heart compels Him to find and rescue the one that is lost.

Jesus' message is clear and transformational for our spiritual walk: in God's Kingdom, everyone matters immeasurably. No distance is too great, no night too dark, no path too treacherous for the Shepherd to tread in search of His beloved sheep.

Let this assurance settle in your soul today: you are never beyond the reach of God's grace. His pursuit is a powerful testament to His boundless love and commitment to every one of His children.

Prayer: Gracious Shepherd, thank You for Your unfailing love that never gives up on me. When I lose my way, Your Spirit draws me back into Your loving embrace. I am awed by the thought that You would leave the ninety-nine to seek and save me. Help me to trust in Your guidance always, to follow Your voice, and to rest securely in Your care. May I remember my worth in Your eyes and live today with the joy of being found by You in the name of Jesus. Amen.

June 14: Strength in Temptation

Scripture for the Day

"No temptation has overtaken you except what is common to mankind. And God is faithful; he will not let you be tempted beyond what you can bear. But when you are tempted, he will also provide a way out so that you can endure it."

1 Corinthians 10:13

Faith is often a path of darkness, and God is the best friend you have on that path. The same message that Paul gives to Corinthians is echoed to every Christian.

This verse takes us to the truth that can be shared with all who face temptation. It is not only an individual but common experience with us all. Accepting that our problems are not ours alone helps us understand that we are not supposed to struggle alone to avoid the problems that torment us and influence our thoughts and emotions.

The truth that God has been faithful to us in temptation is captured here. He is goodness and mercy. He gives the strength to break our chains. He goes over each obstacle separately and drops gaps where they should be so and bolsters our physical and spiritual capabilities to go through the storm. Thus, we are given a double gift, an insight into spiritual truths, and a practical optimism. Every trouble becomes an example and a proof of God's provision.

The faithfulness of God becomes our anchor, and the survival of our faith is the reason to escape. "Way out." This does not mean a partial victory, but the capacity to endure and dominate during it all. The pledge, therefore, is not a call to slumbering but a stimulus that causes us to look actively for the unmistakable mark of God's hand, guiding us in the right direction away from the snares of the tempter.

Prayer: Dear Father, I thank You for reminding us that true peace comes from leaving our problems in Your hands in whatever situation. Let me always be enlightened about finding the way out of each complex case You see. Grant me not to rely on my own wisdom but on Your care and direction. Amen.

Embracing Shiloh:

June 15: Trust in the Everlasting Support

Scripture for the Day

"My help comes from the Lord, the Maker of heaven and earth."

Psalm 121:2

As we face the rising sun and step into the day, our hearts might carry the weight of the unknown, the burden of the unfinished, and the tremor of challenges yet to confront. Yet, in the mists of early morning or the tumult of midday, we are embraced by a truth that anchors us firmly—the unwavering assurance that our help comes from the Lord, the Maker of heaven and earth.

What a profound declaration is found in this verse from the beloved Psalm 121! It is a harbinger of hope and a testament to the eternal steadfastness of a God who is not just a distant observer but a dynamic helper. We remember that the heavens and the earth, the vast expanse above and the intricate detail below, are the works of His hands. When the Creator of all decides to be our ever-present support, what can truly unsettle us?

This day, let every step echo the rhythm of this truth; every breath draws strength from this inexhaustible source. Amid our occupations and preoccupations, we can lift our eyes to the mountains, symbols of might and majesty, and boldly declare that our help is from the One who sculpted their heights and knows their every stone.

Prayer: Heavenly Father, I come before You with a heart full of gratitude for Your never-ending presence in my life. Your creation surrounds me, a constant reminder of Your glory and power. When I lift my eyes to the hills, let me always remember where my help comes from—it comes from You, the Lord, the Maker of heaven and earth. Amen.

June 16: Clothed in His Righteousness

Scripture for the Day

"From the blue, purple and scarlet yarn they made woven garments for ministering in the sanctuary."

Exodus 39:1

The artisans in today's verse crafted these garments with the finest materials—blue, purple, and scarlet yarn. Each component was meticulously chosen for those who would minister before the Lord. These sacred garments were not just articles of clothing. They symbolized holiness, dedication, and the beauty of serving God's purpose.

We, too, are called to be clothed, not in physical fabrics, but in the spiritual tapestry of His righteousness. Ephesians 6 reminds us to put on the full armor of God so that we may stand against the trials of this world. We are to weave our lives with threads of faith, hope, love, joy, and obedience, which are the markers of our service in His sanctuary, the world.

While the priests' garments set them apart, it is Christ's sacrifice that sets us apart. By His blood, we are dyed in scarlet, purified, and made holy. The blue thread represents the royalty of our calling in Jesus as children of the King. The purple signifies our identity as a royal priesthood, privileged to carry His presence wherever we go.

We are called to minister not in a temple made by hands but in the very lives we live. Daily, may we adorn ourselves with compassion, kindness, humility, gentleness, and patience, as Colossians 3 advises. These are the true garments of His disciples.

Remember, you are a walking testimony, a sacred vessel fashioned by the Divine Artisan. Walk in the dignity of your calling, beautifully arrayed in Christ's spiritual garments.

Prayer: Heavenly Father, dress me in Your holiness as I seek to serve You in all I do. May my life reflect the colors of Your love and grace. Guide me to walk in righteousness, wrapped in the fabric of Your wisdom and strength. Let others see less of me and more of You in every thread of my being. Amen.

June 17: Master of the Storm

Scripture for the Day

"The disciples went and woke him, saying, 'Master, Master, we're going to drown!' He got up and rebuked the wind and the raging waters; the storm subsided, and all was calm. 'Where is your faith?' he asked his disciples. In fear and amazement they asked one another, 'Who is this? He commands even the winds and the water, and they obey him.'"

Luke 8:24-25

The disciples in Luke 8 were in the thick of a storm, yet it was more than the wind and the waves that raged; it was their own fear and disbelief.

When they cried out to Jesus, their plea was borne from desperation, yet it brought a divine response. Jesus stood, rebuking the chaos into peace. This wasn't only a command over nature—it was a deep, spiritual lesson unfurled in front of their eyes. He was both the Master of the elements and of their hearts.

Jesus sharply asks, "Where is your faith?" It is a question that resonates through the ages, reaching into our very own circumstances. Where is our faith when we face the inexplicable, the difficult, or the terrifying? Are we to succumb to despair or turn to the one who is Peace?

Jesus' dominion over the natural world is a testament to His rule over our life's trials. Just as the wind and the waves obey Him, so too can the storms within us be calmed by His word. When we anchor ourselves in the belief that Christ is with us, we can find serenity amidst the tempest.

As He beckoned Peter to walk upon the waters—eyes fastened on Him—so He beckons us. Keep your gaze steady on Jesus, the author and perfecter of our faith, especially when the waves rise high. He is not just capable of calming the storm. He is with you in it, teaching, guiding, and holding you afloat.

Prayer: Lord Jesus, amid life's storms, I look to You. Forgive me when my faith wavers and remind me of Your power. Rebuke the winds and waves that unsettle me and command peace within my heart. May I rest in the knowledge that You are always present, commanding even the most chaotic elements of my life into Your perfect will. Amen.

June 18: Gods Handiwork

Scripture for the Day
"For we are God's handiwork, created in Christ Jesus to do good works, which God prepared in advance for us to do."

Ephesians 2:10

One cannot help but stand in awe of the truth that we are His handiwork. But to understand this masterpiece is to recognize not merely the what but the why. We are fashioned for a purpose, created in Christ Jesus for good works.

Imagine a sculpture created with no intent or a canvas painted without vision. This is not so with us. Each of us is a unique expression of divine artistry infused with intention and meaning. Our every contour carved by grace, every hue of personality, every gift and talent are the intentional strokes of the Master Artist's brush.

God prepared these good works in advance, saying, "Walk in them." He has set the path, aligned the opportunities, and equips us with every necessary tool. The good works are for us to write God's poems, His narratives in which we are the main characters, designed to spread His love, mercy, and justice in the world.

This is a communal journey created in Christ Jesus. We are a collective artwork designed to complement one another, to learn, and to grow in unity. When we embrace our purpose, we collaborate with God, and we join in the cosmic symphony of serving His will.

Let this profound truth sink into the very marrow of your bones: you are God's masterpiece, a creation unlike any other, formed by the hands of the Almighty to radiate His glory through your life's works.

Prayer: Divine Craftsman, I am in awe that I am Your workmanship. Help me embrace the purposes for which I was made; to serve joyfully and walk confidently in the good works You've prepared for me. Grant me the grace to see Your artistry in others and to celebrate the vast beauty of Your creation. May my life reflect Your love and mirror the work of Jesus, in whom I have a purpose. Amen.

Embracing Shiloh:

June 19: Spiritual Fruits

Scripture for the Day

"But the fruit of the Spirit is love, joy, peace, forbearance, kindness, goodness, faithfulness."

Galatians 5:22

Paul does not simply create a list of virtues to be admired when he talks about love, joy, peace, patience, kindness, goodness, and faithfulness. He describes the fruit as the product of a life lived by the Spirit.

Consider the first of these fruits: Love. It is not a transient emotion or affection that fades away in time but a solid dedication, just as God's love for us. The sweetness of it brings coolness to tired souls and food to hearts in need of mercy.

Joy comes as a godlike potion that stays even during pain. It does not rely on the situation but on the eternal loving character of God in us. And then comes peace, a tranquility that is within, that remains, though the storm should seek to sweep it away.

Forbearance, or tolerance, helps us to offer grace to others as God offers grace to us. It talks about patience, that does not lose strength. Kindness mirrors the gentle nature of God, a healing touch to a hurting world. Goodness is the virtue of kindness, which reflects integrity in all actions and intentions.

Finally, we get faithfulness – a continuous loyalty and confidence in God that never fades through the hardships we face. It's an affirmation that our anchor stands no matter how life rolls.

These virtues permit the Spirit's transformative force to take shape within us, forming us into Christ's likeness and eliminating darkness with the light of every act of divine love that is carried about by us.

Prayer: Father God, let Your Spirit bear forth more fruits within me. Make in my heart a garden full of love, joy, peace, longsuffering, kindness, goodness, and faithfulness. May I not only know these virtues in words but also in action in the reality of my life, Lord, as Your presence lives and moves in me. May my life be a witness of Your Spirit, showing Jesus to all around me. Amen.

June 20: Divine Defense

Scripture for the Day

"We have a strong city; God makes salvation its walls and ramparts. Open the gates that the righteous nation may enter, the nation that keeps faith. You will keep in perfect peace those whose minds are steadfast because they trust in you. Trust in the Lord forever, for the Lord, the Lord himself, is the Rock eternal."

Isaiah 26:1-4

Picture a city with walls so strong they're made of salvation itself. That's some impressive masonry work, courtesy of God's own construction company — Divine Defense Inc.! And the only keycard you need is righteousness. I hope you've been keeping up with your spiritual fitness, doing those faith-lifts and truth crunches!

Now, let's talk about this perfect peace business. God offers peace like a heavyweight blanket lovingly knitted to keep us all cozy and calm, even when the external world is like a hyperactive toddler hopped up on sugar and late for naptime. The secret to draping that peace around our shoulders? A steadfast mind that trusts in God. It's like spiritual superglue that won't crack under pressure.

Thinking of the Lord as our Rock eternal is also rather encouraging, especially since most of us fluctuate more than a politician's promises before an election! Our Rock does not erode, does not weather away, and certainly doesn't crumble when we cling to Him. And let's face it, sometimes our lives need that kind of stability, especially when we seem to be making decisions with the certainty of a squirrel crossing the street.

Prayer: Heavenly Father, thank You for reminding us that salvation is not just a strong concept but the very walls that protect us. We're talking spiritual superheroes' fortress-level strength! I'm sending up a celestial RSVP as you say, "Open the gates!" and I'm jogging right through—though I might be slightly out of breath, Amen.

Embracing Shiloh:

June 21: Seeing Through the Storm

Scripture for the Day

"My ears had heard of you but now my eyes have seen you. Therefore I despise myself and repent in dust and ashes."

Job 42:5-6

Job's journey was no walk in the park. He had some serious dialogue with the Almighty after what might be called the worst time ever in the history of bad days. His friends had theories, his wife had advice, but in the whirlwind — literally — it was God's voice that redefined everything.

These profound words from Job capture a moment of unparalleled spiritual clarity. It's like the difference between reading about the Grand Canyon and standing on its rim — awe-inspiring reality eclipses second-hand knowledge.

The lesson for us? True understanding of God doesn't come from hearsay or even rigorous study alone; it comes from encounters that resonate deep in our souls. Job is schooled in the most epic way possible, leading to an "I-get-it-now" discovery that's so overwhelming he claims there's a whole lot he's gonna put in the trash. And that's not just his outdated wardrobe, folks!

Let's apply this principle. When life hurls its worst, and friends tote their well-meaning clichés, may we seek the face of God amid the storm. Because when we see God, truly see Him, our world reorients. Our pride melts like ice cream on a hot sidewalk, and humility becomes as natural as breathing.

Job's transformation is both relatable and hopeful. So, let's aim to move from "hearing about" to "seeing and experiencing" the divine in our daily lives.

Prayer: Father in Heaven, I come before You humbled by the story of Your servant Job, who endured much and saw You amid his trials. I confess that often I've relied on second-hand knowledge of You, relying on my own understanding or the words of others. But today, I long for an authentic vision of Your majesty, one that reshapes everything I am, Amen.

June 22: A Thankful Heart

Scripture for the Day

"I will give thanks to you, Lord, with all my heart; I will tell of all your wonderful deeds. I will be glad and rejoice in you; I will sing the praises of your name, O Most High."

Psalm 9:1-2

The psalmist David had a knack for getting to the heart of worship. Here in Psalm 9, he's not just singing a catchy tune about gratitude; he is painting a picture of his whole heart in vibrant, worshipful technicolor. David's heart is like a banquet hall, thrown wide open to celebrate the goodness of God.

When we give thanks with all our hearts like David, we're not leaving room for halfhearted murmurs of thanks or distracted acknowledgments. No, we're talking about a full-blown, all-consuming gratitude fest. Imagine if our lives echoed this kind of thankfulness! Our daily routines would turn into thanksgiving parades, and every little provision would warrant its own ticker-tape celebration.

David's commitment to tell of all God's wonderful deeds is not just a poetic whim—it's a battle strategy against discouragement and despair. When we recount God's faithfulness, we build a fortress of remembrance that stands strong against life's many storms.

And there's joy here, too—pure, unadulterated joy—plus a side order of rejoicing. It's an invitation to the kind of party where everyone ends up dancing with joy because of who God is and the marvelous things He has done.

This kind of praise party starts with the decision to focus the heart solely on the One who deserves all our songs of gratitude. Today, let's join David. Let's recount the wonders God has worked in our lives and let our joy overflow into a melody of praise that celebrates the Most High.

Prayer: Lord of wonders and reason for my song, I approach You today with a heart brimming with gratitude. I declare, like Your servant David, that my thanksgiving will be wholehearted, spilling over every area of my life. I am in awe of Your wonderful deeds and Your unfailing love for me, Amen.

Embracing Shiloh:

June 23: Crafted in His Service

Scripture for the Day

"So Bezalel, Oholiab and every skilled person to whom the Lord has given skill and ability to know how to carry out all the work of constructing the sanctuary are to do the work just as the Lord has commanded."

Exodus 36:1

Bezalel and Oholiab might have been the headliners in this divine construction project, but they were far from being a two-man show. This was a testament to a community where each person's God-given talents were harnessed for a purpose far greater than individual achievement: building a sanctuary where God's presence would dwell among His people.

Reflect on that for a moment. Isn't it awe-inspiring to think that the Creator of the universe gifts us with specific skills and talents? In Exodus, we see God's Spirit poured into hearts and hands, making them capable of creating something holy. It's like God is the ultimate project manager, assigning roles that perfectly fit each person's CV—crafted by Him, no less!

So, where does that leave us? We might not be called to build the Tabernacle, but each of us has been endowed with a set of spiritual and natural skills meant for God's purposes—our own version of silver and gold for the sanctuary. Our daily work, when done for His glory, has as much sacred potential as crafting the Ark of the Covenant. The question is: Are we using these skills to serve God's master plan?

Today, let's embrace the skills God has entrusted to us. Whether you're a spreadsheet savant, a wizard with words, a caregiving champion, or a leader who lifts others, your talents are divine tools. Work with the joy of Bezalel and Oholiab, knowing your part of a celestial blueprint, crafting a life that glorifies the Master Designer.

Prayer: Heavenly Father, I pause today to consider the abilities You have graciously woven into the fabric of my being. Like Bezalel and Oholiab, I want to be attuned to Your Spirit's guidance, using my God-given skills to fulfill Your commands and advance Your Kingdom. Amen.

June 24: The Revolution

Scripture for the Day

"I will be glad and rejoice in your love, for you saw my affliction and knew the anguish of my soul."

Psalm 31:7

To seek revolution is to desire transformation at the most fundamental levels. Psalm 31:7 stirs within us a spiritual upheaval that challenges the very roots of despair. It's a raw outcry from the depths of affliction, met by a love so mighty it sees and knows our inner turmoil and rushes in to rescue us.

The Creator of all does not stand aloof. He isn't blind to the suffering and needs of His children. This shatters the chains of loneliness and distress and sparks a radical rejoicing in His love. God intimately knows the angst of our souls and is moved by it.

His awareness is coupled with action. The psalmist's gladness stems not only from being seen and known but also from the deliverance that follows. There's a divine activism at work in God's love—a holy initiative that charges into the fray of human brokenness.

We are known, truly known—the naked truth of our souls laid bare before divine compassion. To know such love is to rebel against the lie that we are alone in our suffering. It is to celebrate the uprising of hope that God's knowledge of us prompts His hand to work on our behalf.

As you encounter today's trials and triumphs, may you carry with you this proclamation of God's intimate love. May it stir a revolution within your spirit, causing old fears to crumble and new joy to rise.

Prayer: Loving Lord and Architect of my salvation, my heart swells with revolutionary joy in recognizing the depth of Your love for me. You see beyond my facade and into the core of my being—You know my affliction and the anguish of my soul, Amen.

Embracing Shiloh:

June 25: The Cornerstone of Possibility

Scripture for the Day

"Jesus said to them, 'Have you never read in the Scriptures: "The stone the builders rejected has become the cornerstone; the Lord has done this, and it is marvelous in our eyes?"

Matthew 21:42

In the words of Christ, we uncover a motivational gem. The stone originally cast aside, deemed unworthy by the builders, becomes the cornerstone—the essential piece without which the structure cannot stand. Through God's grace, what is overlooked becomes foundational.

Embrace this: your value and potential do not hinge on the world's affirmation. Like the cornerstone Jesus speaks of, your significance is divinely appointed. Rejections and setbacks are not final verdicts; they are the preludes to a greater plan that God has authored for your life.

And the beauty is that God often uses the "rejected stones," the unlikely candidates, the underdogs, to accomplish His most enduring work. The world looks for polished marble, but God seeks willing hearts. Your readiness to serve Him, to trust His vision, can turn what was once dismissed into something glorious and indispensable.

Use this as a springboard today—a reminder that in God's hands, you are more than you seem. Every no, every dismissal, can be a redirect to a divine yes. As you position yourself in Christ, your life takes on the worth of a cornerstone in God's masterful construction.

Let's resolve to see our trials through this lens, to understand that our moments of rejection may just be setting the stage for God's marvelous work. Rest in the knowledge that the Lord's plans are often hidden in the discarded stones of life— ready to become central to His grand design.

Prayer: Father, I stand in awe of the transformation You bring to life's rejected stones. I hold onto the deep truth that what is disregarded by the world can be repurposed by Your hands for a role of unexpected significance. Amen.

June 26: Abiding in Everlasting Love

Scripture for the Day

"As the Father has loved me, so have I loved you. Now remain in my love. If you keep my commands, you will remain in my love, just as I have kept my Father's commands and remain in his love."

John 15:9-10

What an incredible thought! To be wrapped in the same love the Father has for the Son! It's a boundless, and all-consuming love. Jesus extends this invitation as a lifeline—remain, abide, and make your home in My love.

Being loved by Jesus is not a fleeting experience but an enduring state. It's a daily choice to nestle into this love, to let it become the ecosystem in which our spiritual roots grow. This environment of love is where we truly thrive, bearing fruit that can weather every season of life.

Keeping His commands is how we stay plugged into this ultimate power source of love. It's not blind obedience but an active choice to align with love's rhythm. In the same way a trellis supports a vine. His commandments guide us upward, keeping us close to the heart of divine love.

Take a moment to consider: God's love is not dependent on the world's standards. It's not earned by ticking off spiritual checkboxes. It's freely given, but we must choose to stay within its reach.

As you step into today, engage with this: You are deeply loved by Jesus, sustained by the same love that echoes through eternity from the Father. Let that empower you—saturate your actions with grace, embolden your decisions with courage, and suffuse your interactions with kindness.

Prayer: Everlasting Father, how humble I am in the light of Your incredible love—a love that You have extended to me through Your Son, Jesus. I am amazed that You call me to abide in this love, to make it my dwelling place. Amen.

Embracing Shiloh:

June 27: Joyful Journey

Scripture for the Day

"And the ransomed of the Lord will return. They will enter Zion with singing; everlasting joy will crown their heads. Gladness and joy will overtake them, and sorrow and sighing will flee away."

Isaiah 35:10

Here, we stand at the dawn of a new day, contemplating a journey. Isaiah presents us with a vision of the ultimate homecoming, a trek with joy unspeakable and crowned with a beauty that lasts forever. This is the promise to us — not just a destination, but a journey transformed.

In life's hardships and heartaches, keeping our footsteps firm and our spirits high can be challenging. They point to a future where our weariness is not merely relieved but replaced with a cloak of joy.

Visualize walking on a road where the milestones are singing, and the signposts are hope. This is the "Highway of Holiness" God has paved for His people — a road where sorrow is a foreigner and joy is the native tongue. This path is open to the redeemed, to those who embrace the name of the Lord and seek His face.

Let us carry this image with us today: though your journey may weave through trials, you are destined for a celebration that outshines the sun. The gladness that awaits promises to overtake us—not just catching up but engulfing us like a wave, washing away every trace of despair.

Hold fast to the truth that we are ransomed of the Lord, snatched from the grip of the grave, and given a future festooned with joy. Today's motivation springs from this truth, urging us to keep moving forward with assurance that our final chapter is one of victorious rejoicing.

Prayer: Lord, my ultimate Redeemer, with a heart full of hope, I thank You for the assurance of joy that awaits as I journey through life with You. In the shadow of Your promises, I find strength for today and a vibrant hope for tomorrow. Amen.

June 28: Guard Your Heart

Scripture for the Day
"Above all else, guard your heart, for everything you do flows from it."

Proverbs 4:23

Proverbs never fails to deliver punchy, life-altering counsel. In this compact directive, we're told to prioritize the safeguarding of our hearts with more vigilance than anything else we protect—because it is the wellspring of life.

Imagine your heart as a fortified city, the source of all that is good and meaningful in your life. Its walls are strong, not only to keep the world out but to keep the purity and passion within from being tainted by those forces that would seek to diminish its brilliance.

Your actions, your words, and the very course of your life are formed here. So, it's vital to keep watch about what we allow through the gates. It's not just a matter of emotional defense but of cultivating a place from which streams of living water flow—pure, unspoiled, life-giving.

This is no small task. It's a daily undertaking. It's recognizing and resisting the negatives that can seep in and poison our perspective. It's embracing and multiplying the positives that align with divine truth.

As you navigate the complexity of life, remember your heart is the soil for your dreams, the canvas of your creativity, the sanctuary where wisdom whispers. Guard it with intention. Nurture it with truth, and let it be a reservoir from which flows rivers of goodness and light.

Prayer: Almighty and wise God, thank You for the profound wisdom You bestow through Your Word. I recognize the magnitude of the charge to guard my heart, and I invite Your Holy Spirit to fortify its ramparts, Amen.

Embracing Shiloh:

June 29: Cast Your Cares Upon Him

Scripture for the Day
"Humble yourselves, therefore, under God's mighty hand, that he may lift you up in due time. Cast all your anxiety on him because he cares for you."

1 Peter 5:6-7

First Peter 5:6 directs us to submit, an attitude of bowing down under the mighty hand of God. It's in this act of humility that we find the paradox of God's Kingdom: we must go down to be able to go up.

To humble ourselves recognizes our human limits and confesses that we are not the controllers of our destiny. It means leaving our pride, hopes, talents, and weaknesses in the hands of God and believing that His ways and timing are better than ours. Scripture guarantees exaltation in "due time" – a divine lifting us up above the peaks that our own deeds alone could not reach.

The powerful arm of God is not only uplifts—it is also supports, guides, and protects. We are not left in dust and ashes as we lower ourselves. It is the hand that has fashioned the universe that holds us. In humility, we find our true dignity by becoming more like Christ, who "made himself nothing by taking the very nature of a servant" (Philippians 2:7).

Self-reliance is valued in our culture, while God favors those who believe in and rely on Him. Humility is the fruitful earth in which the seed of God's purpose thrives. It is the floor on which a life of spiritual prosperity is laid. We are called to put our anxiety on Him, for He cares with us, to humble ourselves under His hand so that in due time, His power might be manifested in us and through us.

Prayer: Lord of hosts, I decided to humble myself under Your mighty hand. Teach me to set my ego and pride aside to have faith in Your ideal plan and time. In quietness, let me feel Your leading hand, and in temptations, Your abiding grace. Lift me, O Lord, not to a place where I am glorified, but to the elevation of Your glory through my life. In Jesus' name, Amen.

June 30: The Majesty of God's Greatness

Scripture for the Day
"Make every effort to live in peace with everyone and to be holy; without holiness, no one will see the Lord."

Hebrews 12:14

In this verse resides a challenge - dare to seek peace and purity as the doorways through which God can be seen in all His glory. The path to witnessing the glory of the Lord cuts through the heart, asking us to develop a life untouched by the discord that so often characterizes human relations, undamaged by the flaws we might think are unfixable.

The greatness of God is amazing. He personally empowers His child to live the standard of holiness that reflects His character and then leads us to live in peaceful relationship with others.

Our work for peace is not only an outward activity but an inward one. We should unite our restless spirits with the soothing peace of God. Also, the life of holiness is an ongoing realignment towards the divine, peeling off the layers that separate us from His purity.

His greatness is glorified in us when we are at peace with others and when our lives reflect His holiness. God does not want to keep us at a distance but chooses to have a personal relationship with us so that we may grow in holiness and see His majesty even more clearly.

Prayer: O Lord, Your presence is the sweetness that captures my heart and instills my soul with awe. Every atom in the universe vibrates in response to Your power; however, I am here as a witness of Your love and the recipient of Your mercy. Lord, help me live in peace with everyone and strive for the holiness You desire. Amen.

Embracing Shiloh:

July 1: Feeling God's Touch in Every Moment

Scripture for the Day

"A woman came to him with an alabaster jar of very expensive perfume, which she poured on his head as he was reclining at the table."

Matthew 26:7

Today's verse is a picture of love and selflessness, showing how powerful God is in our lives when we come to Him with generosity. The woman in Matthew 26:7 shows her love for Jesus through an act of worship, which was both individual and costly – a real example of Jesus's impact on her life.

The influence of God in our lives can be like this aromatic offering, changing us into something that cannot be but noticed. Like a fragrant scent, His being penetrates all our ways of living, letting its sweet fragrance into the remote areas of our souls. God leads us with grace and love, and our reaction to that care should be like the woman's pure adoring act.

It should be remembered today that every small step we make is a sign of our thankfulness to Him for His miracle initiated in our lives. All that we do can be an expression of love, recognizing the enormous influence of God. His light turns our ways from the shadows. His healing soothes our deepest hurts. His love fills all the emptiness.

Just like perfume's smell fills the room, so does God's presence, impacting our lives, providing a testimony of His eternal faithfulness, and transforming power. In this, we find many motivations in giving Him our best. Just as the woman with the alabaster jar did, we pour sacrificial praise from a heart that His grace has forever touched.

Prayer: My Lord and my Redeemer, I come to You, inspired by the woman's act from Matthew's Gospel, utilizing a valuable perfume to honor You. I am recalling the ways You have made my life different with Your presence, altering my very essence as that perfume altered the same air inside. Amen.

July 2: Fight the Good Fight of Faith

Scripture for the Day

"Fight the good fight of the faith. Take hold of the eternal life to which you were called when you made your good confession in the presence of many witnesses."

1 Timothy 6:12

With the new day unfolding, we are reminded of the continuous struggles through which we tread in our walk of faith every day. Amid the challenges and the chaos, 1 Timothy 6:12 calls us to warrior status, with the command to "fight the good fight of the faith." What does it mean to be a warrior in the spiritual world?

Faith is not a call to arms in the military sense. Rather, it's an opportunity to fight for that which we believe to be true, to defend our beliefs and convictions even when the waves rage against us. We are called to lay claim to the life that will never end, a life beyond momentary fears.

We took our stand for Christ in the sight of many during a moment of decision, or through our everyday actions, which lay bare our root faith. Remember that today. It is our standard in the battlefield of life where truth often struggles with deception and principle with concession.

The good fight carries with it honor. It is good as it is righteous and just, worth all the effort. It is not a struggle that depends on our own power, but it is supported by the divine force which leads and upholds us. The life eternal that we seek is not only a promise of the future but a present reality, which demonstrates itself in peace and hope amid trials.

Pause to think about the parts of your life where you are called to fight this good fight. It might be in hunting down injustice, dispersing goodwill, or maintaining faith when doubts besiege. Every time we select love over hatred, forgiveness over malice, and tranquility over discord, we are moving ahead in this worthy war.

Prayer: Heavenly Father, in this day's quiet, I answer the call to strive with godly might. Give me strength, courage, and wisdom to remain steadfast in times of trials, to cling to the hope of eternal life. Assist me at remembering my testimony of faith, the time I decided to walk with You and to follow Your Word. Let my doings and utterances express Your love and grace, a witness of the hope which is the foundation of my soul. Amen.

July 3: Becoming Righteousness

Scripture for the Day
"God made him who had no sin to be sin for us, so that in him we might become the righteousness of God."

2 Corinthians 5:21

This verse gives an unimaginable exchange – the perfect One took away all our ugly sins so that we, who are unfit, will be covered in the righteousness of God.

By knowing our natural impotence to acquire purity ourselves we grasp the generosity of this gift. By virtue of what Christ suffered, we are accounted as righteous, not through our own righteousness, but through the righteousness of the One who was made to bear our sins.

Imagine the righteousness of God as a glowing robe, a robe that doesn't just wrap but changes. In Christ, we are not only made righteous, but we are born again, into a state of grace that dismisses our history and determines our future.

Let the awareness that you are justified in the sight of God produce in you the behavior required by such a high calling. You are no longer what you have failed to be but what God's grace is for you. When the world wants you to be down, rise in the power that God grants. When allegations are hurled, clothe yourself in the robes of heaven's righteousness, in the knowledge that you are justified by faith.

Pick honesty instead of deception, generosity instead of greediness, love instead of apathy. Keep in mind that you become a demonstration of God's power on the cross, a display of change and life to a world that hungers for both.

Prayer: Loving Father, standing before You today, Lord, I am amazed at the grace of righteousness which You have richly given me. Your Word informs me that Jesus, who knew no sin, was made sin for me so that I might be Your righteousness. To understand this kind of love and sacrifice, I find it wondrous, and so I shall forever be thankful. Amen.

July 4: Grace Through Redemption

Scripture for the Day
"And all are justified freely by his grace through the redemption that came by Christ Jesus."

Romans 3:24

As we greet the day and its many possibilities, pause to reflect on the great gift described in Romans 3:24. We are all freely justified by His grace through the redemption that came by Christ Jesus. What does this truth mean for us in our daily walk?

Justification means to be pronounced righteous in the sight of God. This righteousness is not earned or ever could be earned, but a gift. The gift of free grace is not cheap – it is expensive. It cost Jesus His life, offered in sacrificial love. Redemption is about being bought back, given back to the rightful owner, and being made good again.

Think about "freely by His grace." There is no exchange, no trade, no plea required. Our debt was so huge, but we paid nothing. We don't just stand acquitted but rather loved, embraced, and included in fellowship with our Creator. The freedom that this gives is no excuse to take advantage of but to encourage us to live thoughtfully, cheerfully, and reflects on the favor that was given to us.

Redemption is not only a concept but a living truth. You walk in liberty with God's loving hand leading you. Tripping during life, remember that you are not characterized by your blunders but as one redeemed in Christ.

The grace and redemption that we have received must be the glasses through which we look at the world and ourselves. It emphasizes the fact that nobody is out of the range of the grace of God, so we should give grace to others. In a world of the judgmental, let us be loving, give compassion and forgiveness, and humbly walk with God who has freely given us everything.

Prayer: Gracious Father, I present myself before You with a heart filled with thankfulness as I am made to understand today that I am justified freely by Your grace. The freedom that was brought through Christ Jesus has made me free, and I marvel at Your love for me. Amen.

Embracing Shiloh:

July 5: Peace with God Through Faith

Scripture for the Day
"Therefore, since we have been justified through faith, we have peace with God through our Lord Jesus Christ, through whom we have gained access by faith into this grace in which we now stand. And we rejoice in the hope of the glory of God."

Romans 5:1-2

As dawn touches the world with its subtle warmth, let us open our hearts to the truth found in Romans 5:1-2. Having been justified by faith, we have peace with God through our Lord, Jesus Christ. This must not be an earthly peace, changing with the seasons of life, but a heavenly peace that answers our hearts in any storm.

To be justified by faith is to be brought into right standing with our Creator, not by our works, but by our faith in the work done by Jesus on the cross. It is a trust that declares, "I rely on what I cannot do for myself, and I take hold of what has been done on my behalf." This trust brings us into a state of grace – unearned favor where we now stand steady.

Think about being in His grace. Picture it as a place of assurance that whatever comes your way in life, your closeness with God where we are flourishing with the confidence of God's unfailing love.

This hope is a cheerful expectation of what is to be, a sure glory of God's future revelation. Though the rush of glory has sapped what was and is, bits and pieces of it resurface in moments of beauty, truth, and love that we recognize every day.

Carry this peace and hope with you to all you confront, all you engage. When conflicts occur, be a peacemaker, being conscious of the deep peace given to you. When whispering despair, let loud hope respond. Your faith has unlocked the door to this grace – an infinite spiritual supply that will provide you with the courage, strength, and happiness that you need.

Prayer: Merciful God, With the day to be met, I take with me the priceless peace that I have in You through the Lord Jesus Christ. By faith, I have been justified, and by faith, I enter this new day. This peace is not my own doing but evidence of Your gracious love and sacrifice, the peace that passes all understanding and keeps my heart and mind in Christ Jesus. Amen.

July 6: The Lord of Strength and Peace

Scripture for the Day
"The Lord gives strength to his people; the Lord blesses his people with peace."

Psalm 29:11

In the stillness of this moment, let us turn our hearts to the promise found in Psalm 29:11. The Lord will provide His people with strength; the Lord will bless His people with peace.

Strength and peace sometimes look like travelers from another land, strangers to us in times of suffering or weariness. But this line doesn't speak of a perhaps or has-been. It tells of a gift of godly power and tranquility—freely shared, not deserved, and not depending on the perfect conditions.

What is this power from the Lord? More than muscle. It is an inner strength that steadies when the world around seems to tremble. His strength allows us to remain committed, to suffer in patience, to labor in courage, and to love when love seems hardest to give.

And His peace that surpasses all the peace in the world. It is sacred calm that does not deny the existence of strife but transcends it. The peace of God can still even the most turbulent heart, bringing order to chaos and certainty when doubt looms large.

Power and peace are gifts the children of God inherits. They are part of our spiritual DNA. Let us draw from this fountain of divine supply. When faced with a mountain of adversity, take the strength He provides to scale it. When storms of life harass, grab the peace He offers, knowing it is ours to keep.

May the strength and peace of the Lord be present in every word we speak and every choice we make. May people be amazed, giving us a chance to point them to the One who gives all good things.

Prayer: The Lord of force and rest, accepting the gift of this day, I express my gratitude for You, promising that You will make Your people strong and will bless them with peace. This verse of Psalm 29:11 is reverberating in my soul, in deep appreciation of Your perseverance. Amen.

July 7: Love Beyond Borders

Scripture for the Day

"You have heard that it was said, 'Love your neighbor and hate your enemy.' But I tell you, love your enemies and pray for those who persecute you."

Matthew 5:43-44

The radical words of Jesus found in Matthew 5:43-44 open a challenge: love your enemies and pray for those who persecute you. It is an order that counters human instinct, challenging us to a higher level, reshaping the horizon of love.

This love is not a passive or superficial feeling but a decision of the will. It is the love that calls for the *agape* love of God— unconditional, self-sacrificing, and all-consuming. Loving our enemies is accepting their being human, meaning we would not want them to suffer, and offering them the same compassion we naturally give our friends.

Such love calls for a deep dependence on the strength of God. It is not work we can do alone. But there lies the glory of God's command: it asks us to approach Him and lean out to the deep well of His love, which He releases into our hearts through the Holy Spirit.

We recognize the barricades we have created in our hearts, limits we refuse to venture past, boundaries beyond which we have decided that love does not, may not, or should not go. Let us then present those obstacles before the Lord in prayer asking Him to enlarge our hearts to love like He loves, to fill us with a divine compassion that spills over even towards those whom we find it hard to love.

Meet hatred with love and put cursing to a stop by speaking blessings. Think about the supreme act of love that Jesus showed when He prayed for His enemies, even from the cross. Rebirthing our reaction to our enemies truly reflects God and it might just be the guide that brings them to His love.

Prayer: Merciful Father, In the silence of this morning, the deep words of Your Son Jesus in Matthew echo within me. You fortify me to love more than what fits—widening the limits of my love even to the people who oppose me. It is the divine love that breaks all norms, a radical invitation to Your love for the undeserving, the unlovable, and even the unjust. Amen.

July 8: Surely Goodness and Love

Scripture for the day
Surely goodness and love will follow me all the days of my life, and I will dwell in the house of the Lord forever."

Psalm 23:6

The poet of the psalm, David, creates an image of our life path being attended by God's goodness and love. Reflect upon this promise: that whatever roads we follow and valleys we cross, goodness and love are not just fleeting guests but constant friends.

Neither merit nor our condition is the master of these two; love and goodness are gifts from the Lord reflecting His nature. This confidence helps us look back and see not only the imprint of our own steps but also the proof of God's sustaining grace and faithfulness in every moment, bliss, and ordeal.

How do we "dwell in the house of the Lord forever"? It affirms an everlasting union, a pledge of eternal life with God, having its beginning here and extending to the unbounded horizons of eternity. It is a possession that does not have to wait for the end of our earthly days, but a present truth we walk in with each moment lived in the presence of God.

Embark upon the tasks and interactions of the day with the assurance that goodness and mercy are enveloping you. They are your legacy as a child of God, your spiritual inheritance, the heritage that endures.

Prayer: Lord, my Shepherd, having a heart floating in the loveliness of Your promises, I am grateful that You promise that surely goodness and love will follow me all the days of my life. This knowledge brings me unwavering hope and a reason to hold my head high, regardless of the situation in which I find myself. Amen.

July 9: Cultivating Joy in Labor

Scripture for the Day
"I undertook great projects: I built houses for myself and planted vineyards. I made gardens and parks and planted all kinds of fruit trees in them."

Ecclesiastes 2:4-5

Think about the activities that steal time and power. In these verses from Ecclesiastes, Solomon talks about his numerous undertakings, his quest for achievement, and his contentment in making and doing. However, from his reflections, we also gather that these accomplishments did not satisfy the deep yearning of his soul.

Thinking over our own great projects that we do day after day also forces us to examine the meaning of our work in general. Do we aim to build and plant for our own honor, or are we planting and building as stewards of what we have been given by God?

Solomon's efforts are more than a reminder. Work can also be a form of worship, another way to share in God's creative nature. Yet it becomes really nourishing combined with wisdom to know that without God at the core, all our toil may become emptiness.

The tasks you perform every day, whether they are as big as building houses or as small as the soil in the house, office, or yard, invite God into your work. Search for the happiness and meaning that is connected not with the fruits of work but with doing it and seeing the One in whose presence the opportunity and strength are given.

Prayer: God our Father, I come to You today with my heart full of thanks for the duties that You have placed upon me. Assist me to regard my labor as Your creative might and a demonstration of Your magnificence. While I perform my chores every day, I lead my heart and hands to perform everything with love, commitment, and meaning. Amen.

July 10: Manifested in His Name

Scripture for the Day

"I have revealed you to those whom you gave me out of the world. They were yours; you gave them to me and they have obeyed your word. Now they know that everything you have given me comes from you."

John 17:6-7

In this prayer of Jesus to His Father, He prays for His disciples but not just for them. For us as well. We are those disciples who were picked out of the world to carry the light of Christ within.

The words of Jesus are not just past; they are present. By making known the Father to us, Jesus has given us the grand revelation that everything we have is from God – our gifts, our callings, our very lives. Having known this, how should we live? Our existence must be filled with the appreciation of the joy at the kindness of our Maker, striving to follow His Word as the ultimate response of our realization that we are His.

Meditate today on the fact that you have been personally shown by Christ to the Father. It is unmerited grace that changes life and goes beyond time. You are called forth, blessed to reflect the glory of God by your obedience and faithfulness. Get this revelation-flood within you. It seizes you to live for the eternal rather than for this world, for His glory, not for yours.

Prayer: God in Heaven, I marvel how You have revealed Yourself to me. You have removed the veil, O Lord, through Your Son, Jesus, and let me see Your face, Your heart, and Your love. I thank You for saving me out of the world, for making known the marvels of Your great truth, and for committing to me Your ways. Amen.

Embracing Shiloh:

July 11: Clinging to the Source of Truth

Scripture for the Day
"I have told you these things, so that in me you may have peace. In this world you will have trouble. But take heart! I have overcome the world."

John 16:33

During life, we wade through ups and downs. The words of Jesus in John 16:33 are a comfort in ongoing storms. They are an assurance, giving us peace that is not of this world but from Jesus, the Overcomer.

Today, think about the trouble that you are suffering. That could be personal tests, relationship problems, or bigger worries about the state of the world. Jesus does not dismiss the fact of our struggle but rather, He admits it and at the same time, brings us comfort and triumph in His victory.

By saying that we may have peace "in Him," Jesus calls us to come into a holy space in which, despite the turmoil that may be around, our hearts can rest. This peace does not mean that our problems get erased but that we have what it takes to confront them with a strong spirit and hopeful mind that we are not handling them alone.

For today—and every day—we get comfort from the words of our Redeemer, Christ Jesus. Let's opt to dwell in the victory He has already won. Let's get peace in His presence, courage through His words, and power from His resurrection.

Prayer: Lord Jesus, I breathe deeply and remind myself that You have conquered the world. Among all that is going on, I make a choice to hold on to this truth. I am aware of life's woes, but I refuse to be defeated, for You have promised triumph. Amen.

July 12: In Honor and Love

Scripture for the Day

"Be devoted to one another in love. Honor one another above yourselves."

Romans 12:10

Romans 12:10 is a powerful mandate to adopt an attitude of selflessness that stands against the instincts and values of the society which the world glorifies.

To be devoted to one another in love is the reflection of the love of Christ to people, love that is constant and sacrificial. It is a love that does not diminish with the contrary feelings of people or contrary events but lasts, based on the nature of God Himself. The theological insight here is the image of Trinitarian relations—Father, Son, and Holy Spirit—all perfectly dedicated by love and respect to each other. This is the heavenly pattern that we are required to live in our relationships with others.

But Paul does not limit himself to devotion; he urges us to "honor one another above yourselves," challenging us to put the needs, concerns, and wellbeing of others before our own. That is the very nature of servant leadership that Jesus displayed – "not to be served but to serve." It is a posture of humility, for as we lower ourselves, we lift others up. This call is an offer to embrace the attitude of honor that makes others special, perceiving them as created and valuable in the eyes of God.

While thinking about this Scripture today, prayerfully ask the Holy Spirit to show us areas in our lives where we can grow in our love and respect for each other. We must pray for the grace that the command of love goes beyond intellectual understanding and is lived with courage and consistency, which will turn us into the Christ-loving force the world needs.

Prayer: O God, all-powerful, You who are love itself, teach me to be devoted in love to my brothers and sisters. I wish to cast Your love in all my relationships, to set aside selfish pursuits, and to respect others beyond myself, even while it is costly. Amen.

Embracing Shiloh:

July 13: Growing in Grace

Scripture for the Day

"But grow in the grace and knowledge of our Lord and Savior Jesus Christ. To him be glory both now and forever! Amen."

2 Peter 3:18

Second Peter 3:18 speaks of a lifelong pilgrimage filling our minds and hearts by divine grace. Concluding the second letter from the Apostle Peter, it sums up the entire spectrum of Christian discipleship. It is a divine imperative to grow in two interconnected areas: grace and the knowledge of our Lord Jesus Christ.

This verse associated with the doctrine of sanctification, the process by which a believer is made more holy and more like Christ. Peter bids us to grow in grace before knowledge. The basis of our growth is not knowledge, but the unearned favor of God given us in Christ. This grace is the provision where partaking of Jesus is the best food. All spiritual growth is a product of God's Spirit working within us rather than just human endeavor.

Peter speaks of growing in the knowledge of Jesus Christ. Such knowledge is not just a set of facts. The way the Savior is known is made clear by the fact that that is what makes the change of the heart possible. It invites us to an intimate relationship where the facts of the gospel saturate every part of who we are and drives us to resemble Jesus in our daily lives.

Our growth in grace and knowledge points to an ultimate outcome: the Lord Jesus Christ is glorified. This opens our hearts to the eternal– the glory of God.

With every step we venture in faith to meet the heart of Christ. We should welcome the transforming influences of God's grace and the beauty in knowing the Redeemer better. May He be glorified in our lives.

Prayer: God, thank You for the favor that You have let overflow in my life through Jesus Christ. Your love and mercy are fresh every morning, and I am amazed. I come with Your heart, desiring to increase in the grace and understanding You have made available at no cost. Amen.

July 14: The Greatest Love

Scripture for the Day
"Greater love has no one than this: to lay down one's life for one's friends."

John 15:13

The love of Jesus proclaimed to His disciples is so deep, so great, that it cannot be fathomed. It is deeply personal and intimate. This love is not just a sense of emotion. It's a deed, an act, a supreme sacrifice, a love that Christ Himself will show soon on the cross.

True love is sacrificial. It throws light upon God's love for us in the person of Jesus Christ, who represents this greatest love in His readiness to give up His life for mankind. The cross is the historical and eternal witness of that fact.

We as Christians are not only called to accept this love but also to follow it in our lives. While dying, Christ enacts the selflessness and surrender that we are reflect in our relationships with others. This is not only perhaps dying for someone but rather living a selfless life to the point that we give more emphasis to the needs of others over our own, sacrificing our comforts, time, and resources for the sake of our brothers and sisters.

Think today about the relationships that you hold dear. Reflect on ways in which you can live out this love that is other-oriented, just as Jesus did for us. Let us not lose heart in doing good, for in due time, we will reap if we do not quit. May this greatest love inspire us to serve, to give, to love without end, as Christ in us.

Prayer: My Lord, thank You for the love that You have manifested to me, the love so big that You sacrificed Your life for mine. Your Son, Jesus Christ, and I pray for the grace to do the same in my life. Amen

Embracing Shiloh:

July 15: Joy In Our Eternal Names

Scripture for the Day
"However, do not rejoice that the spirits submit to you, but rejoice that your names are written in heaven."

Luke 10:20

In Luke's Gospel, we see fascinating moment where Jesus shares with His disciples a unique reason for their joy. This comes after 72 disciples have returned, excited since the spirits obeyed them in the name of Christ. However, Jesus turns our attention away from the that to the eternal, from earthly victories to heavenly conquests.

The divine viewpoint gives the Christian's primary source of happiness. Success in this world, spiritual achievements, and what our hands produce are things we should be encouraged by, but they are not the main source of joy in our lives. The recording of our names in the Lamb's Book of Life means our inclusion in God's forever family, our salvation ratified, and our future guaranteed by God's own hand. It is a reason for rejoicing that eclipses all others, that of life with God, secured for us by Christ's sacrificial love.

Deposit this certainty in your heart and be glad in it. Our names written in Heaven signify who we are as Christians, redeemed by His grace. This is a spiritual truth with eternal relevance. In the victories and struggles of today, we should note that the supreme pleasure is in the everlasting truth of our inheritance in Christ.

Prayer: Gracious God, Your love is so intense, and Your promise of my eternal home with You is so comforting. Thank You for the delightful happiness that doesn't come from my deeds but from the certainty that my name is written in heaven, inscribed in the Lamb's Book of Life by Your loving hand. Amen.

July 16: Guiding Paths

Scripture for the Day

"Start children off on the way they should go, and even when they are old they will not turn from it."

Proverbs 22:6

Proverbs 22:6 brings the comfort of a promise allied to a sense of responsibility. It says to us that the seeds we sow in the hearts of the young can flourish, leaving a lifelong legacy of the proper way and moral strength.

To set the children in the way they should go means much more than just a gentle push in the right direction. It includes constant nurturing, demonstrating a way of life and a set of values deeply ingrained by example and teaching. It recognizes the role of the caregivers, teachers, and others in influencing people.

This proverb speaks of the quality of the path we prepare for the next generation. It prompts us to see the tracks we have left in our lives and the markers we leave for others to follow. We need to consider the legacy not only in economic or social terms, but in the knowledge of life transmitted by our parents' acts and words.

In determining the path where we lead our children, bear in mind the north star of love, honesty, faith, and mercy charts the purest course. These are the signs of a trail that, once traveled, is never completely lost, and serve well when the travelers are no longer the kids now but guiding others. The command we give starts from love of the Lord, ensuring that the values we uphold will reverberate through eternity.

Prayer: Heavenly Father, stepping into this new day, I seek the wisdom of Your Word in Proverbs. Guide me to be a light of Your love and the direction to those whom I meet, particularly the children You have entrusted to my care. Make me patient, wise, and gentle in the way I teach and lead them. Amen.

Embracing Shiloh:

July 17: Dwelling in the High and Holy Place

Scripture for the Day

"For this is what the high and lofty One says— he who lives forever, whose name is holy: 'I live in a high and holy place, but also with the one who is contrite and lowly in spirit, to revive the spirit of the lowly and to revive the heart of the contrite.'"

Isaiah 57:15

In the immense glory of His majesty, God proclaims Himself residing not only in infinity but also with those who have humble and penitential hearts. What a God we serve! Glory without measure, but turning up to live in the lowest, most broken of the worst of us. This deep truth tells of a Maker who looks beyond our flaws and chooses to revive hope in a soul that has been broken.

He is the Most High and Lofty One. The word "lofty" does not just denote His position over all but that He is in a state of being that is beyond our human limitation and understanding. However, this very God wants to live in what we perceive as small and worthless places. God works in the extraordinary. But His greatness is also sown by His involvement in the ordinary grain of our daily life.

He revives the contrite, and He renews the lowly. Isn't it comforting that our spiritual strength is revived not by our power but by the soft, comforting breath of the Almighty? He raises the head of the fallen and refreshes the tired soul, showing His strength and His grace too.

Our spiritual attitude of humility and brokenness attracts Him. In our humbling and kneeling, His comforting presence dwells, for His strength is made perfect in our weakness.

Prayer: Oh, Lord our God, I admire Your awesomeness, which dwells in the whole of heaven and the Earth. I am overwhelmed that You decided to live with someone as insignificant as me. I admit that I need You, and I am always in need of Your grace and mercy, Amen.

July 18: Walk in Love

Scripture for the Day

"Follow God's example, therefore, as dearly loved children and walk in the way of love, just as Christ loved us and gave himself up for us as a fragrant offering and sacrifice to God."

Ephesians 5:1-2

As children imitate their parents, we also are to imitate our Heavenly Father. These verses call us to walk the path of love just like Jesus Christ did. This love is an active love that gives itself in sacrifice and service to others.

The love of Christ was an expensive love that took Him to the cross. He yielded His life not out of coercion but willingly, motivated by His undying love for us. This kind of love is termed here as an "odor of a sweet smell," attractive and acceptable to God. The fragrance of Christ's sacrifice went to the heavens, and in this way, salvation dawned upon mankind. This is the example of love that we are called to imitate.

To walk in love is to walk in purpose, to opt for actions every day that are unselfish. It is this forgiving love that reflects how we have been forgiven, and that is kind to others even when they do not return it, that seeks others' good before our own. Such love is basic to the very nature of God, for God is love, and to walk in love is to walk with God.

As perfume fills a room, Christ's sacrificial love fills our lives, changes us, and urges us to give ourselves to others. We are to be the aroma of Christ in a world that is usually contaminated with the stench of self-centeredness and hate. This is no walk in the park; it is a walk of surrender and commitment to live the love that has been poured so bountifully upon us.

Prayer: Father in Heaven, who is love absolute, I am overwhelmed by the way You love me. You identify me as Your child, and in this, I want to emulate Your love without limits. Lord, direct my steps in the love that Christ did—love that led Him to give everything for us. Amen.

Embracing Shiloh:

July 19: The Path to Life Through Obedience

Scripture for the Day
"Keep my decrees and laws, for the person who obeys them will live by them. I am the Lord."

Leviticus 18:5

The Lord does not give His judgments as burdensome laws but as ways of life. This verse speaks a truth that runs like a golden thread through the tapestry of Scripture: obedience to the commands of God relates all phases of our life in every detail.

Our lives are bounded by God, as the gardener builds trellises for the vines. The commandments sometimes seem oppressive but lead us to His light. They are His love expressions for us to flourish and not wither in the chaos of moral uncertainty.

This approach to the law is brightened when we look at Jesus' radical fulfillment of the law in the New Testament. Christ is the ideal personification of obedience, and in His grace, we are also enabled to walk in the way of God's testimonies. Our obedience is not slavish but a joyful reaction to the love shown at Calvary.

The laws were imposed on the Israelites to create a barrier of protection to sustain life and develop a reliance on the provision and goodness of God. We are to follow the instructions of God, understanding that they are designed to save and prosper our souls so that we can live life in Him in His fullness.

My challenge is to ponder God's laws not as fetters but as conduits through which I am led to the very heart of God. I am to be controlled by His word and let Him mold my deeds, thoughts, and personality.

Prayer: Lord, I stand before You in meek acknowledgment of Your rule and love. Thank You for Your mandates, which are not heavy but are my guide my life to You. Assist me in finding Your laws as extensions of Your loving wish to let me prosper. Develop in me an attitude of submissiveness that delights to submit my will to Yours. Amen.

July 20: Trusting Through the Trial

Scripture for the Day
"The Lord said to Satan, 'Very well, then, everything he has is in your power, but on the man himself do not lay a finger.'"

Job 1:12

Reflecting on the book of Job, notably the moment when the Lord permits Job to be tested by Satan, helps us discover that trials are allowed by our all-powerful God, but He also sets boundaries to them. The question is not "Why do trials come?" but "What will I do when they do?"

The experience of Job teaches that suffering is not always the result of sin. It is a fact human existence in a fallen world, yet it rests under the divine lordship of God. When all visible supports crumble, His faithfulness is our fortress. Looking at the enormity of Job's testing, remember that the depth of spirituality is not determined by a lack of adversity but by faith in it.

This passage is more than an example of Job's trust; it is a comfort to my own spirit that, even when the enemy has a certain measure of power. It is limited, designated for a purpose, and always under the sovereign control of God. My Redeemer is the One in control, who sees the end from the beginning, and He will cause my ultimate good.

I am challenged to rethink trials, to consider them an avenue for God's faithfulness to be revealed and my character to be purified. Suffering is not sent by the Lord on a whim. My faith is being shaped into something new – stronger, harder, and more dependent on His grace.

Prayer: Sovereign Lord, I realize that the troubles that sometimes come my way, though confusing, are not greater than You are. Like Job, support me in enduring my tribulations with the undying faith to Your higher knowledge and kindness. Although You consent for some hedges of protection to come down, let me be comforted that nothing reaches me except through Your loving arms. Amen.

Embracing Shiloh:

July 21: Born Anew into Eternal Perspectives

Scripture for the day

Jesus replied, 'Very truly I tell you, no one can see the kingdom of God unless they are born again.'

John 3:3 "

Christ talks of a "second birth," a thought that arrests our ordinary understanding of life. He does not mean a physical rebirth but a spiritual one, showing a change so complete and dramatic that it is akin to a move from non-life into life.

How is being born again understood?

The second birth is created by the Spirit; it is not the offspring of the will of flesh or of man but of God. The change in salvation is so radical that it can only be described in terms of finding a whole new life, just as a baby being born is a new life for a human being. Rebirth is being given new eyes to see truths that we were once unaware of, being part of the world activity not only as the present circumstance but from an eternal point of view. It means new priorities, new values, and new actions. It echoes the prophet Ezekiel's account of receiving a new heart and a new spirit (Ezekiel 36:26).

As you walk through today, keep in mind that "to be born again" is not something that happens once and then is forgotten, but it is a continuous process of development, learning, and letting the Spirit mold you more into the image of Christ. May we all yearn for that fresh outpouring of the Holy Spirit, bringing forth life where there was none, sprouting hope in desolate places, and renewing our minds for the glorious Kingdom of our God.

Prayer: May we all yearn for that fresh outpouring of the Holy Spirit, bringing forth life where there was none, sprouting hope in desolate places, and renewing our minds for the glorious Kingdom of our God. Amen.

July 22: Go Forth with the Good News

Scripture for the Day

"He said to them, 'Go into all the world and preach the gospel to all creation.'"

Mark 16:15

Let us turn our hearts to the command that ignited the early Church's mission and continues with urgency for us today in Mark 16:15. We hear the risen Christ commission His disciples that is timeless, calling everyone to respond.

Christ's command is to "go into all the world." Everything in creation is under God's loving dominion. This commission is not just for the select few, not just for those with "minister" before their names, but for every soul that has experienced the redemptive love of Jesus.

The gospel is the good news of Jesus Christ of salvation, grace, and hope for everyone. It tears apart the boundaries created by states, cultures, and people. It cures and solidifies. We, as believers, are the messengers of this good news of salvation of the story of our Lord Jesus Christ and His life, death, and resurrection.

Do I practice the Great Commission in my life? Not with me giving such good news in words only, but in actions of kindness and love?

We might be the first gospel read by someone that they see. In our homes, workplaces, schools, or online, through our digital interactions, there are opportunities abounding to express and explain the reason for the hope that is in us.

Stepping out into your day, remember that the Holy Spirit has empowered you to be an effective witness. Like the early disciples, you are equipped, not by your might or power, but by the Spirit of the Lord Almighty (Zechariah 4). Therefore, you should not be prevented by a sense of inability but stand up, trusting His call.

Prayer: Almighty God, Lord, give me an understanding of the breadth and length of this call. Implant in my soul the fire to show Your love and truth to others. Give me eyes to behold the opportunities You bring each day to witness Your kind and generous face. Amen.

Embracing Shiloh:

July 23: Gods Mission

Scripture for the Day

"The thief comes only to steal and kill and destroy; I have come that they may have life and have it to the full."

John 10:10

Jesus makes the sharp difference between the enemy's intentions and His mission. The thief is the epitome of all that is bad, desiring to rob us of happiness, crush our aspirations, and obliterate our hope. On the contrary, Jesus comes to give us life and life more abundantly, a life full of purpose, meaning, and contentment.

The contrast is great. It makes us remember that what we confront and go through, the temptations move us away from God. The doubts are the strategies of the enemy to rob our abundant life. Yet Jesus, the Lamb of God, has come to restore us to the right position with God, to return all that had been stolen from us, and to direct us into a life of plenty in all dimensions.

Hold on to this promise closely. Is the thief seeking to take peace, love, and faith from us? We can take comfort in knowing that Jesus had already triumphed. He is our answer and the source of our eternal life. We have an amazing chance to live life to the fullest, not only to exist but to flourish in all seasons.

Look for the change that Jesus provides. Let's drop fears, doubts, and worries and invest our trust in Him completely. Let us accept the life that Christ has given to us and live it courageously, giving to others His love and truth.

Prayer: Heavenly Father, thank You for the truth found in John 10:10. We note that there is an enemy who comes to steal, kill, and destroy, but we are thankful for Jesus, who came to give us life abundantly. Give us the strength to overcome the challenges and temptations that come our way. Fill us with Your Holy Spirit and grant us the wisdom and discernment to recognize the enemy's schemes. Amen.

July 24: The Call of the Faithful

Scripture for the Day
"The Lord had said to Abram, 'Go from your country, your people and your father's household to the land I will show you.'"

Genesis 12:1

In Genesis 12:1, the Lord begins talking to Abram to leave the known world to enter a covenant that would determine the future. The call of God to Abram reminds us of the call to obedience and faith every one of us receives and follow Him to the unfamiliar.

We as believers are often called to venture out of what is unknown, believing He is leading us to a higher purpose. God pushes us to venture beyond what is comfortable, believing in His promises, and the belief that He has a purpose.

Abram's call marks the starting of a faith journey, a divine initiative wherein God invites him into a narrative much bigger than himself. Abram's compliance with no knowledge of the end entails a deep sense of faith in the character of God and His word. He does the same for us.

Here, we are pointed to the process of our life's inquiry and the attentive listening for God, calling us to move. It tells us that walking in faith means leaving something behind—a place of safety, a former identity, or even presumptions of God's design. Obedience involves sacrifice but also untold blessing.

Prayer: Father, I hear You beckoning me like you did Abram. Put into me the courage to abandon the known shores and come into the depth of Your will. Give me the belief to walk into the tomorrow You have for me without holding on to my maps and designs but standing only on Your word. Help me as I leave and reveal Your promises in my life. Amen.

Embracing Shiloh:

July 25: Salvation in No Other

Scripture for the Day

"Salvation is found in no one else, for there is no other name under heaven given to mankind by which we must be saved."

Acts 4:12

Let us be rooted in one name only, Jesus Christ, because salvation is only in that name. This verse tells us that there is no other Savior, no other way to eternal life. In Jesus, our brokenness is healed, our emptiness filled, and our wandering hearts found a real home.

In a world filled with a variety of beliefs and voices that profess to be the truth, hold to the exclusivity of Jesus. He is not one of many alternatives but the only path to reconciliation with God. This truth dictates both a responsibility and a privilege: telling the good news and living His grace in our lives.

As followers of Christ, are to be the salt and light, His messengers of love and compassion. Let us be both brave and unashamed in proclaiming the name of Jesus because it is only through Him that lives are changed, burdens are lifted, and souls are set free. Look for chances to tell His love in your daily contacts as keep in mind that salvation is not a mystery to keep but a gift to share.

Prayer: O Lord, I thank You for salvation present in Jesus Christ and in Him alone. I thank You for making me a new person and bringing me into Your family, which will last forever. Mold me, O Lord, to keep true to this truth and not to falter in my faith. As I go about my daily activities, let me receive the courage and understanding required to spread the gospel to others. May Your name be lifted up and honored in my words and deeds so that many may know the love and salvation in Jesus. I pray so in Your holy name, Amen.

July 26: Devotion in Fellowship and Faith

Scripture for the Day

"They devoted themselves to the apostles' teaching and to fellowship, to the breaking of bread and to prayer."

Acts 2:42

In the early Church, devotion was not only a private affair but also in fellowship with others. In Acts 2:42, they were unwavering, perpetually involving themselves not only in learning but in the true spirit of community life – communion, breaking of bread, and prayer. This verse still whispers to our hearts, bidding us to reclaim the beauty and happiness of a joint faith.

To be dedicated as they were meant to be immersed in the message, to live it, to go all out for the teachings passed down through the centuries, the words of life that the apostles carried. It was meeting with other people who were also believers, not only to be social but as a crucial element of spiritual development. In companionship, we receive the power to meet our trials and enjoy our triumphs.

Sharing meals in fellowship is the act of living life together in its simplest yet most meaningful sense. It reminds us of the fellowship of Jesus' last meal with His disciples as well as many He shared with them in their times together.

Prayer, the breath of the soul, is the thread that knits everything. From the conversation with God, we receive direction, consolation, and the food that sustains our spiritual pilgrimage.

Take inspiration from the early believers to be a faith community grounded in Christ's teachings, knit together through real relationships, rooting in each other's lives, and sustained by prayer without end.

Prayer: Dear Father, I thank You for the gift of Your Word and community of fellowship. While I meditate on the steadfastness of the early church, I plead that You give me the same craving for Your Word, loyalty to fellowship, and passion for prayer. Teach me to search for You zealously, to fill my brothers and sisters in Christ with love, and to live with them in hardships and victories. Amen.

July 27: Born From Above

Scripture for the Day

"Now there was a Pharisee, a man named Nicodemus who was a member of the Jewish ruling council."

John 3:1

Nicodemus, a man of far-reaching influence, sought Christ under the cover of night. His encounter with the Savior reveals a critical spiritual truth: its understanding demands humility and the desire to be changed from within. Nicodemus noted that Jesus was a teacher from God, but as their talk progressed, it emerged that mere intellectual acknowledgment was not enough. Jesus made the way for Nicodemus – and for all of us – to understand the need to be born again, to receive a new spiritual life from above.

Nicodemus' journey helps us realize that what we are, know, or have done in life doesn't link us more to the Kingdom of God. A sincere and humble heart that desires rebirth and renewal through the Spirit is what how divine truths are received. In my life, when what I know is questioned by Jesus' teachings, I too am called into daylight to be reborn to new life into God's Kingdom.

Every day is a chance to allow the Spirit to infuse life. You may seek God's face in the night by asking questions and admitting what you do not know under the gentle guidance of Christ.

Prayer: Kind Lord, I come to You this day when the world is silent, seeking Your knowledge. I recognize that I am ignorant and that my soul needs Your fresh touch. Implant in me, O Lord, a heart that is receptive to Your changing power and lead me by Your Spirit. Amen.

July 28: A Miracle Begins

Scripture for the day
"On the third day a wedding took place at Cana in Galilee. Jesus' mother was there"

John 2:1

Cana at a modest wedding is where Jesus performed His first recorded miracle in public, that of turning water into wine. It is a scene of laughter and merriment. The event reveals the divine power of Jesus and His attention to human requests, even the quite everyday ones, such as the serving of wine at the festival.

Looking at the mother of Jesus, Mary, we see her faith and comprehension of her Son's mission. She identified who He was, His power, and concern for others. It forces me to ask how I handle my problems and weaknesses. Am I giving them to Jesus as Mary did? Do I believe that He is concerned with life details and can transform a little into much?

The miracle at Cana was not just supplying wine. It was an example of the power of change is what Jesus came to give us – to turn the water of our rituals, routines, and expectations into the wine of joy, spiritual fulfillment, and new life in Him. Faith anticipates miracles in the ordinary and looks to find Jesus first in every situation.

May each of my needs, however small and common, remain in Christ, believing that He will perform miracles in them. Let's be open to the wonder of the ways in which Jesus chooses to demonstrate His love to us.

Prayer: Lord Jesus, once again to You I come today. I am captivated by the miracle at the wedding of Cana, as You showed Your compassion and Your power in such an intimate way. Thank You for loving us even at our lowest — when we ignore the faithfulness of love. I believe that You are ever mindful of my needs, and You are orchestrating what ought to be in my life without my knowing. Amen.

July 29: Renewed by His Mercy

Scripture for the Day
"He saved us, not because of righteous things we had done, but because of his mercy. He saved us through the washing of rebirth and renewal by the Holy Spirit,"

Titus 3:5

Salvation is by the grace of God, not by our works or our struggles. That my salvation is a gift, founded on God's mercy, not my worth, results in both relief and humility. It is against the general notion that we must earn our way to grace or labor to guarantee our salvation forever.

The mercy of God is a river, flowing and renewing. The cleansing and rebirth speak of a new beginning, a second life as new creations in Christ. The quickening by the Holy Spirit is a type of continuing renewal born in my heart and seasoned it with divine grace and wisdom.

Every hour of each day, the Holy Spirit is at work within me in such a way as the river molds the riverbank, gently and persistently. It is a symbol that my walk with Christ is not a still pool but a river of life, baptized in the grace of new birth and the constant refreshment that the Spirit brings to me.

Today, I accept this heavenly grace completely, understanding that I am saved, washed, and forever regenerated by love, which hardly can be grasped.

Prayer: Most generous Lord, I am amazed by the merciful act that You show me time after time. Thank You for redeeming me, not because of my works but out of Your mercy. It is an undeserved gift, and in this, my heart sings with thanks. Amen.

July 30: Let Not Your Heart Be Troubled

Scripture for the Day
"Do not let your hearts be troubled. You believe in God; believe also in me."

John 14:1

At a difficult time, Jesus addressed the unrest in the hearts of His disciples. His soft, but forceful talk told them not to let their hearts burn with the anxieties and uncertainties. It challenges me not only to trust in God but also in Him. Jesus provides a place of comfort and peace from the storm.

Belief is more than just recognition. It is an invitation to trust completely and to lean on the reality of Jesus being the way, the truth, and the life. This assurance is beyond my comprehension. It reaches the deepest part of me and quiets my inner storms. When I am facing hardships, when tomorrow is unclear and today is unbearable, these words whisper serene assurance.

Jesus did not guarantee a trouble–free life but His presence as a strong shelter. With Him, I draw courage, peace, and the power to live for another day. This trust is an active refuge in the One who has conquered the world.

May I retain this divine peace as the day unveils its challenges and tasks. May my heart believe that in Jesus, I have an eternal dwelling place, an ever-ready helper, and a strong fortress.

Prayer: Lord Jesus, my Shepherd, and Guide, I approach You with a soul in need of consolation and peace. In a world perplexed with doubts and troubles that I carry heavily, Your words come like a light. "Do not let your hearts be troubled," You told me, and today, I choose to accept this instruction. Amen.

Embracing Shiloh:

July 31: Encounters that Transform

Scripture for the Day
"The Pharisees heard that Jesus was gaining and baptizing more disciples than John"

John 4:1

Reading that Jesus was gaining and baptizing more disciples establishes the way Christ works within and outside the norms of society, touching places and hearts where other religious authorities would not venture. The word going around about the increase of Jesus' influence is the evidence of the power of renewal of His ministry and of His divine call to discipleship.

It marks the dynamic nature of Jesus' mission and how His presence makes hearts come alive, moves borders, and moves beyond the expectations of the religious establishment. God is acting, sometimes in ways or among people we would never have imagined and calls us to center in His expansive love.

Just like Pharisees, we might be tempted to evaluate spiritual growth through worldly success. But the example of Jesus shows that real growth in faith occurs in the places where we don't expect it, in the poor places, and from the ministry of love, without prejudice.

In the present, seek Christ in little signs and wonders unfolding in the humility of goodness, in everyday acts of kindness and love. There is wonder in what God can do in simple ways: maybe a talk, an act of service, or something that is remarkably beyond our imagination.

Prayer: Lord Jesus, You are truly the living water and the fount of all truth. Reflecting on how Your ministry expanded to so many people, particularly those on the fringes of society, makes me think about stepping beyond my own prejudices and comfort zones. I ask You to let me see Your work in the world and grant me the humility to accept Your mission with all my heart. Amen.

August 1: United in Purpose

Scripture for the Day
"So Christ himself gave the apostles, the prophets, the evangelists, the pastors and teachers,"

Ephesians 4:11

Ephesians portrays Christ's wisdom in creating a variety of gifts and roles within His body, the Church. It's not just a network of talents but a divine structure of unity and expansion, both personal and collectively. Christ purposely equips His Church and gives us specific gifts— whether great or small — to achieve His purpose here on Earth.

The roles listed—apostles, prophets, evangelists, pastors, and teachers—serve to work towards a common goal: growing the body of Christ. This helps us understand not only our personal part within God's plan but also the parts that He has assigned to others. Each gift is very important, and no matter what is being done, it will still have an eternal value in God's Kingdom.

The sharing of these gifts is a call to oneness. It connects me to back the others in their God-given place as I try to find and nurture my own. The final purpose is to grow up, achieving the whole measure of the fullness of Christ, as Paul would later characterize it.

In walking with the Lord today, strive for unity with other believers, respecting the different gifts each brings to the table of the Lord. It also evokes a hunger for growth — to intensify understanding, to fortify faith, and to participate more fruitfully in the Church's mission.

Prayer: Father in Heaven, I want to thank You for Your thoughtful design and the unique gifts that each one of us is given. The role assigned to me in Your divine narrative is what keeps me humble, and I want to be Your instrument there. Amen.

Embracing Shiloh:

August 2: Hope Amid Sin and Grace

Scripture for the Day

"Therefore, just as sin entered the world through one man, and death through sin, and in this way death came to all people, because all sinned."

Romans 5:12

Our verse today from Romans shows the birth of the creation of the sinful condition of the human—sin through Adam which is on every one of us. There is a stark reality: Sin is not only an individual action but a collective way of existence, a legacy that appears to be absolute and undeniable.

We do not have to be left in despair. It is not the end of the tale. Then the passage talks about the grace-gift, greater than sin. It talks about the One man who came into this world, Jesus Christ, to defeat sin and death, giving life eternal to those who believe.

This knowledge awakens hope. While the mark of sin is upon every facet of my existence and all that surrounds me, the grace given through Jesus Christ is all the stronger. It is the assurance that in Christ I have also triumphed; in Him I have found deliverance and the hope of a new life.

His grace moves me from a sin heritage to a righteous heritage. This move is not my doing but an exchange made graciously by God at the cross. Even though the world around me is fallen, my journey is lit by Christ's victory that I mine to partake in.

Prayer: Merciful Father, I approach You, fully conscious of the destruction that sin has brought upon this world and within my own life. However, in this I am not hopeless. For in Your measureless design, You have given a cure for sin in Your Son Jesus Christ, Amen.

August 3: Unashamed of the Gospel

Scripture for the Day

"For I am not ashamed of the gospel, because it is the power of God that brings salvation to everyone who believes: first to the Jew, then to the Gentile."

Romans 1:16

This bold announcement by Paul proclaims his unshakable faith in the gospel of Christ. Paul's gospel is not just a set of good suggestions or moral principles. It is God's mighty power, alive and active, saving and renewing all who believe.

A cross seems like a foolish message to some but, it is the highest truth about what God's love and deliverance means. Speaking this takes bravery, especially when one is laughed at, or the opposition is strong. However, the confidence of God's power in the gospel encourages us to be firm in the faith and share it with others with assurance.

Unashamed of the gospel, is not only verbal confession, but a living testimony of the transforming power of God's love. It is taking the gospel to the extreme so that its truth sings through every part of life, from the core of my being to what I present to the world.

It's all about securing the fact that the gospel is for all people without exception. Therefore, I have the confidence to pass it on to others with love, zeal, and a sense of calling, believing that the Spirit of God is at work to help others hear it.

Prayer: God Almighty, I appreciate the strength of Your gospel - the Good News which has changed my life and gives hope to every person who lives on Earth. I plead for the courage of my soul to announce, like Paul, that I am not ashamed of this fact, Amen.

August 4: Faithful Forgiveness

Scripture for the Day

"If we confess our sins, He is faithful and just and will forgive us our sins and purify us from all unrighteousness."

1 John 1:9

God's provision for my sins is transactional. My confession is responded to by His unwavering faithfulness. The Lord is, however, not just forgiving, but He is purifying. He takes away the stains of my sins and making me spotless in His righteousness.

My sins do not define who I am. Confession opens the door to fellowship with God, His invitation to start in His righteousness again. It is a lifestyle of rhythm in the grace of God. If I fail, I can confess. God will forgive me and cleanse.

I therefore do not have to hide my guilt but go to the Almighty in truth and faith. His righteousness is not to penalize but to restore. Each time I come back to Him, humbling myself to ask for mercy and healing, He welcomes me with love and mercy.

Grace has been extended to this day. The promise shall never fail. By confessing my sins to Him, I am empowered by His mercy and purified, ready to go through the day with joy and confidence, to face its challenges and benefits with a clean heart.

Prayer: Loving God, I kneel before You and I understand that I need Your grace. Thank You for Your amazing promise of pardon and cleansing. Help me to confess my sins without fear as You are faithful and just to forgive, Amen.

August 5: When the Spirit Moves

Scripture for the Day
"When the day of Pentecost came, they were all together in one place."

Acts 2:1

There was strong unity and anticipation demonstrated by the believers on the day of Pentecost. They were of one mind, waiting on the Holy Spirit. This breathtaking sight is an embodiment of the fulfillment of Jesus' words, and it shows us how unity and expectant faith allows God to reveal His miraculous power.

Power can be found in gathering in unity with other believers with one aim when we place ourselves in the right place for God to move. Just as the disciples had gathered in prayer, I too, can form a space in my life where the Spirit of God is allowed to flow freely.

The day of Pentecost was a divine appointment, the igniter that changed the early Church, and sent the gospel to all nations. It motivates me to seek God with other people and as in unity we wait for His miracles in our lives. That birthday of the Church on Pentecost motivates us to seek worship and prayer together as interlink with brothers and sisters in Christ.

I raise my heart in hope, knowing that the Holy Spirit, who descended at that time, is alive and well today, enabling, directing, and unifying all who call upon the name of the Lord.

Prayer: Father in Heaven, today, as I call to mind the unity of the disciples and the outpouring of the Holy Spirit at Pentecost, I desire to meet You in my own life. I desire to be of one mind with my brethren, standing together in faith for Your power which continues to move, Amen.

August 6: Diligent in Truth and Grace

Scripture for the Day
"Do your best to present yourself to God as one approved, a worker who does not need to be ashamed and who correctly handles the word of truth."

2 Timothy 2:15

Set amid a world of distractions this verse calls us to make a way that is acceptable to the Lord. Not a journey of quick fixes or shortcuts, but of resilience and honesty. To show myself approved unto God means living a life of discipline and studying, making sure my knowledge of His Word is correct and that my deeds reflect His teachings.

I want to be the worker that fears no reproach, so I need to delve deep into the Scriptures with understanding. This requires and deserves my full attention. And through that, I do not only study for the sake of knowledge but to recognize the intent of God and to show this in my daily living.

It is an active and continuous duty which is born of love for God and His word. It is a challenge that shapes me, strengthens my soul, and prepares me for the hardships of life with intelligence. Though the effort of getting God's blessing may look overwhelming, it is a voyage of grace. In every attempt to comprehend and use His word, He is there, leading and cautioning me with a gentle touch.

Prayer: Holy Father, I am here, today, seeking to know and willing to be enlightened. Assist me in giving my best as I try to offer myself to You as one who stands approved. Give me the intelligence to do right by Your holy Word of truth. My desire is not to be ashamed but to serve You well, working and living to honor Your name, Amen.

August 7: Embraced by Grace

Scripture for the Day
"Therefore, there is now no condemnation for those who are in Christ Jesus."

Romans 8:1

I bask in the light of an astonishing truth: in Christ I am cleared of judgment. This statement rings with freedom reverberating to the core of my being. It is a spiritual emancipation from the shackles of guilt and the burden of previous wrongs. My standing before God is not based on my imperfections but on the perfect love and redemption of Jesus Christ.

As I meditate on this, I am wrapped in the embrace of God's unconditional love. The word "therefore" links the present reality of mine with the earth-shattering events of the cross. In Christ who substituted Himself as a ransom for me I am clean, restored, and blameless. In Him, I find the grace which does not only save but also sustains and transforms me within.

It means I am released from self-condemnation as I turn my heart to the voice of God who declares me righteous. It's a day to identity with how God sees me—a precious child, entirely redeemed and eternally loved.

Absence of condemnation leaves room for the life of peace and fulfilment. I am called to be not a slave of the past but a creator of the future, one that God has molded in His hope and good purposes. It is a life where I am motivated by the Holy Spirit who guides me into all truth and righteousness, and not by fear.

Prayer: O God most gracious, I approach You with deepest thanks, for it is in Christ that I am free from condemnation. In Your Son, You have dressed me in His righteousness and in Him, I have my hiding-place and my power. May You be blessed for the gift of freedom which with I am free of sin and guilt to live. Amen.

August 8: United in Joy and Sorrow

Scripture for the Day
"Rejoice with those who rejoice; mourn with those who mourn."

Romans 12:15

"Rejoice with those who rejoice; mourn with those who mourn" is a holy call to engage in the ministry of compassionate presence – to be with others in their joy and their suffering, knowing that I am not a singular being, but a part of the living body of Christ.

This calls me to rejoice in the victories and milestones of my brethren as if they were mine. Their happiness is not to provoke jealousy in me but to become the source of our shared joy. Similarly, when someone I know is overshadowed by sorrow, I am not called to provide clichés but to sit with them in the depths of their grief, delivering my silent company and comforting shoulder.

By accepting this call, I affirm our mutual dependence on each other. I acknowledge that the Christian walk is one of godly truths and an art of godly love. Christ's heart is found through empathy, demonstrated through His tears of sorrow and how He touched the untouchable and loved those others did not. By following His pattern, I become a version of His love, a channel of His consolation, and a faithful participant in the lives of those around me.

Joy and sorrow are not just emotions but spiritual practices that bring me closer to others and the heart of God. They demolish the walls of egotism and construct the ties of unity in the Spirit. Today, I decide to open my heart and sense the heartbeat of life that pounds in the community of believers, genuinely connecting with them in a spirit of love.

Prayer: All-powerful and all-present God, we thank You for the beautiful complexity of human feelings and the gift of community. Train me to be in the now with others as they experience their heights and depths. Let me have true love and sympathy, and may I genuinely be happy with the happy and weep with the mourners. Amen.

August 9: Gift of Understanding

Scripture for the Day

"What we have received is not the spirit of the world, but the Spirit who is from God, so that we may understand what God has freely given us."

1 Corinthians 2:12

Today, I am reminded of a deep treasure that has been committed to me—the Spirit from God. This is not a spirit swayed by varying values and knowledge of this world but the Holy Spirit, who grants divine understanding and illumination. When I receive Him, I have been granted the power to understand the fullness of God's grace and unnumbered blessings He has showered upon me.

The excerpt from 1 Corinthians kindles in me respect for the ways in which the Holy Spirit acts within, leading me to truth and unveiling the mystery of God's abundant love. I feel driven to retreat from the chaos and noise that rule my days, to be more sensitive to the small, quiet, but everlasting voice whispering wisdom into my inner self.

That which God gives freely is not to be just recognized but is to be fully lived. The indwelling presence of the Spirit strengthens my discernment and I see past the everyday and into the evermore. The power of the Spirit helps me to realize what grace, mercy, and the endless love of God truly means.

Today and every day, I am enabled to allow the Spirit's knowledge to guide my life, to accept the illumination He brings to my life, and to live all it means to be a child of God. The Spirit empowers me in every situation to know what the will of God is, getting me ready to relate to the world from a position of divine wisdom and perception.

Prayer: Father Almighty, I am so thankful for Your Spirit who shares Himself so liberally with us. Thanks for making me realize the depths of Your love and the width of Your blessings. Enlighten the eyes of my heart to realize Your acts in my life and the world around me. Amen.

Embracing Shiloh:

August 10: From Death to Life

Scripture for the Day

"As for you, you were dead in your transgressions and sins, in which you used to live when you followed the ways of this world and of the ruler of the kingdom of the air, the spirit who is now at work in those who are disobedient."

Ephesians 2:1-2

At one time I was dead spiritually, having been caught up in transgressions and sin. I floated in the stream of a world divorced from God, unaware of the true state of my soul. However, this passage is more than a picture of the old me—it is a live image of what I have become due to the mercy and grace of God.

The lifestyle I lead now is characterized by a great change – from the darkness of spiritual death to the light of an eternal life. It is a shift from despair to abundant hope, from bondage to an awesome liberty in Christ. The ways of the world, which seemed so enticing before, are now recognized for what they truly are: paths that run away from the peace and purpose of the Almighty.

This reminder is a double portion of spiritual enlightenment. The feelings of thankfulness and amazement at the work done by God through Jesus elevates my spirit. No longer am I called by my past mistakes but reborn into a cherished child of the Most High, who continuously molds and leads me by His Spirit.

As I accept this, I lead a different life, cherishing the grace that has revived me from my spiritual apathy and to manifest that God's love toward others. Each choice is for me an attempt to mirror the saving power of life that God brings right in front of the dead ways of the world.

Prayer: Lord God, I kneel before You with a thankful heart because of the new life that I found in Christ. You have pulled me out of the darkness of spiritual death and breathed Your life into me. I was captured by sin once, but by Your grace, I am saved, renewed, and alive in Jesus. Amen.

August 11: Sealed Yet Unstoppable

Scripture for the Day

"So they went and made the tomb secure by putting a seal on the stone and posting the guard."

Matthew 27:66

Matthew 27:66 presents us with a strong image. Authorities have sealed the tomb of Jesus to secure it, so that His bones would not be stolen. This act of human intention ignored the intention of God. The seals and guards notwithstanding, Christ's resurrection's power was irresistible. The sealing of the tomb was only a physical act and could not hinder the spiritual fact that Jesus would rise again. This reminds us of the seals we in our own lives – times when obstacles appear to be impassable, and everyone seems to know each of our mistakes or missteps.

As the sealed tomb is closed, it becomes clear that no human force can defeat God's plan. In s similar way, our "seals" and "guards" are such things as doubt, fear, an unforgiving spirit, or a failure to step out in faith. But God's new life is a more powerful reality than any hindrance. Whatever our situation or the world's effort to shut off our hope, the ability of God's power comes, and our final victory is faith in Him.

Stones could never hold Jesus. In the same way, our perceived limits will never bind what God has in store for us. We are reminded that we have access to the same power that raised Christ from the dead. He dwells in us, empowering us to overcome the obstacles we face.

Prayer: Holy Father, You are the God of the unattainable, the One who breaks seals and rolls away stones. I am before You today, knowing You are more powerful than any challenge I encounter. While the guards watched the tomb that could not hold Your Son, may I stand in faith, believing that my circumstances cannot stop Your purpose for my life, Amen.

August 12: Embracing the Mission of Love

Scripture for the Day

"The Spirit of the Lord is on me because he has anointed me to proclaim good news to the poor. He has sent me to proclaim freedom for the prisoners and recovery of sight for the blind, to set the oppressed free."

Luke 4:18

In Luke 4:18, we see Jesus announcing His mission on Earth, a mission that is full of love, piety, and a dynamic desire to bring hope and healing to the brokenhearted, the outcast, and the downtrodden. We are reminded of the challenge to follow the example of Christ in our lives. The same Spirit who anointed Jesus now lives in us, enabling us to continue His mission of spreading the Good News, setting captives free from chains of hopelessness, and bringing light to those in darkness.

Jesus' mission is radical love and inclusiveness. He approached the outcast, healed the sick, and embraced those in despair. His words in Luke 4:18 call us to the same ministry of love, mercy, and justice. Today, I am challenged to find the downtrodden, to speak words of hope to the hopeless, to reach out to people who are caught in the traps of life, and to be a radiant stronghold in a scary world.

Prayer: Father in Heaven, thank You for the model of Jesus who came to bring hope and restoration to a fallen world. As I meditate on Luke 4:18, please enable me to follow Your steps, preach the good news of Your Kingdom, and channel Your love to people around me.

August 13: A Song of Joy and Victory

Scripture for the Day

"The Lord has made His salvation known and revealed His righteousness to the nations. He has remembered His love and His faithfulness to Israel; all the ends of the earth have seen the salvation of our God."

Psalm 98:3

Stop for a minute to meditate on our Lord's constant love and faithfulness. Think of the ends of the Earth seeing God's salvation. God not limited by location, time, or any situation. This line contains an insightful statement about the limitless and everlasting love found in God's salvation.

In any part of the world, you might find yourself, and whatever challenges or successes you have, the Lord in His faithfulness will be with you. He has not left His promises, and neither has He ceased to work deliverance in the lives of those that call upon Him. His love is an anchor in life that holds through any storm, bringing stability and hope.

Israel was loved and shown the faithfulness of God, and you too, are a beacon of His unfailing love to His children. Let this certainty be the rock on which you build your faith and the song of your soul today.

Prayer: Heavenly Father, I kneel before You. My heart is full of thanks, for You are a God of love and faithfulness. Your deliverance is shown throughout the ends of the earth. Amen.

Embracing Shiloh:

August 14: Sowing Seeds for a Harvest of Blessing

Scripture for the Day
"Do not be deceived: God cannot be mocked. A man reaps what he sows."

Galatians 6:7

With the new dawn, let's explore the lesson found in Galatians 6:7. This verse is a clear but gentle reminder of a universal principle in both the physical and spiritual worlds: sowing and reaping.

With every act, word, and thought, we are planting seeds that will eventually grow and bear fruit. We can count on this truth. It teaches us to be aware, to opt for goodness, and to spend our energies on what is right, real, and honorable.

In your life, what seeds do you need to plant? Consider kindness, patience, love, and faith. Be it in your interpersonal relationships, at your place of work, or the silent seclusion of your development—every good seed sown with purpose is a deposit in the future that you want. What you plant in the rich soil of today will flourish into a beautiful tomorrow.

Let us not be tired of acting righteously, for we shall reap at the appropriate time if we do not lose heart. May the wisdom of God not be mocked. The honor He gives us is a heart that seeks to sow right through this day, and all days to come.

Prayer: Gracious God, meditating upon your Word today, I understand the grave duty of sowing good seed that is pleasing to You. I realize that every action has a reaction, and every choice has consequences. Thus, I seek Your wisdom and discernment to sow rightly and grow a life that reflects Your kindness and mercy in me. Amen.

August 15: Strength for the Weary

Scripture for the Day

"He gives strength to the weary and increases the power of the weak."

Isaiah 40:29

In the murmurs of the morning and the peace of night, our spirits can be tried. We can be left trying to find balance in a world that never ceases to ask for more. However, amid this we have a promise from our Creator. Today's verse reminds us that God is an unlimited fount of power. He offers strength to us so that we are not overwhelmed.

The attraction of faith is not in our capacity to suffer but in our readiness to trust the One who can restore our exhausted resources. We are not abandoned when our limbs are quaking under the heavy burden of our fatigue and our hearts are wavering. This verse challenges us to a divine swap – our weakness for His strength.

We lean on His unfailing arms, whether it is physical fatigue, emotional fights, or mental weariness. Admitting our limitations, we open ourselves to the tremendous strength that God generously gives. It is a simple yet profound reality that we don't go this way by ourselves but by the hands of the all-powerful Creator of the universe.

Let this assurance sink deep into your spirit today: He strengthens the exhausted. Your exhaustion is witnessed, your speechless wars monitored, and your silent persistence is seen by the One who gently gives strength to go on.

Prayer: Father, I come before You today acknowledging that I am tired, and I need Your heavenly strength. I am grateful to You for the consolation and hope that is in Your Word, knowing that You care for those who grow weary and uphold the feeble. Amen.

August 16: Trusting the Present to His Care

Scripture for the Day
"Therefore do not worry about tomorrow, for tomorrow will worry about itself. Each day has enough trouble of its own."

Matthew 6:34

In the symphony of life's different duties, the tunes of anxiety sometimes override the serene melodies. Tomorrow, with its mysteries is the ocean where our thoughts will sail, leaving today's shore behind. Still, Christ calls us to navigate the present – to rely on Him in the immediate current of the day's rapids.

Matthew 6:34 is Christ's mild reproof to our forward-focused thoughts. It is an instruction to offload tomorrow's burdens on the shoulders of the Savior who has already walked our tomorrows. Jesus does not waver in the face of the challenges of tomorrow; instead, He teaches us to live in a place of faith and responsibility in every moment.

Our Savior knows that every day comes with its own troubles and leads us as we face them in faith that does not borrow trouble from tomorrow. With this, we find the liberty to focus all our efforts and faith on the faithfulness of God, knowing that just as He has reliably steered us through the waters of the past, He will also guide us through those yet-to-come streams.

As we walk through today, let us not drain strength by worrying over unknown tomorrows. Instead, let us confront today's challenges with grace and courage. Live in the present, wise in the use of your days. Tomorrow will be under the same providential care as it is now.

Prayer: I seek You today amid all the challenges, hoping for the peace that only You can give. As the words of Matthew 6:34 live in me, I ask for faith that will help me battle the temptation of worrying about the unknowns of tomorrow. My heart often gets carried away into the future what-ifs, leaving my current present unattended and full of insecurities. Help me to trust. Amen.

August 17: The Purpose in Our Suffering

Scripture for the Day
"For Christ also suffered once for sins, the righteous for the unrighteous, to bring you to God. He was put to death in the body but made alive in the Spirit."

1 Peter 3:18

Suffering is a part of the journey.

Christ suffered torments and death, not for His sins, but our sins—the unrighteous. His surrender represents the ultimate act of love and compassion known to man. Christ showed the way for us in His suffering, the link connecting the gap between our imperfection and God's perfect mercy. His suffering was not wasted, but necessary for our salvation.

As His disciples, we endure hassles and challenges of life, but our ordeals are shaded by His ultimate sacrifice. This makes our battles meaningful. They are not only problems but chances to make something out of our lives, to approach the divine love that God offers us.

As you move through difficult or uncomfortable situations today, remind yourself that you are in the presence of Christ. Suffering is never in isolation. He has conquered death, and through that, He has gifted us with life. This truth turns our suffering in the world into spiritually sanctifying suffering.

May this thought bring solace to your heart. God will use pain to further bless us in our gifts of salvation, love, and eternal friendship with God through Christ. May the peace that passes all understanding fill your spirit today as you contemplate this holy truth.

Prayer: Lord, I approach You with a thankful heart for the crucifixion of Your Son, our Savior. He – the righteous – who took my place, suffering for my sake, to bring me into Your holy presence. Aid me in recollecting that, especially in rough times, Christ suffered, but His pain was not in vain, and mine will count for His sake as well. Amen.

Embracing Shiloh:

August 18: Sacred Rest in a Restless World

Scripture for the Day

"'There are six days when you may work, but the seventh day is a day of Sabbath rest, a day of sacred assembly. You are not to do any work; wherever you live, it is a Sabbath to the Lord.'"

Leviticus 23:3

In this fast-paced world, where the race to complete tasks and the noise of claims hushes the whispering of the soul, the Lord commands in His wisdom that a day be crowned as a gift of rest. Leviticus 23:3 prescribes a day of sabbath rest, it is a divine remedy for our souls, bodies, and communities.

The rest of the sabbath is an honored time, not only for bodies to rest but for hearts to convene for worship of the Lord. It is a day of meditation, communication with our Maker, and restoration of our souls. This divine pause is a potent reminder of two truths: our worth is not measured by our productivity, and in the stillness of the sabbath, we find a precious opportunity to appreciate the bountiful blessings that life offers beyond work.

Look at this day as a holy present. Allow it to be a page for the Lord to write with soft brushstrokes of His peace, a tranquil tune of orchestral tempos of life! In this interlude, may you have enlightenment, reactivation, and a deepened relationship with God.

Prayer: O, Lord, in this divine moment of silence, I come to You with a heart full of desire for the rest of sabbath in You. I want to find the peace of Your presence where time stops, and Your small, quiet voice is louder than the noise of my active days. I thank You for this holy day, a sign of Your everlasting mercy, where I am told that I am loved not for what I do but for who I am in You, Amen.

August 19: The Call of the Faithful

Scripture for the Day

"The Lord had said to Abram, 'Go from your country, your people and your father's household to the land I will show you.'"

Genesis 12:1

In Genesis 12:1, the Lord begins talking to Abram to leave the known world to enter a covenant that would determine the future. The call of God to Abram reminds us of the call to obedience and faith every one of us receives and follow Him to the unfamiliar.

We as believers are often called to venture out of what is unknown, believing He is leading us to a higher purpose. God pushes us to venture beyond what is comfortable, believing in His promises, and the belief that He has a purpose.

Abram's call marks the starting of a faith journey, a divine initiative wherein God invites him into a narrative much bigger than himself. Abram's compliance with no knowledge of the end entails a deep sense of faith in the character of God and His word. He does the same for us.

Here, we are pointed to the process of our life's inquiry and the attentive listening for God, calling us to move. It tells us that walking in faith means leaving something behind—a place of safety, a former identity, or even presumptions of God's design. Obedience involves sacrifice but also untold blessing.

Prayer: Father, I hear You beckoning me like you did Abram. Put into me the courage to abandon the known shores and come into the depth of Your will. Give me the belief to walk into the tomorrow You have for me without holding on to my maps and designs but standing only on Your word. Help me as I leave and reveal Your promises in my life. Amen.

August 20: Love Manifested in Obedience

Scripture for the Day
"If you love me, keep my commands."

John 14:15

Love is a real sign of discipleship. It is not just a theoretical feeling but a norm that requires actions and expresses the strength of our link to Christ. In the Gospel of John, we hear Jesus speaking to us, His followers, with a profound simplicity that resonates through the ages: "If you love me, obey my commandments."

This verse is a firm reminder that our love for Jesus should be demonstrated in behavior that follows His commands. It fits with the concept that to obey is not a yoke but a happy affirmation of love. It shows the close bond between love and submission.

Christ's commands offer a life path that enriches our experience of God's love and enables us to become vessels of that love to others. They are not mere laws but evidence of how Jesus lived a life of love and that He calls us all to live. We echo His commands in the love that we have been given, a song of devotion that is heard in every loving deed, every pleasant word, every forgiven error.

Let it lead us in our interactions, influence our decisions, and guide us when tested.

Prayer: Gracious Lord, Your Word is a lamp to my feet, and a light to my path. Today, with Your command of love and obedience, I sense Your guiding force as I meditate. Aid me, I pray, to personify this love that calls for action. May my life be evidence of the love I have for You. Amen.

August 21: Love as He Loved

Scripture for the Day

"A new command I give you: Love one another. As I have loved you, so you must love one another."

John 13:34

In the glimmer of dawn, we hear Jesus' words through time straight into our hearts. This timeless call is to practice unselfish love. By loving each other as Christ loved us, we are urged not only to have feelings but to do something – to serve, sacrifice, and give of ourselves in a way that human logic alone cannot fathom.

Kneeling to wash the feet of His disciples, Jesus showed perfect servant leadership. He loved unconditionally and He loved completely. This is the love of God, this *agape* love, we are to imitate. It is more than just putting up with one another or carrying one another's burdens and forgiving as we have been forgiven. It is to put the other person's interests above our own.

While we meditate on the overwhelming love Jesus has for us, the type of love we are called to extend to our brothers and sisters becomes more evident. It is love that goes out, that overlooks the faults and mends the scars.

Let us take on this command as our norm. May we look for ways to manifest that love, pulling from the unyielding spring of grace that Jesus has given us. Loving each other is where we mirror God's love for the world, and we become hope as well as peace temples.

Prayer: Lord, Your love is light even in the darkest night, leading my tired soul home to Your arms. I thank You for providing me with unconditional love in Your son, Jesus Christ. Lord, imprint in my heart His decree to love others as He did, Amen.

Embracing Shiloh:

August 22: In Spirit and Truth

Scripture for the Day
"God is spirit, and his worshipers must worship in the Spirit and in truth."

John 4:24

God invites us into a fellowship that is beyond the material world. This heavenly fellowship is not confined to a place or time and does not depend on human practices; it is as infinite as the Lord Himself.

Worship is more than an act. Each breath and every second offer a chance to glorify the Creator. Through our spirit, worship allows the Holy Spirit to direct our minds, deeds, and will. Worship provides a spiritual connection with God, a guiding factor, to make our walk a godly one, giving our lives heavenly perspectives.

True worship comes near to God in truth, not pretending and being hypocritical, even with our weaknesses and imperfection. The truth is explored in several ways: by God's Word, recognizing reality as God does, and expressing the sincerity of our souls.

In a world of images, where reality is distorted by facades, to worship in spirit and truth is radical and transformative. It asks us to reject the superficial and communicate to God at His most profound level.

As we strive to be one with the Spirit today, let us remove the irrelevant, get rid of obstacles and concentrate our hearts on the reality of God and who we are in Him. Let us be authentic in our worship, going straight from our hearts to God's heart.

Prayer: Most holy and loving Father, in the stillness of this day, I come to You desiring to worship You in spirit and truth. I desire a bond that is not just formal and built on words but one that is in a holy place where my soul unites with Yours. Amen.

August 23: The Promise of the Advocate

Scripture for the Day

"And I will ask the Father, and he will give you another advocate to help you and be with you forever."

John 14:16

In sweet communion of this hour, let us open our souls to the Gospel of John. Here we see Jesus' most personal farewell to His disciples; a message mixed with sadness and hope, reassuring us that He will always be with us, even though He is not with us in the flesh. He pledges the Holy Spirit, the Advocate, to be our permanent helper and guide.

This vow is a light in the dark, a constant assurance that we are not deserted to face the maze of life alone. The Advocate is the constant in our lives, a never-failing source of direction, our present help in our daily struggles and joys. By the Spirit, we always have access to divine wisdom and power, and the certainty of God's presence.

In a panic, it can be easy to wish for a Jesus to physically see, touch and hear. However, His pledge of the Holy Spirit is a promise that goes beyond temporal and physical constraints. The Spirit lives in us, giving solace, giving peace, and developing in us the very nature of Christ.

Today, let's embrace with hope and appreciation that promise. Let us be alert to the promptings of the Advocate inside us and rely upon this divine partnership which enables us to live our faith with trust. May the Spirit direct our feet, control our deeds, and brighten our way with the light of God's wisdom and love.

Prayer: Gracious and Almighty God, in the stillness of this day, I stop to recognize Your wonderful gift – the Holy Spirit, my Counselor. Thank You, Lord for foreknowing the fact that I would need such a Helper, for giving me a Comforter and Guide, who is always at my side, Amen.

August 24: The Creative Spirit of God

Scripture for the Day
"Now the earth was formless and empty, darkness was over the surface of the deep, and the Spirit of God was hovering over the waters."

Genesis 1:2

In the beginning, Earth was a blank canvas covered with darkness, awaiting the voice of the divine artist. Painted by the Genesis story, this powerful image leaves us struck in awe of the magnitude of His presence and of the infinite power He wields. Before anything was, the Spirit of God was there, active, molding, creating order from chaos, and filling the void with life.

Such a scene is not only a historical reflection of the beginning of our world but also of hope and rebirth. It points out that my life can be seen as formless and void, but the Spirit of God is ready to create again. No darkness is too deep that God's transforming light cannot reach it.

Also, God's Spirit desires to bathe the waters of my soul. He lives in the empty places and unshaped corners of my heart, waiting for my call to perform His artistic work. The Spirit of God is stirring to change my life through His spoken Word just as He did the void at the beginning of time.

Today, let us welcome Him into our areas of shapelessness, our voids, and the chambers of our being that appear to be wrapped in blindness. May we release the power of God's creating Spirit that will work freely, forming beauty from ashes, strength from fear and faith from doubt.

Prayer: Creator God, with the dawning brightness on the world, I wonder about the presence of Your Spirit at the beginning of creation. I am amazed by the magnitude of Your strength, and how tenderly You made miracles from nothing, Amen.

August 25: The Living Word

Scripture for the Day

"For the word of God is alive and active. Sharper than any double-edged sword, it penetrates even to dividing soul and spirit, joints and marrow; it judges the thoughts and attitudes of the heart."

Hebrews 4:12

The Bible is not a static book but a living force. It thrives and flourishes in our lives if we open the door. The Word stands as permanence and certainty. It powerfully conveys truth to our internal world, telling us about our intimate feelings and wishes. Inspecting us, it is as exacting and discerning as a physician with a scalpel or an artisan with a tool.

When you study Scripture, you read stories or commandments and dialog with the divine. The Holy Scripture is an instrument that provides instructions, points out mistakes, and brings us peace, but at the same time denies, criticizes, and converts us. It is a mirror that shows us not only who we are but also, by grace, who we are called to be and can become.

Be a passenger and feel the Word of God working in your life. Let it ruthlessly expose your shortcomings, fortify what you already know, and clear out any untruth within you. Take advantage of its tremendous power to become your spiritual source and be changed by it.

Receive it with a sensitive heart that can be touched because, through the Word, we understand God better, conform to His will, and are molded and changed.

Prayer: Heavenly Father, I am grateful for receiving the message of Your Word, as it pierces my soul and spirit and reminds me what truth and grace mean. As I meditate on Hebrews 4:12 today, God, I pray Your words will be the light that leads my feet and a lamp that shows me the things to come. May I let it judge my thoughts and attitudes and be there for me to receive its divine teaching and correction. Amen.

Embracing Shiloh:

August 26: The Power of Righteous Prayer

Scripture for the Day

"Therefore confess your sins to each other and pray for each other so that you may be healed. The prayer of a righteous person is powerful and effective."

James 5:16

Today's reading is an image of a community that our faith beckons us into – a community of openness, help, and intercession. Our walk with Christ is not a solitary journey but one in a fellowship where we can openly talk about our sufferings and victories. On this common ground, our prayers unite with follow believers and are presented before the throne of God.

Let's take comfort that confession is not a process of judgment but a path to healing and liberation. Bearing our burdens together removes the load from our shoulders and enables our united faith with our brothers and sisters to support us. The Holy Spirit enables the corporate voice of the prayers that touch God's heart.

Ponder the strength that springs from a rooted and honest prayer life. Reflect on how prayer has been productive for you in the past and have faith that it will be productive again. Note that by aligning your heart with the righteousness of God, your prayers resonate throughout the heavens and lift His healing touch upon the earth.

When you pray today, do so with confidence and faith, relying on the promise God has given that the prayer of a righteous person is powerful and effective. Embrace the society of faith, getting close to each other in vulnerability and trust.

Prayer: God, thank You for the opportunity to pray, for the open call to come into Your presence bare heartedly. I admit the things that trouble me before You, Lord, and before my brethren. I beg for Your forgiveness and restoration. Lord, I pray for myself and others who need Your touch in their lives. Amen.

August 27: The Blessing of Obedience

Scripture for the day
"So, because Jesus was doing these things on the Sabbath, the Jewish leaders began to persecute him."

John 5:16

Today's Scripture is a powerful portrait of the perseverance of Jesus, doing the will of the Father. Although He knew that He risked being persecuted, Jesus kept healing and spilling His love on the Sabbath. However, Jesus' actions on the Sabbath caused strife among the religious leaders. He stood as a testimony that true faith is not constrained by human interpretation of the law. His efforts make us dig further into our hearts, asking ourselves if what we do is what God wants with mercy or mere compliance of the law.

Living spiritually is to recognize that the path of righteousness is sometimes opposed. There are instances when our commitment and submission to God appear controversial to others. However, Jesus teaches us that the core of obedience is to perform the works of God with love and mercy, even if we are condemned or misunderstood.

During your tribulations, when you are torn between doing what is easy or doing God's will, recall the picture of Jesus healing and serving the sick without hesitation. May it be a light that stimulates steadfastness in your purpose and leads you in the path of Christ, expressing love, mercy, and service beyond human approval.

Prayer: Gracious and loving Father, Thank You for showing in Your Son, Jesus, the fundamental nature of spiritual action. Through misinterpretation and persecution, Jesus followed Your will without wavering. May I have the bravery to walk on this holy path. May I keep Your commandments not in words but especially when it is hard to do so. Amen.

Embracing Shiloh:

August 28: Abide in the True Vine

Scripture for the Day

"I am the true vine, and my Father is the gardener."

John 15:1

The words of Jesus are full of powerful imagery of connection, development, and spiritual growth. Christ proclaims Himself the true vine – a fountain of life and sustenance for all branches that cleave to Him. As a gardener, the Father roots us carefully, with accuracy and intent. Although our lives are closely associated with Christ, we can produce fruit that represents God's glory if only we stay in Him.

The message is clear: outside the vine, the branches do not prosper, not to mention yielding any harvest. The vine provides all life, nutrients, and vigor; thus, it is complete and perfect strength. Think about yourself for a while. Think of how you have tried to live and bear fruit apart from Christ. It is usually characterized by frustration and low results, aren't they? But life in Jesus is a life that thrives, even where you would least expect to find it.

Abiding in Christ is keeping a continuous relationship with Him that does not break and allows His teachings, love, and His Spirit to permeate every part of who we are. It is not a passive existence but rather an active and dynamic one where discipline, pruning, and at times, painful stripping away of the obstacles are involved.

Prayer: God, I am grateful for being grafted into the true vine, Jesus Christ. Assist me in remaining in Him and submit to Your tender pruning. May I be a tree that gives forth abundant fruit of through Your Spirit. Teach me to become one with Your vine and to find in it my sustenance and strength, never seeking to be apart from it. Amen.

August 29: Treasures

Scripture for the Day
"Do not store up for yourselves treasures on earth, where moths and vermin destroy, and where thieves break in and steal."

Matthew 6:19

Often, we find ourselves caught in the endless pursuit of material wealth—possessions that demand our time, energy, and often our very souls. Yet, in His infinite wisdom, Jesus invites us to consider the futility of such efforts. Moths and rust corrupt, thieves menace. Even the most secure of our treasures are not totally safe from the decay of time.

This Scripture compares what is temporary to what is timeless. It nudges us to ask ourselves: What are we accumulating in our lives that holds eternal significance? If our hearts are treasure chests, what are we storing in them that is incorruptible?

Every selfless act of love, every moment of genuine spiritual connection, every sacrifice made in the name of Christ is a coin in the unshakable Kingdom of Heaven. These are the treasures that withstand the test of time, immune to the decay of the earthly realm.

In this timeless lesson, our Savior redirects our gaze heavenward, guiding us to invest in what is unspoiled by death or decay. Let us, then, dedicate this day to amassing wealth not with our hands, but with our hearts.

Prayer: Heavenly Father, ignite within me the passion to seek the treasures of Your Kingdom above all else. Remind me daily that true riches are found not in possessions, but in Your presence. Help me to store up heavenly treasures through a life of service and devotion to You. Guide my actions, that they might reflect the imperishable wealth of Your love. In the precious name of Jesus, I pray. Amen.

Embracing Shiloh:

August 30: Born of Water and Spirit

Scripture for the Day

"Jesus answered, 'Very truly I tell you, no one can enter the kingdom of God unless they are born of water and the Spirit.'"

John 3:5

This verse presents us with spiritual rebirth. In the discourse between Jesus and Nicodemus, the Lord articulates the mystery and the importance of the second birth. This second birth is not physical but a change of heart and mind, through the Spirit. This renewal of the Spirit signifies the start of a new path to eternal life.

To be born of the Spirit means to be purified, to be refreshed and renewed, just like the rain cleanses the earth. Water stands for cleansing, and the Spirit is the wind of God, representing the life of our spiritual being.

A walk with God is not without stumbling blocks or periods of insecurity, but it is characterized by ever-growing changes as the Spirit molds us into who we are meant to be. With this new birth, we leave the old ways behind and rise to live a life of complete trust and surrender under the care and leadership of God.

This is also an invitation to daily renewal, to ceaselessly dip ourselves in the flowing waters of God's Word and presence, allowing His Spirit to bear within us the fruits of a vigorous and fulfilled life in His kingdom. Every day, each person has a chance to manifest the reality of our birth anew in the flesh, and in anticipation of the kingdom to come.

Prayer: Heavenly Father, I stand before You, humbled and awed by the mystery that I am born of the Spirit. I am grateful to You for the gift of spiritual resurrection that You gave me through Your Son, Jesus Christ. Purify me, Lord, as I strive to bathe in the flowing waters of Your mercy. Renew me with Your Spirit. Breathe Your life through my entire being. Amen.

August 31: The Mind of Christ

Scripture for the Day
"In your relationships with one another, have the same mindset as Christ Jesus."

Philippians 2:5

Today, we are gently called upon to cultivate an important spiritual discipline: to have the mind of Christ. The apostle Paul, in instructing the Philippian church, bids us to look beyond ourselves—to consider others humbly and selflessly, just like our Savior Jesus Christ.

Jesus, the personification of divine love, established a model of humility, service, and sacrifice. His attitude was not to advance Himself but to humble Himself for the sake of humankind. Committing to an identical mindset means accepting a lifestyle opposite that from what most people strive for. It is a road of giving instead of taking, of serving rather than being served, of sharing grace as grace has been shown us.

To have the mind of Christ is to look with His eyes—eyes that consider every person as invaluable, deserving of love and kindness. This angle changes how we relate with others, making us speak and act differently and treat conflicts uniquely. It calls on us to be peacemakers and to put the welfare of others first and foremost.

Be aware of this godly mentality in both small actions and major choices. Let us be marked by the humility and sacrificial love that Christ has shown Himself. We thereby not only glorify God but also create a little tiny heaven of our own.

Prayer: Dear Jesus, I want to live Your words and by Your way. Grant me eyes to see that I need to have the same mind You had when on Earth. Help me to love as You have loved, to serve as You have served, and to show grace as You did. Amen.

Embracing Shiloh:

September 1: The Lamb of God Who Takes Away Sin

Scripture for the Day
"The next day John saw Jesus coming toward him and said, 'Look, the Lamb of God, who takes away the sin of the world!'"

John 1:29

With this resounding proclamation, John the Baptist acknowledges Jesus to be the perfect sacrifice for people. Elsewhere the gospel writers describe the scene: the calm Jordan River, the heavens opening with divine light, and the Spirit of God descending on Christ. John, the forerunner, would look up to Jesus, who was the one that satisfied the old prophecies and finish God's plan of salvation.

Jesus, Lamb of God, took the sin of the world upon Him—our sins, our failings, our deepest regrets—and carried this burden unto death on the cross that we may be washed clean and unbound. This is not just a historical event; it is a current reality.

Every day, Jesus comes to us and asks us to notice Him, inviting us to be free from the slavery of sin. It is an offer to drop our baggage at His feet and to enjoy the freedom of His grace. Do not let this moment pass without recognizing the immense sacrifice made in love for us.

Prayer: Gracious and loving Father, I humbly stand before You in gratitude, thinking about the powerful reality that Your precious Son, Jesus, who is the Lamb of God who takes away the world's sin. Your love for me is amazing, a love so deep that You sent Jesus to bear my grief and set my soul free. Amen.

September 2: The Essence of Listening

Scripture for the Day
"My dear brothers and sisters, take note of this: Everyone should be quick to listen, slow to speak and slow to become angry,"

James 1:19

Amid the hurry of today crowded by a thousand voices, where everyone has an opinion on everything, the divine wisdom of the book of James speaks profoundly. It tells us to listen, exercise the tongue's control, and quell the anger that often tries to take over our hearts.

To be a "hasty listener" is to be fast in hearing the words, opening the heart for a deep understanding of others. Listening is an act of respect for the views and experiences of our brothers and sisters. Listening is an act of love.

Slowness to speak is the natural partner of enthusiastic hearing. There is discipline in holding our speech until we have fully considered the words of others and what our own words will sow. Will they be kernels of mercy or cruelty? The space between hearing and response allows wisdom to guide us to say the right thing at the right time.

Finally, being "slow to anger" is the most difficult yet the most freeing. Anger usually comes from expectations not being met or wounded pride. By being patient and understanding, our compassion will extinguish the fire of rage and choose peace instead of war.

Within this trinity of hearing, speaking, and controlling our wrath, we are on the way of modest living and sacred wisdom. Let us strive to live these virtues to glorify God and edify those near us.

Prayer: Father, in the silence of this hour, I seek Your nearness and help. Please assist me in being slow to speak so that I will become a receptacle of compassion and comprehension. Set a watch, O Lord, before my mouth and guard my lips so that my speech is always seasoned with wisdom and that I do not fall into foolish speech because of my lack of checking my words. Calm my anger impulse so that I may show Your mercy and peace in patience. Amen.

Embracing Shiloh:

September 3: The Reign of the One King

Scripture for the Day
"The Lord will be king over the whole earth. On that day there will be one LORD, and his name the only name."

Zechariah 14:9

Today, we look at Zechariah 14:9, that promises the day when the divisions and discord will be replaced by the unity and tranquility of the reign of the one true King. Our present world often looks like a cloth of different colored threads, each pulling at a thread to create its own fabric. Nevertheless, amid the turbulent waves of life, this promise is an anchor to our hope, a pledge of unity under God's rule.

Let this instill in you a faith in tomorrow and a longing to follow what is eternal and not what is passing. Our earthly kingdoms are only for a time, while the dominion of our Lord is forever. Knowing that there will be a day when the Lord will reign supremely over all there is, we can find peace for our souls, and we can be inspired to live a life that reflects the values of His Kingdom here and now.

Let us be the tools of the togetherness that is yet to be. May we have the name of the Lord within us and share the light of His image in our actions, words, and studies. In everything, His love shall speak, His wisdom guide, and His peace triumph.

Prayer: O Lord my God, today I come before You with a heart that overflows with thanks for Your will that brings harmony from discord and order from confusion. I recognize You as the only real King, the master of the whole world. I anxiously await the day when Your name becomes the only one and every creature dances before Your throne in perfect harmony. Amen.

September 4: The Choice of Goodness

Scripture for the Day
"Then Jesus asked them, 'Which is lawful on the Sabbath: to do good or to do evil, to save life or to kill?' But they remained silent."

Mark 3:4

In this passage, Jesus challenges us with a decision that goes beyond the prescriptions of religious law to the heart of morality. It brings home to us is that the heart of our faith is not ceremony but love, mercy, and the value of life. We are not only to refrain from evil but also to be life-giving and shine light in the darkness by showing divine love.

Let's consider the question Jesus asked us concerning our lives. Every day, we must decide—some decisions can determine our destiny, and others become so petty that we do not notice that they are already woven into the pattern of our day. But in both good or bad, life and its opportunities can be neglected.

What does it mean to rescue a life? Sometimes, it's not about heroism. Occasionally, it is words of support for someone suffering, a listening ear for a friend in distress, or actions of kindness for justice in some small way within our communities. Lifesaving is the act of giving to the lives of others and bearing the light of hope and compassion in the world that surrounds us.

Prayer: Dear Lord, today I come before You, moved by Your mighty message to live in goodness and life in every moment. Teach me to see these options on the pure and uncompromising view of Your love as demonstrated through Christ, our Savior. Amen.

September 5: Love That Transforms

Scripture for the Day

"Husbands, love your wives, just as Christ loved the church and gave himself up for her."

Ephesians 5:25

Today's Scripture demands an undying love that is all-absorbing and sacrificing, a love that is a Christian virtue. It is a command targeting husbands in its details, but its spirit spreads gently toward the heart of every believer, female or male, married or single. The principle is unconditional love, which is not contingent upon what we receive but is a product of what we are willing to give: ourselves for the good of others.

Just as Christ sacrificially loved the Church by laying down His life for it, He has taught by living example the highest form of love one gives. This is the love that protects and serves, without desire for recognition or return. It is a love that labors in quiet, unnoticed hours, and holds fast through the most trying tests. It is gentle and nurturing.

Accept the challenge of this Christlike love today. The call to love others as Christ has loved us should be extended everywhere, including our workplaces, homes, communities, and even ourselves.

Prayer: My Redeemer and my God, Your love amazes me; a profound and self-sacrificial love carried to the cross for me. The love You have demonstrated towards me and the instruction to reflect it in my life has left me humbled. Teach me, Lord, to love like You. Grant me the strength to give of myself, to sacrifice without keeping score, and to cherish and honor those You have placed in my life. Help me to express Your love in all my relationships, extending grace, forgiveness, and patience. Amen.

September 6: A Daily Walk in Faithfulness

Scripture for the Day

"I have declared to both Jews and Greeks that they must turn to God in repentance and have faith in our Lord Jesus."

Acts 20:21

Paul's mission statement in our passage for today is the core message of the Good News. Paul did not discriminate in his ministry. He preached repentance and faith to everyone – to Jews and Greeks, to all, pointing out that faith in Jesus Christ was for everyone.

Consider the universality of this message: Paul's words stir in us a calling for a twofold response to the gospel: to repent and have faith. Repentance is what the Bible calls it when we are called to turn from our prior paths that lead us away from God. However, turning away from something is insufficient; we also need to turn towards Someone.

It is the Lord Jesus in whom we are to put our trust. This is the faith part of it – faith in Jesus Christ as our Savior. We believe in Him, not just that He is God but that He can truly save us from our sins and give us a new life, what the Bible calls being "born again."

In life, there are a lot of crossroads choices. The call to repentance and faith is not a one-off but a continuing exercise. We are to renew this commitment, to resolve to refrain from actions, thoughts, and behaviors that do not glorify God, and to place our trust in Jesus anew.

Prayer: Father, I come before You with a lowly heart, seeking Your help to live the truth of today's Scripture. Lead me to reject my old ways that are not pleasing to You and to accept the new path that You have laid before me. I need the grace to repent and the force to trust Jesus, my Lord, in my heart. During the day, let Your Spirit bring Your love and faithfulness to mind. Your Word is a light on my path and a lamp to my feet. In Jesus' name, Amen.

Embracing Shiloh:

September 7: Offering of Praise and Generosity

Scripture for the Day

"And do not forget to do good and to share with others, for with such sacrifices God is pleased."

Hebrews 13:16

Today's verse reminds us that our calling as followers of Christ extends beyond our spiritual growth to actively expressing His love through doing good and sharing with others.

Doing good is a call to action. It requires us to look beyond our needs and desires and to be attentive to opportunities where actions reflect God's goodness. It may be a kind word to a neighbor, an act of service to a stranger, or standing up for someone in need—each instance of doing good plants seeds of God's love around us.

Sharing with others is an extension of our gratitude for what we've received. In sharing our resources, time, and talents, we don't merely give from our abundance, but we participate in a divine economy where love multiplies, and needs are met in miraculous ways. God's pleasure rests not merely in our routine offerings and liturgies but greatly so in these everyday sacrifices—these acts of love and generosity that speak of the grace we ourselves have received.

Let this be a day where we intentionally look for occasions to do good and to share. Envision each act of kindness as a fragrant offering, pleasing to God. Even the smallest gesture can carry immense weight in the kingdom of God.

Prayer: Lord of all generosity, I praise You for Your infinite goodness and the bounty You provide daily. Instill in me a spirit that delights in doing good and a heart that loves to share. May I not overlook the simple ways I can express Your love. Guide me to see those in need and give me the resources and wisdom to support them. Let my life today be an offering pleasing to You, reflecting the sacrifice of Jesus, who gave all for us. Lead me in Your grace and wisdom, and may my actions be an extension of Your benevolence. In the precious name of Jesus, I pray, Amen.

September 8: Remembered Covenant

Scripture for the Day
"Then I will remember my covenant with Jacob and my covenant with Isaac and my covenant with Abraham, and I will remember the land."

Leviticus 26:42

God's covenant, a thread woven throughout Scripture, is a testament to His unending faithfulness and unfailing memory. Even as He spoke to the children of Israel, He assured them that His promises to the patriarchs—Abraham, Isaac, and Jacob—would not be forgotten.

The land and the covenant given by God, symbolize a spiritual truth for us today. Though we may wander and find ourselves in places of spiritual emptiness or confusion, God does not forget us. He remembers His promises and is committed to His covenant with us through Christ.

The reminder of God's faithfulness brings comfort and hope. It calls us to remember our part in the covenant: to live as His people, set apart, walking in His statutes, and observing His commands. Yet, even when we fall short, God's memory and commitment to us remain steadfast.

Let this verse stir in you a profound assurance that God does not forget your life. Your prayers, longings, and hopes are held within the eternal memory of the Almighty. Trust that the One who made the covenant with our ancestors is just as attentive to His covenant with you.

Prayer: Everlasting Father, Your promises are sure, and Your memory is perfect. I thank You for remembering Your covenant with the patriarchs and, through Your faithfulness, establishing a new covenant with us in Jesus Christ. Help me to trust in Your steadfast love and to live in a manner worthy of the calling You have placed upon my life. Thank You for never forgetting me even when I am prone to forget. Uphold me with Your righteous right hand and renew my spirit to walk faithfully in the land of Your promises. In the sacred and precious name of Jesus, I pray, Amen.

Embracing Shiloh:

September 9: Embrace the Father's Discipline

Scripture for the Day
"My son, do not despise the Lord's discipline and do not resent his rebuke, because the Lord disciplines those he loves, as a father the son he delights in."

Proverbs 3:11-12

Proverbs 3:10-11 calls us to accept the discipline of our Father in Heaven, to love His corrections and rebukes for what it is – His great love. As a caring parent corrects the child, out of affection and devotion, so the Lord disciplines us.

Discipline can make people feel despondent, rejected, or misunderstood. However, the Word of God tells us not to despise His correction, for it forms our character and shapes our hearts to His perfect will. While we walk through the changes of life, His chastening is an affectionate guidance which brings us back to the ways of righteousness and wisdom.

The Lord, in great love, chastises us not to condemn but with the goal that we will grow. His discipline is based on the delight that a father has in us, His dear children. Let us not shy away from His reproofs but embrace them as chances for development, improvement, and a closer relationship with Him.

May you be comforted in the realization that the discipline of the Lord is His love poured out on you. Accept it with humility and faith, understanding that with His loving guidance, you are being molded into the person He designed you to be.

Prayer: Merciful Father, I approach You recognizing Your divine justice and love in punishment. Assist me in welcoming Your corrections with a humble heart and knowledge that they are born from Your deep concern for me. Let the process of refining in me produce fruit to Your name. Empower me to follow Your will and give me wisdom to understand the lessons in Your loving chastisement. Thank You, Lord, for the honor of being Your child and for the instruction You bring through Your discipline. In the name of Jesus, I pray, Amen.

September 10: Embracing the Truth

Scripture for the Day

"For I am convinced that neither death nor life, neither angels nor demons, neither the present nor the future, nor any powers, neither height nor depth, nor anything else in all creation, will be able to separate us from the love of God that is in Christ Jesus our Lord."

Romans 8:38-39

Love without condition brings comfort to our hearts, knowing that there is no part of our lives that is not embraced by the love of our Lord. This is a strong proclamation of our Savior's unyielding dedication to us, evidence that there is no abyss that His love cannot span.

Jesus offers a welcome to all souls. He calls us to seek solace and *shalom* – the peace He brings. By receiving Jesus, we are not only stepping into a resting place but also interacting with the image of Shiloh, the fulfillment of the ultimate peace we have been promised and we now embrace. This verse is a commitment, an agreement that even the strongest powers of this world cannot break.

May this guide your day, direct your affairs, and uplift your faith. As we move ahead, may we seek to exemplify His love in everything that we do and think, to be channels of grace in a world that needs embracing.

Prayer: God our Father, thank You for the certainty that nothing can separate me from Your embrace. Assist me to bear this truth in my heart and to come from a place of thanksgiving and harmony. Let Your love direct my every word and action. Make me strong to love others just as You have loved me. In Jesus' name, Amen.

September 11: Hope in Eternity

Scripture for the Day

"He will wipe every tear from their eyes. There will be no more death or mourning or crying or pain, for the old order of things has passed away."

Revelation 21:4

In life we encounter various trials, heartaches, and difficulties that make us feel that the world is indeed heavy on us. However, the promise from Revelation provides us with a look into a future when all sorrow will be over, because that future is held in the hands of our compassionate and victorious Lord.

For the believer, every trouble is short-lived. The sufferings and pains, although actual and sometimes virtually intolerable, are not the last part of our story. Hope is beyond the horizon and is unshakable and unwavering.

God is highly conscious of our pains. He draws near to the brokenhearted. His final plan is restoration and peace. The day will come when He will Himself delicately brush every tear from our eyes, and death and mourning will no longer be.

Once we journey through our current world, let this blessed assurance guide our souls. We are not people without hope but who know that today's trials are the steppingstones to the joy of eternity. The last renewal of God is not very far away, and until that day dawns, go in courage serving others in love and as a witness to the bright morning that awaits all children of God.

Prayer: O Abba, God and Father, Amid the desolation that engulfs me, Your Word is a standing rock of hope. I cling to Your promise in Revelation that there shall come a day when You will wipe every tear away, and the former things will be no more. Keep my heart sustained with the idea of this bright future when all the sorrows disappear and only Your peace will reign. Amen.

September 12: The True Measure of Giving

Scripture for the Day

"Calling his disciples to him, Jesus said, 'Truly I tell you, this poor widow has put more into the treasury than all the others.'"

Mark 12:43

While we race through errands, in which riches and boastful charity often measure one's worth, Jesus changes our attention to a picture of silent, simple giving. He shows an instance that would be swallowed up by the surrounding bustle — a poor widow donating two small coins. Whereas most people gave out of plenty, she gave out of her poverty everything she had to live on.

This act of giving, done through sacrifice, powerfully calls us to a deeper meaning of giving. Our Master does not regard the size of the gifts we have given but the heart from which they are given. She left everything, showing a trust that knew that God would supply all her needs even when she could not see how.

Today, let us think of the widow's mite as a yardstick of our own giving – not only in coin but also in love, time, and service to others. We honor God with our faithfulness by giving our last and believing that God will fill the void. May we be inspired to follow this genuine generosity, giving not from our excess but from the point of real abandon and trust in our Provider.

Prayer: Lord of all abundance, Your teachings constantly reverse the world's wisdom, showing the attractiveness of humility and the power of weakness. The widow's offering is a reminder that what matters is not what I have but how I give that which I have. Direct my heart to be a willing giver, self-giving, which shines with the proof of how much I trust in You to provide for me. Amen.

Embracing Shiloh:

September 13: Laying Aside Every Weight

Scripture for the Day
"Therefore, since we are surrounded by such a great cloud of witnesses, let us throw off everything that hinders and the sin that so easily entangles. And let us run with perseverance the race marked out for us."

Hebrews 12:1

Oh, you who are on your way to Heaven, spend a moment thinking on how this verse gives wonderful encouragement. Imagine the arena where the faithful who have gone before are cheering us from the celestial stands. These witnesses have finished their course, suffered their tribulations, and have received their crowns. Their lives testify that God is faithful and gives grace to endure in hard times.

As a child of God, you are to put off the sin that so easily entangles you and anything that hinders you. Like a runner who removes clothes that are unnecessary to be faster and endure for a long time, so must you cast off the weights that slow your spiritual growth.

Reflect on what hinders you: is it fear, doubt, or an old pattern that doesn't serve your divine purpose? Let it go today. Lay aside this weight, being aware that it is not fit for the race you are running. This course of yours is unique, a way that God has carved out for you to run with faith and devotion.

You are not called to sprint but to run with patience. It is not a race of the swift but of those who keep running even when the road gets steep and the air thin.

Prayer: Father in Heaven, I appear before You this day, recognizing the host of witnesses that have passed before me, their lives a testimony of Your faith. Grant me the power to cast off all that weighs me down and let go of the sin that so easily binds my heart. Amen.

September 14: In Him All Things Hold Together

Scripture for the Day

"Through him all things were made; without him nothing was made that has been made."

John 1:3

In the quiet of this moment, meditate on this Scripture from the Gospel of John. It tells of the all-powerful hand of Christ at work in the tapestry of creation, proclaiming His dominion over the cosmos, the immense galaxies and the complex designs of our DNA.

Consider this, dear friend: If all things were made by Him, your life was also designed purposely by Him. You are not an accidental creation but a deliberate work of the Creator that made the stars and the universe. The identical power that called light out of night gave birth to your essence and supports your every moment.

Remember that no molecule in this multifaceted world escapes Jesus' creative work and sustaining care. In God, all things hold together— every challenge, every joy, every dream, and every sorrow— when life seems incomplete or disorganized.

Being a member of His creation, you are called to co-labor with Him in making order, beauty, and goodness in the places and lives surrounding you. It is a great honor to be a colleague to the One who is the conductor of the world symphony and to contribute your notes to the melody He created.

Prayer: Lord Jesus, Author of Heaven and Earth, I am amazed at Your marvelous creation. I embark upon this day with the knowledge and source of all things being You. Your hands created the world, and Your breath makes me live. Amen.

September 15: Founded on the Rock

Scripture for the Day

"And I tell you that you are Peter, and on this rock I will build my church, and the gates of Hades will not overcome it."

Matthew 16:18

Within your quiet space, turn your thoughts to the powerful words Jesus spoke in the Gospel of Matthew. Christ shared a profound truth to Peter, outlining the unshakeable nature of the Church that would rise from the revelation of Jesus as the Christ, the Son of the living God.

As a follower of Christ, you are a living stone in this spiritual building. The Church is not merely a stone-and-mortar structure, but a vibrant body of believers founded upon the rock-solid confession that Jesus is Lord. It is a testament to faith's victory over darkness and stands firmly against the trials and tribulations of this world. The gates of Hades represent the forces of opposition or anything that seeks to attack or bring about the destruction of the life and vitality of the Church. Those forces shall not prevail.

As you face adversities of life that threaten to shatter you, remember that Jesus' declaration over His Church includes you. You are a part of a divine legacy designed to withstand, endure, and emerge victoriously. In recognizing Jesus as the cornerstone, find the strength and stability for your own life.

Embrace this truth with courage and conviction, for the same power that raised Christ from the dead is at work within you and the body of believers worldwide.

Prayer: Almighty God, my Solid Rock, and Foundation, I stand in gratitude for Your promise that the gates of Hades will not overcome Your Church. As a member of Your Church, founded upon the rock of Jesus' Lordship, I am humbled and emboldened and give thanks this day and every day moving forward. Amen.

September 16: The Living Word

Scripture for the Day

"For the word of God is alive and active. Sharper than any double-edged sword, it penetrates even to dividing soul and spirit, joints and marrow; it judges the thoughts and attitudes of the heart."

Hebrews 4:12

Today, it is important that we understand the great truth that the Word of God is not a set of fables or bygone wisdom. It lives to change and renew. Hebrews 4:12 teaches that the Word of God is active and powerful.

This Word is unlike any other—a blade sharper than the sharpest, able to cut through the polish of the surface, peeling back the layers of the facade of our outer selves, revealing our true intentions and condition of our hearts. It knows no hidden mysteries. It reads our innermost thoughts and searches out the very core of our hearts.

This piercing action is in love to make us closer to the heart of God. When we allow the Word to lead, correct, and mold us, we find our spiritual purpose.

How wonderful that in this spiritual operation, the Word is the scalpel and the surgeon, Jesus, the Living Word working in us. This should bring us a great deal of comfort and inspires us to look for the transforming work of the Word daily in our lives.

Prayer: Dear Lord, As I stand in front of your living Word today, grant me the grace to receive its active working in my life. May You make my heart be soil-like, well-prepared for the sowing of Your truth. Allow Your Word to pierce through my shields, to the point of separating the soul from the spirit, to show me the areas of my life where I need Your healing touch and heavenly insight, Amen.

September 17: Children of God

Scripture for the Day
"Yet to all who did receive him, to those who believed in his name, he gave the right to become children of God."

John 1:12

In our hearts amid the clatter of worldly concerns, how often do we yearn for a true sense of belonging? This promise from the Gospel of John speaks to our deep longing.

At first glance, we might pass over the enormity of what it means to be given "the right to become children of God." But pause and let that reality sink in. It is not by bloodline, nor by the will of the flesh, nor by human desire, but by God's will that we are born into His family.

In ancient cultures, to be named a child of a king was to be bestowed with honor, status, and inherent worth. How much greater, then, is the honor given us through believing in the name of Jesus, that we are called the children of the Creator of the universe? This is not a right that can be earned by merit; it is given out of the boundless grace that flows from the heart of God.

Receiving Christ and believing in His name is not merely a mental decision but a deep, life-changing trust—a relational bond. Through this bond, we find our identity, which forever alters how we see ourselves and how we interact with the world and with God. Our status as God's children means intimacy with Him, access to spiritual riches, and an imperishable inheritance.

To be called children of God also means that we grow in the likeness of our Heavenly Father. As we walk in faith, we are gradually transformed, bearing the family resemblance of love, mercy, and righteousness.

Prayer: Abba, Father, how stunning it is to stand in the truth that I am Your child. I confess that at times I live beneath my privilege, forgetting the dignity and worth You've accorded to me through Christ. Today, I receive wholeheartedly the truth that in believing in Jesus, I have been given the right to become Your child, Amen.

September 18: Hearts of Good Soil

Scripture for the Day
"Others, like seed sown on good soil, hear the word, accept it, and produce a crop—some thirty, some sixty, some a hundred times what was sown."

Mark 4:20

In a world of instant results and a cult of productivity, the sower parable challenges us to look at our receptiveness to the Word of God. In the different types of ground Jesus depicts, the good soil serves as a motivating image of our spiritual life.

The good soil is the hearers of God's Word who not only hear but receive and absorb it into their lives, allowing it to take root and grow. To receive the Word is more than consent; it is a response of obedience and taking root in every part of the life.

The interesting thing about Mark 4:20 is the crop harvest interval – a yield of be thirty, sixty, or a hundred times. It implies variance in the fruitfulness even among the recipients of God's Word. This might symbolize the variety in our talents, chances, and phases in life. Our growth in God is not of rivalry but a personal walk of faithfulness and development of the gifts God has given to each of us, and that we must encourage one another rather than compete.

Let us review the condition of our hearts. Do we resemble rich soil that allows the Word of God to go deeper and take root? It is not passive waiting but active making—taking away stones of hardness, pulling weeds of distraction, and watering the seed with the Spirit.

We are to be a people of depth and fulness, which comes from a consistent and faithful immersion in the Word of God. Let us be receptive to the diverse and slow ways God wants to bring about changes and growth in us.

Prayer: O Sower from heaven, Your Word is the seed of life, and I want to be good soil in Your hands. I desire to hear Your Word, receive it, and let it be fruitful in my life. Assist me to endure and to await the development, to welcome the silent and productive times, believing that You are refining me. Amen.

Embracing Shiloh:

September 19: A Great Multitude

Scripture for the Day

"After this I looked, and there before me was a great multitude that no one could count, from every nation, tribe, people and language, standing before the throne and before the Lamb. They were wearing white robes and were holding palm branches in their hands."

Revelation 7:9

Picture a scene so huge, that it reaches beyond the ability of humans to understand. This vision from Revelation 7:9 gives us a picture of God's promise fulfilled.

In our world, often marked by discord and divisions, this Scripture is a comforting and hopeful message that the Kingdom of God is beyond all boundaries. It unveils a reality where our national language and cultural differences are no longer sources of division but aspects of a divine quilt reflecting the multi-faceted Kingdom of God.

This group is depicted as standing before the throne and before the Lamb, Jesus Christ, united in worship and mission. They wear white gowns representing purity and triumph and carry palm branches, the traditional symbols of peace and victory.

What do we do with this today? We, as believers, are to carry this reality into our places and be instruments of reconciliation and sowers of peace. We are summoned to respect the image of God in every person, close gaps, rejoice in diversity, and show the oneness that Christ has bought for us with His blood.

While we look forward to and labor in receiving the complete revelation of God's Kingdom, let us come close to our brethren of every nation, tribe, people, and tongue in love, humbleness, and honor. Let us hope for the day that we will be part of the great multitude to glorify Him eternally.

Prayer: Heavenly Father, The vision of the great multitude standing in unity in front of Your throne, Lord of all nations and people, leaves me breathless. I feel joy in my heart and hope for the time when all the barriers will break under the pressure of Your Majesty, Amen.

September 20: Faith in His Word

Scripture for the Day
"'Go,' Jesus replied, 'your son will live.' The man took Jesus at his word and departed."

John 4:50

The encounter between Jesus and the royal official in the Gospel of John is an illustration of faith that is simple, yet extraordinary. The official comes to Jesus, desperate for his dying son to be healed. He had likely heard about Jesus' miracles and now, clinging to hope, he stands before the One he believes can save his child. The response of Jesus is direct and unfaltering, "Go, your son will live." It is a declaration that demands a response.

The royal official didn't request additional assurance, sign, or wonder. Instead, he "took Jesus at his word" and departed. His faith wasn't rooted in evidence he had witnessed with his eyes but in the trustworthiness of Jesus' words. This scenario starkly contrasts Thomas' later declaration in the same gospel, where he insisted on seeing before believing.

There is a great truth here: faith is not about seeing proof first but about taking Jesus at His word. The royal official believed the word of Jesus was as good as the manifestation of the miracle itself. This is the essence of faith—complete confidence in Jesus' promises, even when physical evidence is absent. It reminds believers that the object of faith is not the outcomes we seek but the person of Jesus Christ Himself.

This faith was honored, for as the official returned home, his servants met him with the news that his son was alive and well. At the very hour Jesus had spoken the words of healing, the boy's fever left him. The official's faith in Jesus' word resulted in the miraculous.

In our lives, we often face situations that seem desperate and hopeless. We cry out for a sign or a miracle, yet the call of Christ is the same now as it was then: "Take me at my word." Be strengthened by the conviction that Christ's word is trustworthy.

Prayer: Lord Jesus, where so many voices compete for my attention, let me hear Yours with clarity and take You at Your word. Like the royal official, help me to trust in Your promises, even when the waters of life are turbulent around me. Let my faith not be contingent on signs and wonders but rooted in the reliability of Your character and the truth of Your Word. Amen.

Embracing Shiloh:

September 21: The Unfailing Compassion

Scripture for the Day

"And he passed in front of Moses, proclaiming, 'The Lord, the Lord, the compassionate and gracious God, slow to anger, abounding in love and faithfulness,'"

Exodus 34:6

Today's Scripture portrays our Creator in the experience of Moses – a man who was so bold that he dared to request to see God's glory.

During this moment, the Lord refers to Himself as compassionate and gracious. These are more than adjectives but are expressions of divine love and compassion towards us. The compassion of God is His emotional reaction to our pain and suffering, whereas grace is His unearned blessing instead of condemnation. Being merciful is one part, and being gracious is another. However, God proclaims Himself to be both, a living example of His comprehensive benevolence.

The Almighty is "slow to anger," a saying that gives comfort to us. How quickly do we respond in anger or unhappiness? However, we encounter God not as a harsh judge awaiting our next blunder but as a patient parent, helping and forgiving us repeatedly.

The passage goes on to say that what the Lord abounds in love and faithfulness. Love is the very essence of the character of God; it is limitless and never-ending. His faithfulness is boundless, like the universe. He is unchanging and eternal. It is a powerful reminder that even when we are faithless, He remains faithful. He cannot deny Himself.

Let us come to this day strengthened by the fact of God's character. His pity means He knows our frailties and difficulties. We have undeserved access to His grace. His patience allows us to be genuinely transformed. His love keeps us, and His faithfulness ensures we are never forgotten.

Prayer: Graceful Lord, I come to You this day under the fresh mercies You have declared. How humble and uplifting, compassionate and gracious You are, Lord. I want to learn in Your presence and to use these aspects of Your character in my daily life. Amen.

September 22: Embraced as Family

Scripture for the Day
"Whoever does God's will is my brother and sister and mother."

Mark 3:35

In the outstretched arms of Jesus, we find a welcome that goes beyond bloodlines. The invitation to be a part of His family is amazing. Most of the time in life, belonging is conditional, and acceptance depends on our doing something. Jesus offers a different way - obedience to God's will.

This is a comforting and yet challenging truth. It is comforting because it is not dependent on our status, achievements, or the family we were born into. Challenging, because doing God's will involves surrender—a journey of continual transformation and growth.

Doing God's will involves listening to the voice of the Holy Spirit, aligning our hearts with the heart of God, and living out the two greatest commands: to love God and to love others. And in that obedience, we find a connection to Jesus that is as intimate and real as any family bond.

Being part of this divine family carries with it not just a name, but also a purpose. It means setting aside our own desires to seek out the things that matter to the heart of our heavenly Father. It's about being united with our spiritual brothers and sisters across the globe, engaged in the eternal work of the Kingdom.

As we meditate on this Scripture today, let us embrace Jesus's radical inclusivity. He doesn't seek servants to decree orders to; He desires family to walk with Him. Our Lord wants everyone to have the closest of relationships with Him, by aligning their will with His.

Prayer: Gracious heavenly Father, Thank You for the beautiful reminder that through Christ, I am embraced as part of Your divine family. Your Word touches the deepest part of my longing for belonging and affirms my place at Your table. Lord, help me discern and do Your will with joy and perseverance. In Jesus' Name, Amen.

September 23: The Manifestation of Love

Scripture for the day

"And he has given us this command: Anyone who loves God must also love their brother and sister."

1 John 4:21

The tapestry of our faith, woven with threads of divine commandments, reveals a clear and compelling pattern. In his epistle, John doesn't merely suggest but clearly states that our love for God is incomplete without a corresponding love for our fellow human beings. This isn't a suggestion; it's an indisputable mandate, shaping the essence of Kingdom living.

This is a key part of the Christian life. God is love, and those who abide in love abide in God, and God abides in them. Love is not merely an attribute of God's character; it is His very essence. When we love—as He loves—we are aligned with the divine nature. It is no longer simply an act we perform but a reflection of the relational nature of God Himself.

What does this love look like in practice? It is patient, kind, void of envy, and not boastful. It reflects the sacrificial love of Christ on the cross—a love so robust that it willingly endured hardship for the sake of another. Such love cannot be siloed into mere emotions or private expressions of piety. It must spill over into the way we treat every person we encounter.

In John's vision, the community of faith is a constant echo of Jesus' love. Love becomes the criteria by which the truth of our faith is measured. To profess love for God while neglecting to love others is to walk in contradiction. Love is not merely what God does—it is who God is. And since we are made in the image of God, to love is our most authentic expression.

Prayer: Loving Father, Your command is clear, and Your desire for me is that my love for You would be made complete in my love for others. Please pour Your love into my heart through the Holy Spirit so that I may truly love my brothers and sisters. Stitch my life into the fabric of Your Kingdom, where love is the thread that binds all virtues together. Amen.

September 24: A Chosen People, A Royal Priesthood

Scripture for the Day

"But you are a chosen people, a royal priesthood, a holy nation, God's special possession, that you may declare the praises of him who called you out of darkness into his wonderful light."

1 Peter 2:9

This verse defines the incredible identity that has been bestowed upon us as followers of Christ. We find not only our purpose but also our heritage and our calling. Wrapped within these words is a revelation of what God has done for us and what He has called us to be.

We are "a chosen people"—this is the radical declaration of our essential worth to God. The world often equates value with productivity or success. God's economy operates differently: we are chosen not because of what we have done but because of His great mercy and love. This choice reverses the order of the world. We are not valued because we are successful, but our success in God's eyes comes because we are valued and loved.

To be "a royal priesthood" elevates our calling, for it speaks of both kingly authority and sacred service. As priests, we have direct access to God, made possible through the sacrifice of Jesus Christ. We are called not to offer sacrifices of blood and grain but to offer our very lives as living sacrifices—our worship, our service, our love—as a spiritual act of worship.

As we reflect upon this truth today, let us recommit to embodying this identity. In a world aching for authenticity and hungry for hope, our lives can serve as beacons of His light, drawing others towards His love and declaring His majesty. Our story now is to live out this high and holy calling, to be the hands and feet of Jesus, our Great High Priest, and to walk in the authority and humility of our anointed roles.

Prayer: Almighty God, I stand in awe of the identity You have graciously bestowed upon me. To be chosen, royal, holy, and treasured surpasses my understanding and humbles my heart. Lord. Help me live out the full implications of this divine calling. May I embrace my identity as a member of Your royal priesthood, sharing Your light and love with a world in darkness. Amen.

Embracing Shiloh:

September 25: The Lord Delivers Us from Fear

Scripture for the day
"I sought the Lord, and he answered me; he delivered me from all my fears."

Psalm 34:4

Every dawn whispers the possibility of newness, but with the light our hidden fears may also find a voice. Today, let us dwell on a powerful truth from the psalms—a truth that reveals God's tender nearness and His transformative might.

In Psalm 34, we meet David, a man familiar with fear. Yet, through heartfelt seeking, he discovered the secret to overcoming: the Lord Himself. The psalm does not say God gave David temporary relief or simple coping mechanisms. No, it says God delivered him "from all [his] fears." The Lord's intervention is total, removing not just the consequences of fear but it's very presence.

The original Hebrew for "sought" resonates with intensity—it is an active, purposeful search. It was not a casual glance toward God but a yearning pursuit. David knew to whom he must turn. The Lord's response is equally intense: "He answered me." The Creator of the universe is attentive to our calls. He is the Answerer, the Deliverer.

When we are caught in the snares of our anxieties, it's a comfort to know that our deliverance lies not in our strength but in our surrender, not in our trying, but in our trusting. Every fear that whispers in the shadows is silenced when faced with the One who is Light.

David speaks of a mutual relationship: we seek, and God answers. This dynamic interaction reflects the covenant love of God—the God who promises to be near, to listen, and to save. He's not a distant deity but a relational, personal one. Our deliverance from fear is rooted in God's power and His desire to be intimately involved in our lives.

With this divine assurance, let us cast aside our hesitation and earnestly seek the presence of the Lord, for in Him is the fullness of peace, a sanctuary for our troubled hearts.

Prayer: Gracious Father, today, I come before You, echoing the truth that King David discovered—that when I seek You, You are there to answer me. In Your vast, unfathomable love, You deliver me from the quagmire of my fears. There are times when shadows of doubt, worry, and anxiety eclipse the joy of Your light. But I choose this day to seek You earnestly, to lean into Your Word and hold onto it as a lifeline amid my storms.

September 26: Walking Humbly in Love and Justice

Scripture for the Day
"He has shown you, O mortal, what is good. And what does the Lord require of you? To act justly and to love mercy and to walk humbly with your God."

Micah 6:8

Micah 6:8 is a poignant command, a trumpet blast calling us to the essence of what it means to be a follower of the one true God. Justice, mercy, and humility are the characteristics of a life lived well before Him.

The term "acting justly" refers to living in a way which allows a person to know what is right and what is wrong only by God's standards and not by the constantly changing morals of society. It means to uphold truth, to protect the weak, and to maintain honor in all our dealings. Justice acts in the character of God, the evidence for the world of His uprightness.

Loving mercy is the same as sharing graciousness and pity. Justice is a simple concept; the idea that all people get what they rightly deserve. Still, the call of mercy is more significant, making it a demand to feel the act of forgiving, to take pleasure in the show of grace, even when it is most undeserved.

This verse distills the essence of true religion: Pleasing God is not in ceremonies or exterior displays of piety, but in the right, merciful and humble state of our hearts and actions. Our task is to reflect the heart of Jesus who incarnated each of these demands perfectly.

The prophecy of Micah, as followers of Christ, is no suffocating prescription but a joyful call to live a full life in Him. Now, let us start with these holy imperatives written on our hearts.

Prayer: Heavenly Father, I stand before You, overwhelmed by Your glory and touched by Your grace. Your Word in Micah 6:8 resonates heavily in me—Your will for my life. I request the grace to act justly, to be equitable and upright in my actions, and to reflect Your justice in the world around me. Help me stick with what is right even when the waves of injustice strain me to go with them. Amen.

Embracing Shiloh:

September 27: Stirring Up the Deep

Scripture for the day

"For I am the Lord your God, who stirs up the sea so that its waves roar—the Lord Almighty is his name."

Isaiah 51:15

Among the silent splendor of spiraling galaxies, within the huge open space of the universe, the omniscient Creator who dances with celestial bodies speaks to me. Ponder the sea, the wild force of nature, with waves sounding the earth's pulse. He is the master of these waves, dictating upon the waters with sovereign might. But in boundless kindness, He stretches His hand to me.

The majestic nature in the character of God is a never-ending source of inspiration. The power that God displayed through nature is not only the show of might but is the opportunity to contemplate the One who is the Lord of the storm and the Giver of peace. This same God, who fashioned the planets and sculpted the canyons, knows me by name and owns me. How can I not wonder and draw power from His world?

In every move of life's stormy waves, I am reminded that the Lord Almighty is His name. He is unwavering, and His support is the foundation of my faith. Amid the chaos, His sovereignty is my refuge and solace. This truth is the foundation of my every day with Him. There is a deep assurance in believing that the One who churns the sea is also the One who calms my heart.

Prayer: Heavenly Father, Lord Almighty, Your name is a stronghold where I find safety. In the grandeur of creation, in the roar of the waves, I see Your power, and I stand in awe. As You stir up the sea, stir up my heart today. Awaken in me a deep reverence for Your Majesty and an unshakeable trust in Your sovereign care. Amen.

September 28: Peace, Be Still

Scripture for the Day

"He got up, rebuked the wind and said to the waves, 'Quiet! Be still!' Then the wind died down and it was completely calm."

Mark 4:39

Opening my eyes, to a new day, the words of Mark 4:39 wash over me with refreshing power. It's a divine reminder that in the chaos and confusion that life might present, there is a Savior who not only walks alongside me but has command over the elements themselves.

Picturing the scene of that stormy Galilean Sea, I imagine the disciples, battered by the relentless wind and waves, frantically striving to keep their boat afloat. I have felt like them during life's tempests, attempting to take control, bail out the water, and somehow tame the untamable. And just like them, forgetting who is in the boat with me.

Jesus, in His divine calmness, rises and speaks words of peace—a simple command, "Quiet! Be still!" That still resonates with the power to silence my fiercest storms. Here, indeed, is a overpowering truth: If Christ can bring quiet to the roaring waters, how much more can He bring peace to the storm in my heart? It encourages me to seek Him before I attempt to fix things myself. His authority which reigns over creation is the same authority that reigns in every aspect of my life.

In the quiet aftermath of His command, the disciples were led to wonder, "Who is this? Even the wind and the waves obey Him!" This moment of miraculous tranquility leads me to think about in a renewed way the awe-inspiring authority of Jesus Christ in my life. Do I allow His peace to rule in my heart, no matter the circumstance? Today, I resolve anew to surrender to His command, to trust His presence and power within my own personal storms.

Prayer: Lord Jesus, amid life's storms, Your voice still carries the power to bring peace. I come before You this morning, seeking tranquility amid turbulence, seeking Your command to be echoed in the situations that I face. Help me remember that You are in control, that You are present, and that nothing is too difficult for You. Amen.

September 29: Living with Eternity in View

Scripture for the Day
"When the Son of Man comes in his glory, and all the angels with him, he will sit on his glorious throne."

Matthew 25:31

We anticipate Christ's celestial kingship and judgment, a drama where the eternal story attains its apex when the Son of Man's comes, not as a lowly servant but in radiant glory.

In this passage, the focus is the Second Coming of Jesus, when the fullness of God's Kingdom will be set up as He sets reclaims the world and establishes His eternal rule. The glorified throne of the Son of Man is an image of His authority. That is not meant to create fear but to form the personality and lifestyle of His followers. Reflection is not enough. The judgment to come must incite action guided by Christlike love and compassion. What are we doing to prepare ourselves and others for this day? What of the unsaved?

The picture of the King in His splendor makes me realize that every day is a chance to minister, to sow seeds of love, and to reflect the gospel through my life. What then shall I do, knowing that my Lord would come back? Does the idea of His coming inspire me to love people more, share His love more freely, and forgive more readily? The rule of Christ is at hand, and its implications are as practical as they are profound. This prompting requires me to be watchful, steadfast, and diligent in my course of righteousness and service.

Prayer: Lord Jesus, You are the King who comes, the Judge who arrives, and the summit of every expectation. I am overwhelmed by Your promise that someday You will come. Your Word vibrates within me, producing the wish to see You enshrined in glory and generating a strong desire to be recognized as one of Your loyal servants. Amen.

September 30: Embracing the Heart of God's Commandments

Scripture for the Day
"Do not think that I have come to abolish the Law or the Prophets; I have not come to abolish them but to fulfill them."

Matthew 5:17

In this passage, Jesus talks about continuity and achievement but not of nullification. The idea that Christ came to destroy neither the law nor the prophets but to fulfill them leads to the perfect unity of God's redemption plan.

In this single statement lies a key theological insight: The spirit of the Law is reflected in Jesus, and the prophecies are fulfilled in Him. He is the link that completes the puzzle, the section that makes the story complete. The life, death, and resurrection of Jesus transform the moral and ceremonial code of the Law from a list of burdens into a relationship with God through the Messiah.

This forces me to rethink the concept of biblical commandments; they are not outdated orders but expressions of God's character and will that are best observed in the life of Jesus. It calls me to see beyond the letter and catch the spirit to pursue not only obedience but the heart of God in His statutes. How can I exemplify the same righteousness to which the Law pointed as Jesus did?

This day, therefore, is a call to walk in the righteousness of which Christ bore witness, a righteousness that is a product of love for God and for neighbor. It is a summons to follow the obedience to an entirely different depth, an obedience out of gratitude for the grace manifested in the fulfillment of the Law by Christ. It is not an obedience to earn love but to answer to it.

Prayer: Heavenly Father, as the new light of morning chases away the shadows, so Your Son, Jesus Christ, illuminates the true meaning of Your Law and Prophets. I thank You for not abolishing but accomplishing what I could never do on my own. Help me to live in the fullness of Your commandments, seeing in them Your love and holiness embodied in Christ. Amen.

Embracing Shiloh:

October 1: The Liberation of His Presence

Scripture for the Day
"I sought the Lord, and he answered me; he delivered me from all my fears."

Psalm 34:4

Through the intimacy of prayer, when the honest soul looks for the whisper of the divine, we participate in a holy interchange where our vulnerability meets His greatness. The psalmist's experience is not only historical poetry but a timeless call to us. Amid turmoil and noise, we are invited to a sanctuary, a place where the finite speaks, and the Infinite listens.

The psalmist refers to his act of seeking the Lord, an active pursuit of divine companionship. Seeking is a deliberate movement toward God. What does this quest produce? A solution – a reply from the Creator Himself, assurance that our whispers do not die out in empty space.

Our fears are not small in His eyes. Instead, we are set free from their tight grasp. The psalmist does not say that we shall never feel fear. Instead, there is deliverance in seeking, in calling on the Lord. When our fears are surrendered to the One who is the author of our destinies, these fears do not determine where we will end up.

God desires to be known and to relate to His children. God is faithful to act when we seek Him with honest hearts, bringing out our Father's caring response. It is proof that we are not by ourselves and that our spiritual path is a path of fellowship, not isolation.

Prayer: Father in Heaven, at this moment when everything is silent, I seek You. I need Your grace and Your peace. Thank You for the assurance that when I seek You with all my heart, You are not a silent observer but the ultimate answer to my prayers. Amen.

October 2: If God is for Us

Scripture for the Day

"What, then, shall we say in response to these things? If God is for us, who can be against us?"

Romans 8:31

Amid the swirling eddies of life's complexities stands an immovable truth, a beacon in my moments of doubt: if God is for me, who can really stand against me? This statement is not an empty spiritual boast but a confident testimony of faith.

In the eighth chapter of Romans, Paul draws out the pattern of God's intent for us – adoption, salvation, calling, justification, and glorification, which is finalized by the great question of who can oppose us if God Himself is for us. This issue is not only a challenge but gives deep comfort. In a world that is often an adversary, it is a wonderful reassurance that the Creator of the universe is on my side.

The implications are enormous. When we are faithful, God is faithful to us so that no enemy can stand against us. This does not mean a life free from persecution or opposition, but rather that, in the big picture, no adversary has the last word over my fate.

Paul's theology is not a concept. It is a living, breathing revelation that in the spiritual ecosystem, the believer is never outnumbered, never outgunned, for the Almighty Himself carries them. The protective love of God surrounds, strengthens, and fills with bravery, even in the face of the most frightful of life's adversities.

Prayer: Gracious Father, I find my strength in the question Paul asked, which resounds through the ages into the reality of my day-to-day existence: If You are on my side, who can be against me? In this profound truth, I find comfort that with You as my defender, no foe—at whatever level—can change the destiny You have created for me. Amen.

October 3: At His Command

Scripture for the Day

"At the Lord's command they encamped, and at the Lord's command they set out. They obeyed the Lord's order, in accordance with his command through Moses."

Numbers 9:23

In the vast wilderness, the Lord led the Israelites in every move. This pilgrimage was more for the soul than the body to teach trust and obedience. The cloud during the day and the fire at night served as not only navigation aids but also a physical representation of the Lord's presence. Amid doubt, His presence was the foundation upon which they could depend.

This story from Numbers is carved with a timeless truth that is applicable in all cultures and generations – the need to obey the will of the Lord and let Him lead, either through time of waiting or instant change. The itinerary of God's people was characterized by obedience to God's timing; they moved only when He would say or stayed as He decided. In this obedience, they found their purpose and provision.

The lesson is important. God is supreme, and He has absolute power. In addition, He is not far and removed. He is close to the day-to-day life of His people. The commands of the Lord are filled with His wisdom and understanding of what is good for us.

In my present life, this passage calls me to ponder my journey. Am I willing to wait when God has not given the go signal? Could I rely on His timing to pack up the camp and depart when His call was undeniable, even if I had no idea where I was to go?

Prayer: O Lord, lead me to sleep in Your masterful will, walk in Your way, and sit on Your command. Assist me in recognizing Your leading and in following without wavering. I seek to act in accordance with Your will just as the Israelites followed the movement of the cloud and the fire, aware that Your presence is both my way and my fortress. Amen.

October 4: A Chosen Servant

Scripture for the Day
"Here is my servant, whom I uphold, my chosen one in whom I delight; I will put my Spirit on him, and he will bring justice to the nations."

Isaiah 42:1

In a world full of turbulence and cries for justice, this divine announcement of Isaiah remains a light of hope. A servant of God, sustained and directed, comes as the personification of divine intention and delight. The promise of the Spirit of God resting on Him guarantees that His mission would not be by human ability but empowered by God Himself. This servant does not just carry local or temporal justice but global justice, spanning nations, races, and generations.

These lines are messianic hope lived; they are addressed to every one of us. By embracing Christ, I am also called to be an instrument of justice in His hands. To be filled with the Spirit is to participate in the healing of all things in a mercy-filled, eternal justice.

This prophecy reveals the attitude of God toward the world and His will to restore it. The servant nature of Christ points us towards a justice that is not vengeful but one that restores what is right, which corresponds to God's intention of *shalom* – peace and wholeness for all creation.

Prayer: Merciful Lord, I humbly stand in thankfulness for Your servant, Jesus, who is Your love and righteousness. I am motivated by Your Spirit, who dwells in me now and empowers me to participate in Your work of redemption in the world. May I also be an axe of Your justice, supported by Your hand and set apart for Your use. Amen.

October 5: None Righteous, Yet Redeemed

Scripture for the Day

"As it is written: 'There is no one righteous, not even one.'"

Romans 3:10

This verse pulls aside the veil of human fate. It levels the field, indicating that I cannot earn righteousness by my actions or moral character. The truth of Romans confronts me that everyone has sinned and failed to do what is required by God's standards.

From this reality check, the beauty of the gospel glows the brightest; the gospel does not start with the greatness of humanity but with the greatness of divine mercy. The great spiritual truth begins with the magnitude of our need and the depth from which His grace is reached down to us.

Although I am totally unrighteous, I have been imputed with Christ's righteousness. This is the foundation upon which our salvation is built like a great building, as explained by the Apostle Paul. From this we learn the beauty and power of a salvation that is not deserved but given.

Prayer: Holy Father, in Your truth, I see that I am not righteous. My heart wanders off, my will fails, and my deeds are not enough. But in Your infinite grace, You have opened a way of righteousness that does not depend on human perfection but is given through divine provision.

October 6: The Unseen Movement of the Spirit

Scripture for the Day

"The wind blows wherever it pleases. You hear its sound, but you cannot tell where it comes from or where it is going. So it is with everyone born of the Spirit."

John 3:8

Like the wind, the Holy Spirit is constantly here, and His movement is often shrouded in mystery, but it is also powerful and purposeful. We do not see where the wind starts or ends, but its power is visible in leaves that flutter and waves on the ocean.

For centuries, theologians have discussed the work of the Holy Spirit in the lives of believers. The Spirit gives life to the heart and animates us. He lives within us, directing, sowing knowledge, and, in some cases, leading us down unforeseen paths. However, to recognize the leading of the Spirit, it is often good to retreat from the noise and carping that seems to define our everyday life.

Jesus speaks of this movement in John 3:8. He describes the movement of the Spirit as the wind - unpredictable, invisible, but definitely real and working. The Spirit's operation is not within the scope of human understanding. However, by giving up this need to control, we let the Spirit of God take our lives toward something far beyond our power.

The life of the Spirit is not aimless. In contrast, it is a path of faith, of readiness to turn away in God's direction, to be enlightened by the Spirit. That which is born of the Spirit is alive in the most profound sense – infused with the divine Spirit, contributing to the continuing formation and rebirth of the world.

Prayer: Heavenly Father, open my heart's ears to hear Your Spirit's song. Teach me to accept the movements of Your Spirit in my life. May I find the freedom of not knowing all but being wholly bound to You, who leads me through every unknown way. Teach me to dance to the beat of Your will, embracing the divine current that takes me wherever You want me to be. In Jesus' name, Amen.

Embracing Shiloh:

October 7: The Currency of Heaven

Scripture for the Day

"And without faith it is impossible to please God, because anyone who comes to Him must believe that He exists and that He rewards those who earnestly seek Him."

Hebrews 11:6

Hebrews 11, transports us into Faith's Hall of Fame. Today's focus gets to the heart of our relationship with God. This is not based on mere wishes or mindless hope; it is a faith that recognizes the truth of God and His attributes.

To approach God, we must believe that He exists. This belief is more than intellectual agreement but a conviction that molds our entire life. It recognizes God as the Creator, Sustainer, and Lord of all. Secondly, we rely on His goodness. He is not just a God of remote judgment but One who actively rewards those who seek Him earnestly.

God does not just want us to know about Him. He wants to have a relationship with us. But such a relationship should be based on faith. This faith is pleasing to God because it is proof that we love and honor who He is and what He has promised. It is an acute dependence on God even when the situations are hard to comprehend.

The verse demands a sincere search, not a mere look at the sky in the morning. To seek God earnestly is to set our course on our spiritual journey, to synchronize our lives with His will, and to continue after Him with intent.

Faith is the currency of the heavenly realm through which we receive from God—not as a transaction but as a relationship. Faith is the channel through which we get direction, supply, and the final gift of His companionship.

Prayer: Almighty Father, I come before You today, humbly recognizing the vastness of Your existence. I believe You are who You say You are, and You do what You promise to do. My heart rejoices in the assurance that You are there and that You reward those who earnestly seek You. Amen.

October 8: The Spirit of Truth in Us

Scripture for the Day
"But the Advocate, the Holy Spirit, whom the Father will send in my name, will teach you all things and will remind you of everything I have said to you."

John 14:26

As Jesus was getting ready to leave the world, He promised His followers that the Holy Spirit, the Helper, would be sent in His name. This Helper is not a concept or a power; He is the third Person of the Trinity, the Spirit of Truth.

The Holy Spirit's role is manifold. He is our teacher who leads us gently into all truth. He does not speak for Himself but whispers the deep secrets of Christ, making the complex things of faith understandable to our finite minds. While the world provides conflicting stories and philosophies, the Holy Spirit holds us in truth that never changes.

The Holy Spirit is also our divine Reminder, helping us remember the words of Christ. How many times have we stumbled upon the right verse, remembered a sermon, or come across something that lights our way in moments of decision or anguish? This is the power of the Holy Spirit.

The Trinitarian doctrine revealed in the Bible may be abstract at times, however, we find that this verse makes it quite understandable. The Holy Spirit is God's ongoing working in us and through us. This is the very essence of a God who is not far but instead, always close to us and active in our encounters, educating, advising, and leading us to Himself.

The promise that the Holy Spirit will guide us into all truth in an ongoing learning and growing process in our faith. That is why our spiritual journey is dynamic, with the indwelling Counselor guiding us into deeper understandings of God and how we are to live.

Prayer: Strengthen me to depend on Your guidance every day. As I navigate the complexities of life, remind me that I am never alone. Your presence is a constant source of comfort and direction. Let Your truth resonate within me, transforming my actions, thoughts, and desires to align with the will of the Father. Amen.

Embracing Shiloh:

October 9: Crossing Over to Life

Scripture for the Day

"Very truly I tell you, whoever hears my word and believes him who sent me has eternal life and will not be judged but has crossed over from death to life."

John 5:24

Today's Scripture is about transformation and transition. It speaks of a profound change that happens not in the distant future or at the end of our earthly existence but the moment we believe—the immediate transition from death to life.

The phrase, "very truly I tell you," captures Jesus' earnestness in ensuring that we grasp the certainty of His promise. This is the bedrock of our faith. Believing in Him is not just intellectual assent, but a heartfelt trust in God and His sent Savior, Jesus Christ.

Jesus' words are not merely informative but performative; they enact what they announce. To hear His word and believe is to experience a resurrection of the soul, a passage from the dead end of sin to the boundless realm of eternal life. There's no waiting room for judgment. Instead, there's an immediate life in its fullness—a life characterized by a relationship with God that death cannot sever.

This Scripture does not only offer a future promise but a present reality. Eternal life in John's Gospel is not simply unending life, but life with God that starts now and carries on throughout eternity. Judgment is fundamentally altered for believers—we will not face condemnation because the verdict has already been given in favor of those who trust in Christ. In this, we see the interplay between divine justice and human responsibility—God's gift of salvation and our response to believe.

The assurance of "crossing over from death to life" is of immense comfort and motivation. It is a call to live out this new life here and now, allowing the reality of what we will fully experience in eternity to permeate our decisions, our relationships, and our sense of purpose.

Prayer: Lord God, I stand in awe of Your magnificent promise that by simply hearing Your Word, repenting of my sins and believing in You, I've been granted eternal life. I am humbled by the depth of Your love and the assurance that I have crossed over from death to life. Amen.

October 10: The Promise of the Spirit

Scripture for the Day
"And afterward, I will pour out my Spirit on all people. Your sons and daughters will prophesy, your old men will dream dreams, your young men will see visions."

Joel 2:28

The prophet Joel speaks God's promise: His Spirit will be poured out on all flesh. This spiritual flood represents more than just a drop of spiritual experience. It is about plenty, about saturation, about a holy flood that will reach all people. In a world of many divisions, this pledge is a symbol of unity and fraternity. Age and sex will not matter, as every person will witness the completeness of God's presence.

The Spirit of God enables people from all backgrounds to prophesy, dream, and have visions. This is not only about forecasting the future but about speaking the prophetic word. Dreams and visions in this light are representative of godly communication calling ordinary people to be a part of the extraordinary encounter with the divine.

Joel's prophecy, validated in the events of Pentecost as recorded in the book of Acts, signals a revolutionary change from the ritual-based Old Testament to a Spirit-in-dwelling New Covenant. It disrupts social norms, for in this new economy of the Spirit, all are called, all can participate.

By the Spirit of God, we are enlightened to His will, enabled for service, and become a community amid diversity. The Holy Spirit's presence in the lives of the believers is a preview of the coming Kingdom, in which God's will is done perfectly, and His purposes are fully realized.

Prayer: Sovereign Lord, You are the Life giver and the Hope of all things. In Your shadow, I stand in awe of Your promise to pour Your Spirit upon all flesh. In Your creative space of infinity, You have called me to be a recipient of this divine gift. Amen.

October 11: Despite the Giants

Scripture for the Day

"And they spread among the Israelites a bad report about the land they had explored. They said, 'The land we explored devours those living in it. All the people we saw there are of great size.'"

Numbers 13:32

The difficulties of what lies ahead can make a person retreat into fear and uncertainty. The spies' report in Numbers 13 indicates that fear can distort the facts. The land was extremely fertile, but the report was not about the blessing but the obstacles – the "giants" in their way.

Often, we behave in the same way, fixated on our giants, the obstacles in our professional life, personal goals, or spiritual path. Giants like these can make our faith in the promises of God look small. Yet, even in this daunting report, we are reminded of an overriding truth: Our God does not cower before the enormity of our challenges.

The Israelites' eyes left the view of the faithfulness of God for their current worries, leaving a blindness that we also share. The giants in the land were not accidents. They were there for a reason – to show God's power and strengthen His people's faith.

The fear that dominated the faith of the Israelites is like a looking glass of our own spiritual struggles. We should realize that no giant is beyond God's power to provide victory. In the face of our fears we know that nothing is impossible to Him who leads us.

Prayer: Heavenly Father, today, my own giants are before me, pressing me with their shadow. However, I decided to cling to Your promises, knowing You are bigger than any hindrance I encounter. Forgive me for the occasions when fear has reduced my faith. Amen.

October 12: Our Eternal Help

Scripture for the Day
"I lift up my eyes to the mountains—where does my help come from? My help comes from the Lord, the Maker of heaven and earth."

Psalm 121:1-2

The mountains of our trials seem to loom before us. We look straight up to the horizon for help. The psalmist reminds us of an essential truth: our aid is not rooted in the shifting dunes of this world but in the unwavering character of the Lord, our God.

Changing our gaze from the hurdles staring us in the face to the Almighty Creator who made our paths is fundamental to faith. Every mountain we face, whether a challenge to our faith, a test of our will, or a trial in our lives, is a chance to recall the source of our help. It comes from the Lord Himself, who is always there as a source of help when we need it.

God's help is constant. This psalm is statement of God's watchfulness; it is a chance to feel His great care. God, the Creator of heaven and earth, is personally involved in our pilgrimage.

By saying, "My help comes from the Lord," the psalmist affirms that God is not a distant onlooker but an active participant in our lives. This truth comes with a pledge. Our Lord will never leave nor forsake us in all our trials. He, who is called faithful and true, always sees us.

Prayer: When I look up to the hills, may I be consumed with an unwavering assurance that You pay attention to me. When doubt darkens my way, when the climb seems too steep, remind me that You are the Creator of all, and nothing is beyond Your power. Amen.

Embracing Shiloh:

October 13: Upheld in Love

Scripture for the Day

"But you, dear friends, by building yourselves up in your most holy faith and praying in the Holy Spirit, keep yourselves in God's love as you wait for the mercy of our Lord Jesus Christ to bring you to eternal life."

Jude 1:20-21

My spiritual walk is an active one. Faith is a structure that is not built by wood or stone, but by my trust and belief in the Lord. Each prayer, study of His word, each act of love is like a stone building up is how the Spirit builds this castle known inside me.

What should I do to create this faith? Praying in the Holy Spirit. Communion with God provides me the power and understanding to grow further in my belief. This holy conversation with God is irreplaceable, as it breathes life into my spiritual life, a life sustained by the vast and generous love of God.

Keeping myself in God's love means residing in His eternal care and provisions. It gives order to my deeds and thoughts to do His will and to dwell in His grace and mercy. This reminds me of the importance of being watchful and faithful in my relationship with the Lord as I wait for the great mercy of our Jesus Christ.

While awaiting Him, I do not just sit idle but engage in a patient expectation which leads me towards the hope of eternal life. This hope is not in fear but is a powerful hope that shapes my spirit, worship, and love.

Prayer: Heavenly Father, I come before You in the quiet moments of this day, seeking the strength to build up my faith through Your Holy Spirit. Guide my hands as I work on the living temple of Your presence within me. Let my prayers be the mortar that binds my actions to Your will, and may my heart be steadfast as I abide in Your encompassing love. Amen.

October 14: Faith Unveiled

Scripture for the Day
"He could not do any miracles there, except lay his hands on a few sick people and heal them."

Mark 6:5

Mark tells us of a place where the world's Savior, the embodiment of power and grace, "could not do any miracles there." This isn't due to a lack of ability but to a lack of something deeply human – the people's faith.

The revelation in this verse is twofold. It underscores the critical nature of faith for the working of miracles and displays God's respect for human agency. Even the Sovereign Lord, who spoke the cosmos into being, chooses not to override the faithlessness of His people. The Son of God honors the freedom He has gifted to humanity, even when it constrains the flow of miracles.

God's power and human responsibility dance together in a divine harmony that honors both His omnipotence and our free will. Where there is faith, there is fertile ground for miracles, for the hand of God moves freely and His purposes are fulfilled.

In my own walk with the Lord, I am encouraged to examine the state of my faith. What miracles is Jesus willing to perform in and through me if only I would believe? Where might I have been skeptical or dismissive of His power? My intention today is to throw open the gates of faith and welcome with open arms our miraculous God who desires to work within my breath and being.

Prayer: Lord Jesus, I am humbled by the lessons of faith from Your time in Nazareth. Teach me to always welcome You with a heart full of trust and expectancy. Forgive me for times when my doubts have silenced the symphony of Your works. Amen.

Embracing Shiloh:

October 15: Steadfast in Perseverance

Scripture for the Day
"Do not be afraid of what you are about to suffer. I tell you, the devil will put some of you in prison to test you, and you will suffer persecution for ten days. Be faithful, even to the point of death, and I will give you the crown of life."

Revelation 2:10

There are stretches where our faith seems to face trials by fire. But within the heart of this smelting process lies an invitation to a deeper trust in God. Revelation 2:10 comes as a tender but firm whisper to our spirits amidst the noise of our trials - it speaks of persecution, but it also promises victory.

Fear has no place in the heart of a believer. Our Almighty God, who knows the end from the beginning, has declared that He has prepared a crown of life for those who endure. The "ten days" of suffering mentioned are symbolic of a temporary period, emphasizing that earthly struggles, however intense, are but for a moment compared to eternity.

Suffering is not an absence of God's love but a part of the Christian journey that refines us. Every challenge we face is an opportunity to demonstrate the firmness of our faith and be fortified further by God's mighty presence.

Drawing strength from the Lord during such times means leaning into the Scriptures, clinging to the promises of God, and nurturing an unwavering conviction that God's goodness supersedes the present discomforts. To be faithful unto death is to acknowledge that our lives are not our own but a testament to the eternal life and glory that await those who remain steadfast in Christ Jesus.

Prayer: Heavenly Father, I come before You today with gratitude for Your Word, a lamp unto my feet and a light unto my path. In the face of my trials, I choose not to fear, for Your perfect love casts out all fear. Help me stand firm in the faith, knowing that these momentary afflictions are pale compared to the eternal weight of glory that You have prepared for me. Amen.

October 16: The Lord Goes Before You

Scripture for the Day
"The Lord himself goes before you and will be with you; he will never leave you nor forsake you. Do not be afraid; do not be discouraged."

Deuteronomy 31:8

Life is unpredictable. We can be fearful and discouraged. Yet today's Scripture offers reassurance: God is not only our front and rearguard but also the architect of our past, present and future.

Deuteronomy 31:8 declares God's active headship as our partner in all our life circumstances. The Lord is not a distant spectator but a concerned and active guide. He does not only observe our journey but also maps the direction and travels with us in every step.

The promise that He will never leave us nor forsake us contradicts every whisper of desertion we might hear in our lonely hours. This assures us that God does not go away when the road becomes difficult. This is the time when His presence shines the most. It is a timeless certainty locked in the nature of the Almighty Himself.

We exist in a time characterized by fear and misery, but the verse helps us to resist them. It tells us to remember: In front of us walks the Creator of the universe, and behind us follows the Savior of the world, and in us lives the Spirit that has raised Jesus from the dead. Consequently, we may advance with faith in the assurance of God's constant direction and unfailing partnership.

Prayer: Gracious Lord, As I put my foot on today's road, I hold on to Your assurance that You are with me. Thank You for going ahead, for making the way, and for Your comfort that I am never alone. All my fears are removed, and all discouragements will end as I put my confidence in Your everlasting faithfulness. Amen.

October 17: The Value in His Eyes

Scripture for the Day
"Are not five sparrows sold for two pennies? Yet not one of them is forgotten by God."

Luke 12:6

We can fall into a vicious circle of thoughts like "Oh no! I am just one among the million of others. I am unnoticed and insignificant." In the meantime, our issues can appear huge and threatening, requiring immediate attention without any help. We can feel entirely alone. Overall this, I hear God's voice as He speaks through creation and Scripture in one clear message, reminding me of my invaluable sonship in the eyes of the Lord.

The economy of God is not akin to ours. He is not concerned about materials, such as money. Rather, He considers many other values: attention, love, and care towards other people. He has an unlimited supply of these.

Because God is present everywhere, every creature is remembered by God. In this moment, Jesus invites us to look to the stars in the sky and then to look at God beyond our poor world. Just like nothing evades the sight of the Almighty God, nothing about you should escapes His gaze.

Prayer: Dear Lord, in the splendor of Your goodness, the realization of my actual value dawns on me. Amid Your great creation, You see me, know me, and fully attend to whatever concern or need I have. Guiding the sparrows as they fly from pillar to post in the shadow of Your sight, God, supports me in granting the safety of your holy watchful eye. Amen.

October 18: Illuminated Paths

Scripture for the Day

"Those who are wise will shine like the brightness of the heavens, and those who lead many to righteousness, like the stars for ever and ever."

Daniel 12:3

In the celestial ballet of the night tracing silk paths, the stars became beacons to sailors, symbols of freedom for enslaved people and inspiration for poets. Their never-ending beams are a visual opera of hope in all-encompassing darkness. Daniel, a prophet who looked beyond his stormy days, speaks of a glory that is compared to these heavenly bodies—a light promised to the wise and people who bring others to righteousness.

The wisdom that Daniel talks about comes from a spiritual understanding based on knowing the Lord. It discovers the truth, behaves righteously, and goes with God. It is aware of the eternal dimension of earthly life. This text introduces us to this wisdom, ensuring that we become the channels that will allow us to share and reflect the light of God's truth in a world clouded by the darkness of confusion and despair.

The calling to lead many to righteousness is the calling to win people to the Lord and engage them in discipleship. It is a life lived that attracts others to godly love through words, actions, and things done. It is a consolation that our labors have an eternal value and are recognized by God Himself. Our work is not fruitless; every change in each heart creates a part of God's Kingdom.

Prayer: God who is eternal and knows all, You who have set the stars in their courses and given them their place in the heavens, guide me to be the lamp of wisdom which shall shine in these dark nights of this world. Amen.

Embracing Shiloh:

October 19: Blessed and Broken for a Purpose

Scripture for the Day

"Taking the five loaves and the two fish and looking up to heaven, He gave thanks and broke the loaves. Then He gave them to His disciples to set before the people. He also divided the two fish among them all."

Mark 6:41

Mark 6:41 shows a moment of divine provision and a powerful lesson about the Kingdom of God. Jesus, faced with a hungry multitude, takes the little that He has — five loaves and two fish, provisions that seemed insufficient — and He makes it enough. More than enough for all to be fed.

Jesus looks up to Heaven — a gesture of His dependence and trust in the Father. He gives thanks — a response of gratitude before the miracle even unfolds. And then He breaks the loaves, a step of intentional fracturing that unexpectedly precedes multiplication.

In our lives, we often feel like those loaves and fishes. Our resources, abilities, and even our very selves can seem so small and inadequate to meet the needs around us. Yet in Jesus' hands, what is blessed and broken is turned into abundance. It is not in our wholeness but often our brokenness through which God's power is made manifest. It is not our fullness that God needs but our offered emptiness.

Our sufficiency does not come from us but from Christ. When we offer what we have to God, however meager it may seem, and allow Him to bless it and break it, we can trust that He will use it. As we yield to His purpose, we find that brokenness in the Kingdom of God often leads to blessings for us and those we serve.

As Christ's contemporary disciples, we are entrusted with the blessed and broken bread of our lives. We are called to distribute it, to share the grace we have received, given to the hands of Jesus. There will be enough. There will even be surplus, a satisfying fullness that flows from the miraculous hand of God.

Prayer: Lord Jesus, who multiplied loaves and fishes, multiply the gifts I bring to You. I offer my life, with all its weaknesses and insufficiencies, to Your divine hands. Thank You for looking up to the Father, blessing what little I have, and breaking it so that it may be used to feed needs around me. Amen.

October 20: Sanctified by Truth

Scripture for the Day

"Sanctify them by the truth; your word is truth."

John 17:17

While moving through the chaos of our everyday existence, we can get lost in the racket, demands, and constant flow of information trying to claim our attention. In this digital age of opinions, theories, and narratives, Jesus's prayer in John 17:17 sounds with deep meaning. He prayed for our sanctification, a spiritual process of being set apart for God's purposes. He points us to the medium for this transformative work: truth, which is contained in God's Word.

Sanctification is not just a moral improvement but a continuous process that makes us conform more to God's will and His character. This process of dwelling within the Bible is not simply about reading words; it is about interacting with the living Word of God, that transforms our minds, cleanses our hearts, and reforms our lives.

In meditating on this insight, let's bear in mind that truth is not a theoretical idea. It is personified in Jesus Christ, who declared, "I am the way, and the truth, and the life" (John 14:6). In the process of searching for truth through prayer, contemplation of Scripture, and obedience to the commandments of God, we become more and more like the image of Jesus and the values of God's Kingdom are integrated into us.

The truth is the transforming fact that transcends our knowing and acts. It forms our relationships with others, determines our choices, and serves as the lodestar for an existence that is lived according to the divine.

Prayer: Father, I approach You with an open heart to Your Word and Your truth. Sanctify me through Your truth; Your Word leads, shapes, and sanctifies me for Your divine purposes. Teach me to search for You each day, live in Your Book's depths, and make Your Word change me inside. Amen.

Embracing Shiloh:

October 21: Lessons from a Tale of Two Lives

Scripture for the Day

"There was a rich man who was dressed in purple and fine linen and lived in luxury every day."

Luke 16:19

In the heart of our faith lies the awareness that our life on earth is a mere speck in the vastness of eternity. Today's Scripture draws us to a parable told by Jesus—a story that contrasts the eternal destinies of a nameless rich man and a poor man called Lazarus. The rich man, adorned in luxury and comfort, lived a life oblivious to the needs around him, particularly of Lazarus, who sat aching for the scraps from the rich man's table.

This parable isn't just about wealth and poverty. It's about how we respond to the divine obligation of compassion and human connection. Our relationship with God is deeply intertwined with how we treat those He loves. In the rich man's case, his wealth became his fortress and his heart, an island. He feasted sumptuously, clothed in splendor, yet outside his gate lay a man whose name means "God has helped." But the rich man had not.

From the tale told by Jesus, we learn that our earthly choices have eternal ripple effects. Our prosperity and success aren't condemned but are given so that we can be stewards of God's grace, sharing with those in need. This parable calls us to be mindful of the Lazaruses at our doorsteps, those longing for compassion, for somebody to acknowledge their dignity as children of God. We are reminded that to ignore them is to ignore God Himself.

As we ponder this message, let us turn our hearts towards the divine directive to love our neighbors. Let us be individuals who do not merely dress in fine linen but clothe ourselves with the love of Christ, which exceeds any earthly wealth.

Prayer: Heavenly Father, I come before You today, reminded of Your immense love for all Your children. Your Word in Luke 16:19 speaks to the core of my being, nudging me to recognize the Lazaruses that You place in my path. Open my eyes, Lord, and soften my heart. Amen.

October 22: The Foundation of Our Salvation

Scripture for the Day

"They replied, 'Believe in the Lord Jesus, and you will be saved—you and your household.'"

Acts 16:31

Acts 16:31 declares an important message of the Christian gospel in one single potent sentence. "Believe in the Lord Jesus" is a message to trust, an invitation to faith, and a promise of salvation. These are beliefs about Jesus and the beliefs in Jesus Himself—as Lord and Savior.

In the context of Holy Scripture, belief is more than an intellectual assent; it is a disposition of the heart, soul, and mind. It is complete trust in the work and person of Jesus Christ. The assurance tagged to this faith is salvation—a change that involves pardon for sins, being reconciled with God, and the promise of eternal life.

The theological understanding of the text focuses on the grace of God. Salvation is not by our works but by our faith in what is given to us. The grace that saves is not private; it reaches outside personal circles to "you and your house," extending the promise of salvation to anyone who would believe.

This personal and social dimension of faith and salvation calls us to be messengers of this good news, spreading the pledge of salvation to our relatives, friends, and society. Our faith is not an inactive seed but a growing tree, always reaching for others.

Today, let this Word of God stir in you the humility of being a recipient of the grace and joy that comes from its assurance. Consider the miracle of faith that not only saves you as an individual but also can change people around you.

Prayer: Father, I approach You with a heart of thanks for the wonder of simplicity and the depth of the gospel. I put my faith in the Lord Jesus Christ, not just in words but in the totality of my existence. I believe in His work on the cross, His resurrection, and His dominion over me. Amen.

Embracing Shiloh:

October 23: Eternal Life Through Jesus

Scripture for the Day
"Jesus said to her, 'I am the resurrection and the life. The one who believes in me will live, even though they die.'"

John 11:25

The poignant declaration of Christ to Martha amid her grief over the death of her brother Lazarus speaks volumes to us today. Jesus does not merely give life; He is life itself. This profound truth reorients our perspective—not only on death but on our daily living.

Believing in Jesus is not just looking forward to an afterlife. It is experiencing the fullness of life now, with hope that transcends the grave. In John 11:25, we are reminded that our faith in Christ breaks the chains of death's finality. Even in death, believers have a continuous relationship with the Almighty, promised through Jesus' resurrection power.

The very presence of Jesus sustains our spiritual vitality as the "resurrection and the life." Our trust in Him is not mere belief in an event but a complete reliance on the person of Christ, the Son of God, who has conquered death itself. There is comfort in the assurance that our physical death is not the end but the doorway to eternal communion with God.

Prayer: Heavenly Father, thank You for the gift of Your Son, Jesus, who is the resurrection and the life. I believe in Him and the eternal promise that even in death, I shall live. Thank You for the hope that I carry every day, no matter the challenges I face. Help me to live in the confidence of the eternal life promised to me, and may this assurance shape my every action, thought, and word. Amen.

October 24: Eternal Presence, Timeless Salvation

Scripture for the Day
"Very truly I tell you," Jesus answered, "before Abraham was born, I am!"

John 8:58

The "I am," Jesus declares His preeminence before time, linking us to the divine reality that Our human history does not bind Him.

These words bring us to the reality of Jesus as the Son of God, the "I Am". In the original Greek text, Jesus uses the name God revealed to Moses in Exodus 3:14, "I Am Who I Am," symbolizing pure existence and unchangeable truth. He is that 'I Am' who remains unchanged throughout time.

This reflection is a source of comfort to me: that the One who came before Abraham dwells with me. This very Jesus, who covers all eternity, is with me now. He is in the moments of the rising sun, the bustling day, the quiet night. He is in the laughter, the tears, and the silence.

My life is built on a foundation which lies even before the stars with Jesus as my cornerstone. His being is a provider of an everlasting hope that leads me away from the temporary cares of my life to an assurance that goes beyond time.

Living in Him, I realize that my spiritual descent is from the belief of Abraham and the eternal truth of God Himself. He, the "I Am," calls me daily to be a part of His eternal character, including salvation, grace, peace, and a relationship that will endure after the universe burns itself out.

Prayer: I come before You, O eternal God, the great "I Am," who exists before all time, with a heart full of thanks. Like Abraham, I desire to live by faith, believing in Your promises that resound in eternity. Amen.

Embracing Shiloh:

October 25: Ignited by the Spirit

Scripture for the Day
"All of them were filled with the Holy Spirit and began to speak in other tongues as the Spirit enabled them."

Acts 2:4

They were united and waiting as instructed by Jesus, and the mighty Spirit descended. Imagine the scene: a breath of wind, flames, and a multi-ethnic logic of God's miracles burst out. The sense of the power and presence of God was vastly overpowering! This scene captures not only the birth of the Church but the intimate call to each believer, me included, to be constantly refilled and rekindled by the Holy Spirit.

The Holy Spirit is not confined to spatial or cultural boundaries. The Spirit overcomes such boundaries, making it possible for the Word of God to be understood even behind the most persistent fences. The way the Spirit spoke through the disciples, I am also enabled to communicate and live out the gospel in ways that are relevant to those around me.

This Pentecost moment means that we all are indeed poor vessels, the Holy Spirit can fill and use us. Whether we hold lineages or are naked, we place ourselves in His hands. It forces me to be sensitive to the Spirit's activity in my life, letting my words and deeds rise above my weaknesses so that God may work in me.

May this Scripture witness that the same Spirit which came down upon the disciples at Pentecost can come upon me now, filling me again with spiritual gifts, courage, and heavenly language of love.

Prayer: Father, I embrace the Holy Spirit, who energizes my life with His power, grace, and love. I am amazed at how your Spirit changed ordinary people into fearless preachers of Your word. On this day, I seek a new filling of the same Spirit to kindle my heart afresh. Amen.

October 26: A Community of Faith

Scripture for the Day

"Those who accepted his message were baptized, and about three thousand were added to their number that day."

Acts 2:41

Can you believe that a single message – the gospel of Jesus Christ – made three thousand hearts accept the truths? It is truly a miracle.

At this point in history, the early Church grew exponentially, not due to human planning but by God's miraculous work through the Holy Spirit. The message of Jesus' death and resurrection pierced their hearts, and they responded by faith. It reminds me that my message today needs to remain as powerful and urgent as ever.

Publicly testifying to their purity and new beginning, the new Christians became instant members of a new community, a family of believers. As a modern disciple, this assures me that I also belong to this eternal community, linked not by nationality or culture but by the Spirit and our common faith in Christ.

Today, I am encouraged to participate in this divine fellowship, sow into fellow believers' lives, and welcome the nourishing fellowship of my local church. Just as the early church, I have been entrusted with the gospel's message, bringing new life in Christ to those who would listen.

Just as the numbers were added to the church then, even so, I pray for the growth of the Kingdom now—not just in numbers but in souls brought to the love and truth of Jesus Christ, resulting in lives forever changed.

Prayer: O Lord, gracious and Almighty, I am brought low by the activity of Your Spirit in the early Church but uplifted by Your constant promise to build Your Church throughout the ages. I am grateful to You for the same message of hope that sounds as loud today as it did then—the gospel of Jesus Christ, my Redeemer. Amen.

Embracing Shiloh:

October 27: The Unfolding Revelation

Scripture for the Day
In the past God spoke to our ancestors through the prophets at many times and in various ways."

Hebrews 1:1

The words of Hebrews 1:1 begin the overarching narrative of God's unfurling revelation of Himself to us, His dear creation.

Reflect on how God, in His grace, chose to reveal His purpose and character through the prophets—this divine tapestry woven with diverse threads: dreams, visions, and words, each representing a unique contribution to comprehending His will. The voice of God was heard through Moses' law, Isaiah's prophecies, and the psalmists' songs. They were parts of the cosmic puzzle; they gave directions and warnings and showed the way to salvation.

However, this was not the end of His communication. Hebrews states that God has spoken concerning the Son, Jesus Christ, the greatest and complete self-disclosure in these last days. The prophets spoke parts of the truth, whereas Jesus is the whole truth.

God of the ages did not become silent but took the form of flesh among us, leaving no room for misunderstanding or distortion of His final message. In Jesus Christ, I see every law, prophecy, and psalm fulfilled. I see God's face reflected in Him.

Prayer: Eternal Father, I thank You for Your different and many ways of addressing people throughout the centuries. Thank You for the prophets who heard Your voice with great attention and passed Your message from generation to generation. Amen.

October 28: Walking in Truth and Love

Scripture for the Day
"Because of the truth, which lives in us and will be with us forever."

2 John 1:2

John's truth is not an abstract concept but intimately connected with Jesus Christ—who is the Way, the Truth, and the Life (John 14:6). In Him, we put our faith, and His truth dwells in us. This in-dwelling truth also stands as a witness of the love of God. In Christian life, love and truth are one, as they are in Christ's person and work.

This truth being in us daily reminds us that we are not lost in the sea of relativism or confusion. We, the followers of Christ, have a constant, fixed compass and guide. The truth of Christ, being in us, helps us to see what is right and wrong, what is light and what is darkness, and what is real and what is illusion.

Let's reflect as we meditate on the Scripture, how this living truth is molding our lives. Does it help us to make our choices, support our connections, and lead our purpose in this life? Do we allow Jesus the truth itself to lead us to love, goodness, and a truth witness of the gospel?

The loving comfort "will be with us forever," also takes us to a never-ending fellowship with the divine. Such an eternal view brings hope to us in suffering and power in doubts.

Prayer: Thank You for the truth of Your Word that You have sown into the depths of our hearts. This truth does not remain static but lives and moves within us, leading us in Your ways. May Your Holy Spirit make this truth increasingly real to us each day, that it would change our lives, and that we would be signs of Your love and grace to those around us. Amen.

Embracing Shiloh:

October 29: Eternal Life in Knowing God

Scripture for the Day

"Now this is eternal life: that they know you, the only true God, and Jesus Christ, whom you have sent."

John 17:3

According to Jesus, eternal life is not simply a hope to be fulfilled in the future; it is a present reality in the relationship of the Father and the Son. It is about God, how to know Him, truly and intimately.

This statement demonstrates the biblical aspect of the dynamic power of knowledge. It isn't just consciousness of His being or a recognition of His reign. It is to be in a deep personal relation with Him, characterized by love, obedience, and acknowledgment of His grace in Jesus Christ.

Eternal life begins not when we leave this earth, but when we know God through His Son. The Greek word of "know" implies a relationship and an encounter. This knowledge is a process of maturing in faith, love, and comprehension of His divine nature, defining our lives and values.

This Scripture teaches that eternal life is available due to Jesus Christ—what He is and what He has done. Through Jesus, we see God in all His fullness but in human form, sent for our redemption and as the bridge to a restored relationship with the Creator.

How does this personal knowledge of God reflect in our daily lives? Do we want to grow nearer to Him? Do we let our understanding of God shape the values that we hold, the choices we make, and the things we do? Do we invite others to know this truth and the life it offers?

Prayer: Dear God, we approach You with hearts thirsty for a more profound understanding of You. We thankfully acknowledge the gift of eternal life, to which You have enabled us through Your Son, Jesus Christ. Aid us in understanding this profound aspect that knowing You is to have this life eternal in this life and the life forthcoming. Amen.

October 30: Abiding in Truth

Scripture for the Day

"To the Jews who had believed him, Jesus said, 'If you hold to my teaching, you are really my disciples.'"

John 8:31

My heart is captivated by the simple yet profound condition Jesus places before those who believe: "If you hold to my teaching." This "if" is a gate that leads to a journey of true freedom. Holding to Jesus' teachings means that my belief is not just a fleeting thought or a momentary agreement; it is a daily walk, a process of learning, applying, and living out the truth of His words.

This journey is not always easy. The world offers countless paths, each proclaiming its own form of truth, but these are often marked by chains disguised as freedom. Yet, as I walk in Jesus' teachings, despite how countercultural it may be, I find freedom that the world cannot give nor take away. For His words are spirit and life (John 6:63), and they guide me into the light of His presence where there is fullness of joy.

Holding to His teachings sets me apart. In a shifting world, His Word remains constant and secure. When I diligently apply His words in my life, I am an authentic disciple—I am not just passing through this life but thriving, rooted deeply in His everlasting truth.

Prayer: Dear Lord, Your words are the bread of life, and today, I come before You humbly, asking for the strength to hold to Your teachings truly. Let my faith be more than words; let it be an active pursuit of Your truth. Help me to understand and live according to the principles You have taught so that I might not only call myself Your disciple but live as one. Amen.

Embracing Shiloh:

October 31: The Unity of the Divine

Scripture for the Day
"I and the Father are one."

John 10:30

In the Gospel of John, Jesus states a foundational truth of Christian theology—His unity with God the Father. The oneness that Jesus speaks of is moral, intentional, and His nature as God – it expresses the common essence and existence with the Father. This unveils the mystery of the Trinity: though the Father and the Son are separate Persons, they are one in nature and substance.

It ensures that we see the Father when we look at Jesus. When we follow Jesus, we follow the Father. Unity assures us that the redemption, grace, and truth in Christ are truly God's redemption, grace, and truth. It emphasizes the level of His connection with us, that He humbly closes the gap between the divine and the human, providing a way for us to experience this divine unity through the indwelling of the Holy Spirit.

Reflecting on the penetrating, mysterious words spoken by Jesus, I consider this unity's profound impact on my spiritual journey. Jesus, as one with the Father, is the perfect image of God's love, power, and wisdom. In Him, I perceive the unseen in God seen, the indescribable made real, and the far in Him brought near.

In a modern-day world where I am constantly pushed to be independent, this text challenges me to seek my identity and purpose in the relationship provided by Jesus with the Father. It calls me to bring my life into harmony with the divine order and to achieve inner unity in myself—my heart, soul, mind, and strength—aimed at one goal, sustained by the teachings of Christ, and animated by the Holy Spirit.

Prayer: Father, I am in lowly worship of this mystery that Jesus and You are one. Assist me in understanding how great this unity is and bring me into unity with You. Thank You for showing Yourself in Your Son, giving me a way to understand and relate to You. As Christ reflects Your heart, may I also reflect the heart of Christ in my thoughts, words, and deeds. Amen.

November 1: The Light of the World

Scripture for the Day
"Again Jesus spoke to them, saying, 'I am the light of the world. Whoever follows me will never walk in darkness, but will have the light of life.'"

John 8:12

From John 8:12 a profound truth is found – Christ is the light in our darkness, a guiding star that shows the way, driving away any shadow we may meet.

For the disciple of Jesus, it is a conscious choice to move out of darkness into His marvelous light. It is not just an acknowledgment of His teachings but living according to His ways, seeking His wisdom, and letting His truth shine in us. Jesus is a never-ending light that outshines the flickering dim lights that would lead us off our path.

Christ, the light of the world, enlightens our intellect to understand the deep mystery of faith. In Him, we see God's definition of love, mercy, and sovereignty. Jesus is the personification of the Word that reveals God's plan to us. We testify of His grace by embracing the light of Christ into our lives. It is not only about dodging the darkness but being bearers of His light, radiating His love to the rest of the world.

Let's choose the light of life then. May our actions reflect His light so that others see His radiance in us.

Prayer: Heavenly Father, I come before You, hungering for the light of Your Son, Jesus Christ, to beam into my heart. In You, not only is the light of my way placed, but also the light of my spirit. As I enter this day, I pray for Your grace, so I walk behind You, never to cross into the darkness of fear or doubt. Amen.

November 2: One in Christ Jesus

Scripture for the Day
"There is neither Jew nor Gentile, neither slave nor free, nor is there male and female, for you are all one in Christ Jesus."

Galatians 3:28

In this beautiful stanza, God's proclamation of oneness and equality overrides all possible social divides. Galatians 3:28 bids me to see beyond stereotypes and constructs, calling me to find unity in Jesus, in whom these differences do not matter.

The Apostle Paul pleads with us to see how faith in Christ has the power to transform. At the foot of the cross, the ground is level, and the grace of God is indifferent. It does not recognize any race, status, or sex. This Scripture reveals God's redemption and the universal reach of the gospel. We are dressed in Christ as believers, and our identity in Him becomes the predominant feature that characterizes us.

The truth revealed in Galatians allows me to cultivate a spirit of brotherhood and sisterhood towards all those who are in Christ. The Church, the body of Christ, is made up of different members, each uniquely empowered and equally cherished by God. Our unity in Jesus is not of sameness but of a symphony, like the different instruments each playing their separate parts but together.

May this settle deeply in my heart as I meet my neighbors, friends, and strangers. Our diversity is beautiful, worship in harmony that reaches the heavens when we, as one, recognize one Lord and Savior.

Prayer: God, You are generous. Your love knows no boundaries, extending even to distances that people have created. I am profoundly grateful for the reminder in Galatians 3:28 that in Christ, we are all one. Amen.

November 3: The Assurance of Eternal Life

Scripture for the Day

"Whoever believes in the Son has eternal life, but whoever rejects the Son will not see life, for God's wrath remains on them."

John 3:36

John 3:36 has both a sad and an optimistic statement about eternity. This Scripture offers us a choice. The question is whether belief or rejection is the solution with regarding belief in the Son, Jesus Christ.

It speaks about the importance of faith. Believing in Jesus is more than intellectual assent. It is also a trusting surrender to His loving lordship, a confident reliance on His saving grace. This belief is the very thing that connects our human deficiency and God's promise of life.

This verse isn't only about the future. The eternal life offered is not only a utopia somewhere in the sky. It starts right now, right this moment. Jesus' life brings meaning to our everyday life, even in the mundane things, that become uplifted by a divine purpose that Jesus gives. Eternal life begins with the knowledge of God and His Son, that gives purpose to the relationship between life and death.

However, to those who reject such this offer, this verse is a powerful warning that they remain under God's wrath. The intention is not to generate fear but rather to inspire acceptance of the gospel's invitation. This admonition is twinned with an open door of hope to all who would believe and a warning to those who do not.

Prayer: Father, how glorious is Your love that You should grant us eternal life through Your Son, Jesus Christ. The certainty of Your Word fuels my wonder and gratitude that through believing in Jesus, life eternal is not only a promise for the future but a present reality. Amen.

Embracing Shiloh:

November 4: Chasing After the Wind

Scripture for the Day
"I have seen all the things that are done under the sun; all of them are meaningless, a chasing after the wind."

Ecclesiastes 1:14

Today I meditate on the sage advice from the book of Ecclesiastes, penned by the wise and wealthy King Solomon. Having the availability of every pleasure that he could imagine and being able to satisfy every wish, he found them to be a striving for the wind, vain and empty.

It can be easy to get lost in the maze of life, scouring for those items that promise happiness and fulfillment. We sweat under the sun, looking for success, appreciation, and comfort, thinking that having them will bring us satisfaction. But Solomon reminds us that all these things are temporary and do not fill the deepest yearning of our hearts.

Solomon isn't criticizing work or pleasure *per se*, but he is wondering about their meaning. The key to understand that true purpose and meaning are found not under the sun but beyond it. They are in God, who provides meaning to every undertaking by aligning them with His will and purpose.

Chasing after the wind reflects the human condition, the hollowness felt in the life that is lived for life itself and not for the timeless and immovable things. The wind is itself a product of God, unseen and untamed. My comprehension and effort can never entirely catch or hold the divine intent. This is a recognizing that this world is not the final goal, good as it is. God has much more. This is only the beginning.

Prayer: God, I admit that I am like Solomon in so many ways – I pursue the joys and achievements of this world far too often. Thank You for the reminder today that the absolute satisfaction is You. Give me grace to understand what is essential in my life and to put my best into the eternal, not just the temporal. Amen.

November 5: The Vision of Purity

Scripture for the Day

"Blessed are the pure in heart, for they will see God."

Matthew 5:8

In the noise of life's distractions, the quest for purity might seem daunting, almost old fashioned. Yet, nestled within Christ's Beatitudes speaks a promise—a vista of the divine for those whose hearts are undivided. – To be pure in heart is to be single-minded in our devotion to God, purging our intentions not merely of moral blemishes but of the clutter that stifles our spiritual vision.

The purity Christ speaks of goes beyond ceremonial acts or surface goodness. It demands a deep cleansing from the idols of our affections—those things that we elevate above our Creator. It is about sincerity, an internal consistency where our outward actions mirror an undiluted love for God and a genuine compassion for others.

It is in this crucible we are refined and prepared to see God, not with physical eyes, but with the eyes of faith. It is a reminder of what the psalmist declares, "Who may ascend the mountain of the Lord? Who may stand in His holy place? The one who has clean hands and a pure heart" (Psalm 24:3-4). To "see God" is not to claim a literal vision but to experience His presence in an intimate and life changing way.

Prayer: Heavenly Father, I seek the blessing of a pure heart. In a world brimming with impurity, help me anchor my heart to You. Cleanse me from inside out, that my desires, thoughts, and actions may reflect Your perfect love. By Your grace, strip away the distractions that blind me, and lead me into the spiritual clarity that beholds Your presence. In Jesus' Name, Amen.

Embracing Shiloh:

November 6: From Fear to Faith

Scripture for the Day
"Then he climbed into the boat with them, and the wind died down. They were completely amazed."

Mark 6:51

In the sea of life, which is by its nature turbulent, storms come, and winds howl. Sometimes, our boats, our very lives, appear ready to sink under our trials and troubles. We fight with the oars, strive against the waves, and sail through the night, lonely and feeling overwhelmed.

In Mark 6:51, the disciples in such a state, pulling the oars in the face of adverse wind. But the scene changes entirely as Jesus walks upon the water and approaches the boat. He brings an end to the wind. The disciples' amazement attests to their growing recognition of who Jesus is and what He can do with the chaos ready to overwhelm us.

This portion is a powerful witness to the lordship of Christ over the natural and the supernatural, over the external and the internal storms of our life. On His entrance, peace prevails. The winds of concern, uncertainty, and fear are dispelled.

The stilling of the sea is not just a miracle. It is a picture of the power of God and the perfect peace Christ gives. In biblical symbolism, the sea often represents chaos and sin. The dominion of Christ over the sea stands for His power to defeat sin and chaos in our lives, too. The receding wind mirrors the silencing of our fears when we see and feel the presence and power of Jesus.

As Karl Barth referred to these miracle stories as signs of the Kingdom of God –when the divine plan breaks through into the human setting. The Jesus walking on water represents not only a disruption of the natural order but also a promise that the Word of God is alive even when all else seems to be dead.

Prayer: We thank You, O Lord, for Your Word that guides us into peace amid the storms of life. Considering the peace that Jesus brought to His disciples on the sea, we ask You to sail the vessel of our hearts. Calm the turmoil of our fears, insecurities, and doubts. Reveal to us that You are the Lord of all creation and that no wind or wave can stop You. Amen.

November 7: The Path to Reconciliation

Scripture for the Day
"If your brother or sister sins, go and point out their fault, just between the two of you. If they listen to you, you have won them over."

Matthew 18:15

When misunderstandings and representations can quickly transform into long lasting hostilities, Jesus helps us understand a way of love that considers the weaknesses of our humanity. In the Jesus' approach to solving conflicts, there is great wisdom.

Jesus outlines a way to allow gentleness, patience, and courage to start a conversation meant for healing. It is an instance that allows grace to win. Jesus emphasizes the concept of privacy and respect, providing the sinner with dignity and not publicly exposing the person to embarrassment. This kind of direct communication embodies the scriptural call to "speak the truth in love" (Ephesians 4:15).

The Greek word for "won over" is also translated as "gained," meaning, recovering an impaired relationship is a profit to the Kingdom of God. This captures the heart of God, who wants unity and peace rather than division and prolonged strife. In this peacemaking, we liken ourselves to Christ, the ultimate Reconciler.

An easy road or way towards reconciliation does not exist. Spiritual insight is needed to see that every person we meet is the made in the image of God.

Prayer: God, Your wisdom surpasses our human mind; Your ways make us righteous and loving. Thank You for the word and gift of Your Word that is a lamp to our feet. Bestow on me the power and poise to come to my brethren with humility and peace. Let me sustain the love and honor that glorifies You and strives to heal what has been hurt. I pray in the name of Jesus, Amen.

Embracing Shiloh:

November 8: Rock of our Salvation

Scripture for the Day
"Then Moses raised his arm and struck the rock twice with his staff. Water gushed out, and the community and their livestock drank."

Numbers 20:11

Numbers 20 intensely shows God's provision and the necessity of relying on His trustworthiness. The Israelites needed water, and Moses, as their leader, sought help from God. In an outburst of wrath and impatience, Moses hit the rock instead of speaking to it as was ordained by God. However, in such an act of disobedience, God still demonstrated His mercy and grace by giving water to His people.

The provision of God is not bound to our actions or righteousness. It comes from His bountiful love towards us. In the same way, water came out of a rock to quench the thirst of the Israelites. And blessings flow in our life from God, no matter how much we falter.

This passage stresses the role of obedience and trust in the promises of God. Having steadfast faith in Him, we are confident He will meet all our requirements at His perfect time. May this story symbolize that God is always faithful even when we trip up.

Prayer: Father, thank You for Your eternal provision and faithfulness in our lives. Aid us to have faith in Your vow to provide for our needs and to depend on Your timing, even when we do not comprehend. Pardon us for those moments when we have acted out of haste or unbelief and enable us to live in Your will. In the name of Jesus, we pray, Amen.

November 9: Taste and See

Scripture for the Day
"Taste and see that the Lord is good; blessed is the one Who takes refuge in Him."
Psalm 34:8

In Psalm 34:8, David calls us to experience the goodness of the Lord for ourselves. Tasting with the lips helps us enjoy the full flavor of food; likewise, we are invited to taste and see that the Lord is good. This knowledge of God's goodness is not just about intellectual knowledge but also the personal experience with His love, mercy, and faithfulness.

The sanctuary of the Lord provides us with peace and protection. He is our refuge during troubled times, guide in moments of vulnerability, and consistent companion on life's journey. We are rewarded with a goodness beyond human comprehension as we allow our hearts to open to Him and seek His face.

Upon the servants of the Lord, many blessings are revealed. We are provided with His love that never fails, His grace, and His provision when we seek refuge in Him. Every day, it wafts the aroma of the Lord and invites us to taste the Lord's goodness, renewing our faith and strengthening our bond with Him.

We shall taste the sweetness of His person and rejoice in His goodness, for they who hide in Him are truly blessed.

Prayer: Father in Heaven, we are grateful to You for Your goodness and faithfulness that never grow weak. Teach us to enjoy and live out Your love and grace. Help us to hide in You, receiving consolation and rest in Your company. May Your favor flood our lives as we believe in all Your promises that never falter. Amen.

November 10: The Greatest Commandment

Scripture for the Day

"Jesus replied: 'Love the Lord your God with all your heart and with all your soul and with all your mind.'"

Matthew 22:37

Amid the chaos of the voices claiming to know what matters most in life — power, riches, fame — Jesus' words come as the cooling salve. The Greatest Commandment is a rule and a way to a changed life. Loving God with all the heart is to synchronize every pulse of the human heart to the divine rhythm of His love, to let our soul echo His glory, and to submit our thoughts under the headship of His truth.

The demand to love God with all our minds is the call to an integrated life. Our hearts, where our emotions and desires dwell, must be so interwoven with His that our love for Him soon dims any other love. This is the place of surrender where we discover the love we have been seeking.

To love God with all our souls is to lay our very self before Him. Our soul is our life and what makes us individuals. Giving our souls to God is like declaring, "Here I am, with my past, present, and future – use me for Your glory."

We learn to love by loving; we comprehend by doing. This commandment is not burdensome; it's freedom. It liberates us from the bondage of smaller things and points toward the final source of joy, peace, and satisfaction.

Prayer: Heavenly Father, we respect Your infinite love for us. You call us to love You, not as a heavy command, but as an opportunity to know the abundance of life in Your company. Teach us to love You with our hearts, souls, and minds. Amen.

November 11: Heavenly Ascension

Scripture for the Day

"After he said this, he was taken up before their very eyes, and a cloud hid him from their sight."

Acts 1:9

As we look at the remarkable scene described in Acts 1:10, Christ's ascension is much greater than simply moving to Heaven; it is the final expression of His earthly ministry and divinity. It marks the beginning of a new chapter for the disciples who witnessed it and for all believers.

Jesus' ascension to heaven shifts Christ's presence to a more spiritual presence that goes beyond the physical side. Just as Jesus was lifted up, we too are called to set our minds on things above, where Christ is seated at the right hand of God.

Christ's physical absence further intensified the apostles' faith to travel to almost every part of the world and spread the gospel quickly. And this marvelous occurrence of the Spirit passing unto them propelled them to become witnesses with their whole lives transformed. Just like our spiritual forefathers, we, too, are given the privilege and responsibility of being the apostles of our generation, making disciples out of all nations, tribes, and tongues.

Prayer: Heavenly Father, Our minds filled with wonder and reverence, we humbly cast our hearts forth to salute the glorious spirit of the Messiah as He ascended into the heavens. We ask You to accept our worship, and as Your Spirit is always with us, even to the end, bless us now and forever. Amen.

Embracing Shiloh:

November 12: Living Waters of Faith

Scripture for the Day

"For even his own brothers did not believe in him."

John 7:5

Jesus, the epitome of the Godhead's love and truth, could not easily be separated from the thorn of unbelief, not even by his kin. Our faith sometimes does not have the support of the people around us. It gives us the strength needed in our faith journey, a strength that Jesus personified, but others near us can be untouched.

The lack of belief in Jesus' divine mission by His family suggests that the personal character of faith is not through flesh and blood relationships but only between a person directly with God.

Just as Jesus persevered, bound by His divine mission, even when his brothers were skeptical, our obligation is to maintain faith that refuses to die despite being doubted by others, even those closest to us. Let us seek the living water of faith that Jesus talked about, waters that will overflow from within and provide us with an everlasting reservoir of strength and resolve. And if those we love and care about don't believe, we bring them before the Father in prayer, asking Him to speak to them.

Prayer: O, Father, in the silence of this hour, I realize that I am not always hearing faith around me. In this example, I follow Your Son, Jesus; He carried on His divine mission, although most people did not believe in Him, including His own family. Please help me to hear the inner voice of faith as I meet life's challenges. Amen.

November 13: Embrace the Refiner's Fire

Scripture for the Day
"Dear friends, do not be surprised at the fiery ordeal that has come on you to test you, as though something strange were happening to you."

1 Peter 4:12

Suffering can be a source of divine testing and spiritual refinement. The Apostle Peter writes to early Christians, warning them not to be astonished by their trials. The fiery ordeal refers metaphorically to the intense persecutions that Christians experienced, but it extends to all forms of trials in life.

The message is clear: adversity is not an glitch in the believer's journey but an expected path leading to maturity. When we encounter trials, it's not a sign of divine displeasure but often a means of spiritual growth. Just as gold is purified by fire, our faith too, can be refined and strengthened through difficulties.

Recognizing trials as a part of God's transformative process helps us approach our own fiery ordeals with a spirit of perseverance rather than defeat. Accepting this, there is a call to solidarity with the global body of Christ, many of whom suffer for their faith. Our struggles, then, not only develop personal perseverance but also connect us more deeply with our brothers and sisters in faith across the world.

Prayer: Precious Lord, as I read the words of 1 Peter 4:12, I am reminded not to be startled by the challenges and trials that come my way. Heavenly Father, I humbly accept the refining process that You lovingly administer through life's fiery ordeals. Amen.

Embracing Shiloh:

November 14: The Heart's True Nature

Scripture for the Day

"Nothing outside a person can defile them by going into them. Rather, it is what comes out of a person that defiles them."

Mark 7:15

This verse from the Gospel of Mark is the deeply significant saying of Jesus that turned traditional religious thinking upside down. Here, Jesus questioned the leading cause of purity and impurity. He changes the focus to the heart—the source from which our words and deeds come.

Doctrinally, this verse reflects on the teaching of inner purity and the importance for meaning and thoughts. It warns against believing that the spiritual state can be retained simply by doing rituals or eating the right foods. But Jesus teaches us to see the real source of defilement, which is inside us, is in our hearts and minds.

By recognizing this, we are called to a transformation of another kind, something that goes deeper than the surface, reaching into the very depths of our soul. Self-punishment is not the process needed but an inward journey, demanding complete openness and readiness to face and the have the inner self changed.

Pause to ponder to think about your thoughts, words, and actions. Do they reflect the purity Christ calls for? This awareness of self leads us to ask God's grace to cleanse and renew our hearts so that what comes out of us may be beautiful and authentic – bringing honor to God and benefiting others.

Prayer: Lord, as I ponder the profound truth of Mark 7:15, I recognize that nothing outside me can stain my soul; rather, what comes out of my heart is most crucial. Forgive me Lord because the fact is that most of the time the words and the actions of mine do not reflect purity, which You want. Amen.

November 15: All Have Fallen

Scripture for the Day
"For all have sinned and fall short of the glory of God."

Romans 3:23

Romans 3:23 tells a deep and humbling truth – none of us is sinless, and all of us fall short of the glory of God. Indeed, this verse is a grim reflection of our human weaknesses and the common human nature we share. However, this common failure is more than just a confession of sin. It is a call for our need for grace.

Here is the basis for understanding the universal nature of sin and, more importantly, the universal reach of God's redemptive plan. It makes it all square, so to speak. Because all people are equally in need of God's grace, there is no place for arrogance.

This verse flows directly into the gospel as it is immediately followed by the verses that assure us of our justification by grace through faith. It offers a beautiful ray of hope: although we are imperfect, we are not unlovable or irredeemable in the eyes of God.

As Christians, we don't focus on our worthlessness. Rather, we stand in awe of the great love and grace He shows us. We may fail, but in God's mercy, His glory is even more shown in raising us up and restoring us.

Prayer: Gracious and loving Father, as I reflect on the truth of Romans 3:23, I recognize my faults and imperfections. I realize that I fall short of Your glory every day in so many ways. But I am also overcome by Your unlimited grace that spans that divide. Amen.

Embracing Shiloh:

November 16: Trust in the Light of Your Love

Scripture for the Day

"Let the morning bring me word of your unfailing love, for I have put my trust in you. Show me the way I should go, for to you I entrust my life."

Psalm 143:8

In the peace of the dawn, the world remains quiet for whispers of the divine. In a passionate appeal, the Psalmist prays that God's steadfast love may be his refuge throughout the day. In search of relief, his soul seeks the Lord to find meaning and refuge.

This one verse of Psalm 143 speaks of day-by-day reliance on God that starts anew every morning. The psalmist recognizes God's love as unchanging and goes after it in the morning. But his faith is active, a conscious, dynamic decision in which a person trusts the help of God during the day's obstacles and trials.

In these instances, the phrase "unfailing love" is not a hollow cliche. The original Hebrew equates this term with *chesed*, which is indicative of love, kindness, mercy, and loyalty. It is a love rooted in the covenant, a promise that God will always act in accordance with His character, which is consistently good and loving toward His creation.

Having this verse internalized, let's greet each day with faith in God's everlasting love. This confidence holds us tightly so that even in doubts or uncertainty, we don't live the day in solitary but with the continuous love and guidance of the Creator.

Prayer: My Lord, in the hush of this fresh morning, I stop to remind myself of Your unceasing love. I am grateful to You for the night that is gone and for the new mercies with which morning dawns again. Stepping into this unfolding day, Lord, may I do so with a strong faith in Your sovereign grace.

November 17: Proclaim His Greatness

Scripture for the Day

"Declare his glory among the nations, His marvelous deeds among all peoples."

1 Chronicles 16:24

In this exuberant verse, we hear King David's song of thanks as the Ark of the Covenant is brought to Jerusalem. He urges the assembly of Israel to celebrate the glory of the Lord with the world, to talk about the miracles that have marked the history of a chosen people, and the love of their God. Praising God's glory is confessing His supremacy, glorifying His grace, and witnessing to His wonderful works.

This verse makes an important point about us being believers. The God of Israel is not the God of a single nation or people but the whole world. Our Christian testimony is based on the stories of God's amazing ways in the history of humankind and our own lives. All these are threads in the beautiful tapestry that showcase God's marvelous deeds.

David's appeal is universal, surpassing all the barriers of race, nationality, or social status. In this sense, it is a timeless call to worship, continuing to reach us now with the same intensity. Contained in this message is the duty of a living testimony to the God we worship—a life that demonstrates His glory through our words, deeds, and actions.

Together, we declare the glory of God, joining centuries of people who have taken the Lord as their refuge, redeemer, and reason for joy. This is an active, an ongoing mission. With technology, international travel, and multicultural communities, we have been given unprecedented chances to declare His greatness in every direction, loudly and lovingly.

Prayer: Heavenly Father, Your glory is unending, going beyond time and space, and Your wonders surpass anything we could ever imagine. Today, I wonder at what You have done, and with a thankful heart, I proclaim Your greatness over all the earth. Make me a bold preacher of Your glory. Amen.

November 18: A Sacred Assembly

Scripture for the Day

"On the first day of the seventh month hold a sacred assembly and do no regular work. It is a day for you to sound the trumpets."

Numbers 29:1

This tells about the Lord's instruction to keep what later became the Feast of the Blowing of Trumpets. It was a period of rest with the sound of trumpets that called them to remember their God. The celebration became Rosh Hashanah, celebrated by Jewish people as the New Year, a time for self-reflection before the advent of the new season.

Spiritually, the sounding of Israel's trumpets mattered a lot. It was a power source, bringing people together, warning of a change in situation, danger, or announcing proclamations and declarations. This tone reflects a call to arms or a call for people to be alert for events and worship. It reinforced that God was the hub of their culture.

In this era of technology where one is subjected to many forms of media, a sense of balance must be found to create an environment for health, peace, and prosperity. The basic principle here is to designate consistent times of adoration, intentionally pausing regular employment and activities. In the spiritual sense, this sort of stop is both a form of worship and a pacemaker of sorts to regulate our heartbeats and maintain inner peace.

This Scripture invites us to find our "trumpet sounds" - those practices and moments that draw our attention back to God amid our busyness. It prompts us to create regular intervals for rest and reflection, to recalibrate our lives to the resonating frequency of God's presence and guidance, allowing us to march to the rhythms of His grace and perfect timing.

Prayer: God, In obedience to Your word, I seek to carve out sacred space and time to pause, remember, and worship You. Like the trumpets that sounded in the days of old, let Your voice resonate within me, calling me into Your presence. Amen.

November 19: United in Divine Purpose

Scripture for the day
"Therefore what God has joined together, let no one separate."

Mark 10:9

On a journey of faith, there will always be a time when we see the reminder that we are not alone. The symphony is not created by just one person/instrument but by many with different instruments playing together. The beauty of Mark 10:9, is that it significantly goes beyond the boundaries of family relations, although it primarily addresses the marriage covenant that seeks God's blessing.

The passage more broadly refers to the idea of covenant. It is through voluntary choice that humankind is granted life. In biblical tradition, a covenant is more than a contract. It is a promise made before God, whose covenants reflect His undivided commitment to humankind. While a routine covenant is in force between people who either get married, form a treaty or business relationship, when God is involved, there is a far greater dimension. A marriage vow that asks for God's blessing for example, takes on greater meaning because His ideal is shown and His everlasting love and mercy are manifested.

While many experiences today glorify individualism and a state of independence, Jesus urges us to be mutually dependent and collaborative. We are obligated to protect what God has joined together, faithfully following His divine plan. It is a responsibility to keep a covenant to improve life with dignity and, most importantly, live confidently and honestly.

Today, as we reflect on this verse, may we ponder how we strengthen those ties and savor the links God has set in our lives. Are we exploring our relationships with mercy, cooperation, and faithfulness? Are we aware of the creative unity the Lord endowed the whole world to foster and complement us all?

Prayer: God, I kneel before You with a heart overflowing with thanks for the great gift you have given me – the refuge to find the unity of my being. With humility and absolute awe, I acknowledge that what You have brought together is a spiritual connection of two people and a reflection of Your love and reason for being. Amen.

November 20: Embracing Daily Surrender

Scripture for the Day
"Then he said to them all: 'Whoever wants to be my disciple must deny themselves and take up their cross daily and follow me.'"

Luke 9:23

By making such a pressing call, Jesus deals with a couple of principles which challenging and transformative. Through this, we understand that we are the ones that need to change and not the world around us. Being a disciple means constantly denying yourself and perpetually surrendering to Christ. The cross, a symbol of agony and suffering, becomes a paradoxical symbol of freedom and assurance when take it up as Jesus took it upon Himself.

The instruction to follow Christ is an enormous challenge. Jesus tells us to discard ego and the deceitful thoughts of being powerful. To carry our cross, then, is to believe in God's plan not in our power but on His wisdom and might. This means that what we perceive as our desires, dreams, and goals cease to be as we see His will for us the only focus.

To deny oneself is also to open oneself to the identity found in Christ. We see it in losing our life, for Christ's sake. The paradox is clear: we are born into eternal life by surrendering that which we have exalted, giving what we received, and dying to self.

Prayer: Father, I come to You today standing by Your side and jumping to action because of Your inspiration to take up my cross. From my heart, I yearn to be Your follower, not just a disciple in formality but in deed. I turn my back on me to go Your way, the example of unselfish love. Amen.

November 21: Rooted in Christ

Scripture for the Day

"So then, just as you received Christ Jesus as Lord, continue to live your lives in him"

Colossians 2:6

In Colossians 2:6, we get a phrase from the Scriptures that summarizes our experience of God in our faith journey: "When we have accepted Jesus as our Lord, it is only the beginning of our journey." It's a continuous process of abiding in Him, of yielding your life to Him so that His presence can fill every part of your life. Just as a tree gets its nourishment and its stature from its roots, we are called to remain rooted in Christ and be built up in Him.

The message of this phrase refers to the power change one discovers when one's life is devoted to Jesus. When we take His invitation of forgiveness, we become a vessel of a wholly new and changed person. God becomes the ground where our attractive personality, high values, and meaning towards life have been rooted.

Let us consider the depth of our Christian roots. Are we fully immersed in His love and favor and standing firm in His grace or have we allowed the world's excuses to be our excuse for shifting ground? Let us renew our promises with Christ, shunning the influence of the world and growing in His character.

Prayer: Dear Lord, I thank You for the gift of Your Son, Jesus Christ, my Lord and Savior. Help me, O God, to truly live my life in Him, rooted in His love and grace. May His teachings guide my decisions, His example shape my character, and His presence fill me with peace and joy. Grant me the strength to remain steadfast in my faith, building my life upon the firm foundation of Christ. May Your will be done in all things, and Your name be glorified. Amen.

Embracing Shiloh:

November 22: Fixing our Eyes on Jesus

Scripture for the Day

"Fixing our eyes on Jesus, the pioneer and perfecter of faith. For the joy set before him he endured the cross, scorning its shame, and sat down at the right hand of the throne of God."

Hebrews 12:2

This verse is at the heart of our faith's storyline – we are to run with a steady gaze, looking to the One who provides us a path to go. He does not only lead the process of our faith but becomes its way bearer and the finalizer as well; He authors and executes our salvation. Jesus Christ is the source of our strength, genuine compassion, and hope.

The significance of Christ in our lives is fundamental. He is the pioneer who walks before us and carries the torch to show us the way He obeyed the will of God with unceasing faith and trust in Him. Our undisputed Leader remains to accomplish the task until we become molded into His image through His shaping, using our struggles and pain. He always shares this burden with us when we experience the ups and downs in our journeys. By not looking at what happens but focusing instead on God, we refine our thoughts to continue with His wishes and cultivate hope to overcome any obstacle.

Through the cross and the shame of it, Jesus revealed the height of His love for us. His decision to endure the one-way ticket to redemption and setting us a sacred example of serving others and self-denial is timeless. As we, too, encounter trials and difficulties, let us reflect on what He did for us; only then will we be able to gather the strength to overcome sin and death, which He drowned in the darkness of His sacrifice.

Prayer: Dear Lord, as I cast myself before You today, I am humbled by the fact that I am fixing my gaze upon Jesus, who is both the forerunner and the finisher of my faith. Through all the rough times and uncertain events of my life, please, dear Lord, lead me towards Him, the One who will give me strength and hope to move forward. Amen.

November 23: Seasoned with Salt

Scripture for the Day

"Salt is good, but if it loses its saltiness, how can you make it salty again? Have salt among yourselves, and be at peace with each other."

Mark 9:50

In the bustling kitchen of life, our actions and words are ingredients that add flavor to the world around us. Mark 9:50 is a potent reminder that we, as children of God, are called to be the salt of the earth. But what does it mean to have salt among ourselves? Salt preserves, heals, and seasons; similarly, our presence as believers should act to preserve truth, offer healing through our compassion, and season our surroundings with the love and wisdom of God.

When Jesus applies the metaphor of salt, He teaches that it is not just the taste of salt that matters but most importantly, the way we maintain godliness in a world where this nourishing commodity can sometimes appear to be lacking or even completely contaminated with sin and sadness. To this effect, the Christian charge is not simply contributing to the decay, but countering it by continuously being His example.

Salt must remain salty to be effective and retain its distinctive quality. How do we maintain our saltiness? It's in our daily communion with Jesus, our willingness to foster the fruits of the Spirit within us, and our unrestrained commitment to live out the gospel in thought, word, and deed.

The latter part of the verse, "and be at peace with each other," is a testament to the harmony that should exist among believers. Peace is the climate in which the saltiness of our faith thrives; it's through peaceful cooperation that we enhance the collective effort to season our world with the hope and grace of our faith in Christ.

Prayer: Heavenly Father, You are the source of all purity and the provider of peace. Instill in me the essence of Your divine Spirit so that I may be an agent of Your preservation and grace in this world. In Jesus' name, Amen.

November 24: Fear Not, Little Flock

Scripture for the Day

"Do not be afraid, little flock, for your Father has been pleased to give you the kingdom."

Luke 12:32

Amid the tumult and uncertainties life presents, Luke 12:32 comes quietly as a whisper from God. Jesus says we are a little flock, an endearing term that signifies care, closeness, and shelter. It is the image of the shepherd-king who leads, nurtures, and protects.

The order of Jesus to "fear not" is not just a call to tranquility but an invitation to faith in the provision of the Father. It is paired with an extraordinary reason: the Father's delight, His divine joy, to give us the Kingdom. The Kingdom of God is not bought by our labor; it is given by His grace and good will.

This verse is a foundation of our relationship and possession by Christ. However, the Kingdom is not restricted in by geographical realms but rather is a representation of God's rule and reign in the hearts and lives of believers. It is a present reality where justice, peace, and the Holy Spirit's power are manifested. It also contains a pledge of the future, which will be revealed in the coming of Christ.

He tells us that in this gentle reign, we do not have to fall into the slavery of fear. Fear usually attacks our peace and hides the true form of God. However, the nature of our heavenly Father is that of a bountiful bestower who enjoys favoring His children with great abundance.

Prayer: Dear Father in heaven, I cling to You gently saying, "Do not be afraid, little flock." Your sound chases away the dark clouds of my fear. Thank You for accepting me into the fold of Your beloved and for the consolation that You are my Shepherd and my King. In Jesus name, I pray. Amen.

November 25: Stand Firm in Freedom

Scripture for the Day
"It is for freedom that Christ has set us free. Stand firm, then, and do not let yourselves be burdened again by a yoke of slavery."

Galatians 5:1

In Galatians 5:1, the Apostle Paul shows that through Christ's sacrificial work on the cross, we have been liberated not only from the bondage of sin but also from the oppressive yoke of legalism and self-effort. The freedom Paul speaks of encompasses our deliverance from trying to earn God's approval through a list of rules and regulations.

This spiritual liberation illustrates the transformative nature of the gospel. It is an release to live a life guided by the Holy Spirit, that blossoms in love, joy, peace, and other fruits that come with living under the canopy of grace. Our freedom in Christ is not merely freedom *from* something—it's also freedom *for* something. For righteous living, for serving others in love, for bearing one another's burdens, and so fulfilling the law of Christ.

Yet, Paul's call to "stand firm" recognizes that the pull of old bonds is potent. It acknowledges that the Galatian believers—and we, too—are prone to reverting to familiar chains, whether legalistic practices, habitual sins, or group pressures. Therefore, the apostle calls us to vigilance and perseverance, so that the freedom bought at so great a price is not squandered.

Standing firm is active and dynamic. It involves daily decisions to live in the Spirit's power and to refuse to submit again to the yoke of slavery—whatever form it might take.

Prayer: Lord God, Author of my liberty, I thank You for the freedom that Christ's sacrifice gained for me. Because of Jesus, I am no longer entangled in the chains of sin and death. I ask for the strength to stand firm in this freedom, to live a life that honors the gift You have given. Amen.

Embracing Shiloh:

November 26: Peace with God Through Faith

Scripture for the Day

"Therefore, since we have been justified through faith, we have peace with God through our Lord Jesus Christ."

Romans 5:1

In the dense forest of human striving, the clear stream of divine truth runs deep and fresh: we are justified by faith, so we are at peace with God. Romans 5:1 is a testimony of this most sublime spiritual truth. Theological reflections coming from this one verse can be soothing to any troubled heart as it captures the essence of the Good News.

Justification is a legal word, meaning our acquittal on all charges. It is the judgment that although all are sinners and imperfect, we are justified before God. Our steadfast Advocate is Jesus Christ who accomplishes this on His own merit, not because of our efforts or moral achievements. This justification is immediate, the moment we believe, ratified by the divine Judge.

The peace referred to here is not a surface tranquility and is not only the absence of conflict. It is the tranquility as of an unmovable rock that only comes from a right relationship with God. It is inexplicable to man. This peace is our shelter, our anchor amid life's chaos, simply because it is rooted in Christ Himself.

This verse is a lovely call in a world sorely fragmented and driven by strife, reminding us that our primary conflict, our estrangement from God, has been resolved. Our faith in Jesus has closed the gap, quieting the noise of judgment and allowing us to enter into God's presence with the assurance of beloved children.

Prayer: Lord of Peace, what depth of grace do You have, that You justify the sinner and bring him to peace with You. This gift was obtained at the highest cost—Your Son's sacrifice. I am eternally thankful for this. I am grateful, Father, for the faith You have given me, a conduit through which Your righteousness comes. Aid me to cling to this grace, to value the peace I have with You, and to walk in the truth of my justified status. Amen.

November 27: The Blessings of the Beatitudes

Scripture for the Day

"Now when Jesus saw the crowds, he went up on a mountainside and sat down. His disciples came to him."

Matthew 5:1

In Matthew 5:1, we witness a moment of divine invitation, as the disciples drew near, eager to receive the teachings that would illuminate paths and transform lives. Imagine sitting at the feet of Jesus, observing as He calmly takes His seat, the natural amphitheater framing His figure against the open skies. The mountain becomes a metaphor for our own spiritual ascents, places where we withdraw from the clamor of the world to seek the presence of the divine. To gain wisdom, we are to climb higher, closer to the heart of God, where the air is pure and the perspective clear.

It is here in the quiet of our hearts away from distractions we can hear Shiloh's voice most profoundly. Every word that falls from His lips is a beatitude, a blessed statement, a revelation meant to lead us closer to the Kingdom of heaven. Jesus invites us, just as He invited the disciples, to a higher plane of existence where the spirit, not the flesh, is nourished.

So today, let us find our own mountainside moments, those sacred spaces of solitude where we can contemplate His words. There, we engage with the beauty of Christ's teachings, allowing them to mold our hearts, guide our actions, and fortify our commitment to walk in His ways.

Prayer: Heavenly Father, I seek Your presence on the mountainside of my spirit today. Lead me above the lowlands of distraction and earthly concern. As I draw near to You in this moment of reflection, let Your words of life resonate within me. May Your Holy Spirit guide my steps so that I might walk in the blessedness of Your teachings and radiate Your love to others.

Embracing Shiloh:

November 28: Standing Watch in Expectation

Scripture for the Day

"I will stand at my watch and station myself on the ramparts; I will look to see what he will say to me, and what answer I am to give to this complaint."

Habakkuk 2:1

The act of standing watch reflects an attitude of active waiting—a deliberate positioning of oneself in anticipation of God's voice. Habakkuk's example teaches us that in the throes of uncertainty and in the silence that follows our fervent prayers, we are to prepare our hearts to receive divine direction. It reminds us that spiritual vigilance is not a mere duty but to be in expectancy of God's assured response.

Let us learn from Habakkuk's resolve by standing firm in our faith, fixed upon the ramparts of hope in our Savior. The practice of waiting on the Lord is not inaction. Instead, it's a statement of faith in the One who is above time and circumstance—assuring us that our waiting has its rewards in His perfect timing.

We wait, in expectation knowing we are not forgotten by our Maker, that every moment of silence is pregnant with divine purpose, and that every instance of watching is an episode drawing us closer to the heart of God. Stand your watch with conviction and prepare to embrace the wisdom that comes from above.

Prayer: Heavenly Father, I am on the ramparts of Your promises today. In the waiting, cultivate in me an expectant heart. Grant me the patience of Habakkuk to stand my watch with confidence in Your supreme rule. Breathe Your words into my spirit so that I may discern Your will. Help me to remember that Your silence is not absence—teach me to trust in Your perfect timing. In Jesus name. Amen.

November 29: Anointing in Faith

Scripture for the Day
"Is anyone among you sick? Let them call the elders of the church to pray over them and anoint them with oil in the name of the Lord."

James 5:14

Speaking of trials, the book of James tells that there is strength in united prayer and anointing. However, what is the meaning of anointing? In Bible times, anointing with oil was an emblem of separation, sanctified for a divine purpose. It was a concrete representation of God's blessing and presence.

However, the anointing James mentions is more than ritual. It is an outside manifestation of internal faith and trust in God's healing hand. Do we seek the prayerful support of our faith community in our times of illness, whether it is of body, mind, or spirit? Do we permit ourselves the vulnerability to be anointed, not with oil only but with grace of God?

The anointing brings us into the holy place where heaven meets the earth, where we confess our weaknesses and how greatly we need God to help us. In this expression of faith, we realize the completeness of God's love for us, which goes beyond our physical conditions and revives our tired souls. It is an impressive representation that we are not left alone in our misery. The submission is an expression of humility in allowing others to serve us as we in our turn, will serve them.

As we meditate on this passage today, let's practice our spiritual discipline of asking our community for help and allowing the healing power of collective faith and prayer come upon us, believing in God's undying love and mercy.

Prayer: Father, I come to You this day begging for Your comfort and healing. I appreciate the prayers of my fellow brothers and sisters in Christ, as Your servant James has commanded. O Lord, as I am anointed, it shall signify the anointing of Your Holy Spirit. Let this remain a sign of Your covenant of health and comfort. Amen.

November 30: Blessed with Every Spiritual Blessing

Scripture for the Day
"Praise be to the God and Father of our Lord Jesus Christ, who has blessed us in the heavenly realms with every spiritual blessing in Christ."

Ephesians 1:3

Ephesians 1:3 opens with an outburst of praise, a doxology that sets the tone for the spiritual truths unpacked in the epistle. It serves as an exuberant declaration of the spiritual wealth possessed by believers in Christ. Paul recognizes that in the heavenly realms, not bound by time or space, we are granted an inheritance that is both vast and eternal.

This verse is drenched in theological significance. It explains the scope of divine blessing – it is all-encompassing, and nothing is withheld. The "heavenly realms" indicate a spiritual dimension that goes beyond our mortal existence. This moves our perspective from the transient to the eternal, from earthly trials to heavenly triumphs.

The blessings mentioned are spiritual, setting them apart from material or earthly favors. They include redemption, forgiveness, wisdom, and the seal of the Holy Spirit, to name a few. These are gifts that fulfill the deepest needs of the soul; they are not vulnerable to economic shifts, social status, or personal capabilities.

These gifts have their source and substance in Christ, signaling that it is only through the intimate connection with Jesus that one truly experiences this bounty. It's in relationship to Him that we find the origin and fulfillment of every good thing we've been given.

Prayer: Blessed Father, I come before You with a heart full of gratitude for every spiritual blessing. You have spared no expense, withholding nothing from me through Your generous grace found in Christ Jesus. I marvel at the riches of Your kindness, which You lavish upon me each day. Help me to understand and embrace these spiritual blessings more fully, to live in the reality of Your provision that equips me for all things. Amen.

December 1: The Armor of God – Our Daily Strength

Scripture for the Day

"Finally, be strong in the Lord and in his mighty power."

Ephesians 6:10

We live in a world that often challenges our peace and serenity, pushing us into battles we feel unprepared for. However, we are not left defenseless. In the words of the Apostle Paul, we find a powerful appeal that uplifts and fortifies our spirit.

This Scripture is a reminder that our strength does not come from within ourselves but from the Lord. In our own strength we falter, but when we put on the full armor of God, we stand firm against the trials and tribulations of life. This armor is not forged of steel or leather but composed of spiritual virtues: truth, righteousness, peace, faith, salvation, and the Word of God, which is the sword of the Spirit (Ephesians 6:14-17).

Being ever vigilant in prayer, constant in faith and steadfast in the truth of the gospel, we are called. We win our spiritual fights not by human strength but by divine might. In this light, strength in the Lord refers to our weakness and His supremacy. It is a submission to His cover of protection that encircles and strengthens us.

We should be encouraged that the mighty power of God is not abstract—it was demonstrated in Christ's resurrection and is available to us daily through the Holy Spirit. This passage in Ephesians reinforces the truth that we are engaged in spiritual warfare and our adversary, the devil, is real. But so is our victory in Christ.

As we wear this spiritual armor, let us walk confidently in the knowledge that we are not alone; God's presence is our constant source of strength.

Prayer: Heavenly Father, I come before You in humble acknowledgment of my need for Your strength. I put on Your full armor today – the belt of truth, the breastplate of righteousness, the shoes of peace, the shield of faith, the helmet of salvation, and I carry the sword of the Spirit, which is Your Word. In Jesus' name, Amen.

Embracing Shiloh:

December 2: An Invitation to Communion

Scripture for the Day
"Here I am! I stand at the door and knock. If anyone hears my voice and opens the door, I will come in and eat with that person, and they with me."

Revelation 3:20

Even on this beautiful day, our Savior's quiet, incessant knocking can be easily missed. Revelation 3:20 is a beautiful statement of Christ's personal and intimate longing for fellowship with us. This is a standard interpretation of this verse as the call of the Lord to the people to let the heart open to His presence in the heart.

The image of Jesus standing at the door of our hearts symbolizes the importance of our free will; He does not force Himself in but waits for the invitation. The spiritual awakening is initiated by a determination of will, not only to hear the voice of Christ but to do open the door. The promise is an intimate communion of life that is represented in the sharing of a meal, which in ancient Near Eastern culture, was an honored sign of friendship and unity.

Theologians call this "divine hospitality" in which God Himself is both the guest and the host. He knocks to be with us and then He feeds us. However, this divine hospitality is more than just about our being nourished; it is at the same time a call for us to open our hearts to others, to pass on the grace we receive to those among us.

You are only a welcome away from your spiritual sustenance. Christ comes not for judgment or punishment, but for the fellowship of His love. By opening the door, a closer relationship with Him begins, characterized by daily meetings and conversations in prayer and Scripture.

Prayer: Loving Savior, who stands waiting by the door of my heart, I hear Your knock today. With a grateful heart, I swing the door open to bid You welcome. I am blessed with Your modest request to come into my life and be with me. Aid me to listen for Your voice amid this tumult of the world. Teach me to be hospitable towards Your Spirit and all others, giving the same grace and love that You abundantly give. Amen.

December 3: Authentic Discipleship

Scripture for the day

"Not everyone who says to me, 'Lord, Lord,' will enter the kingdom of heaven, but only the one who does the will of my Father who is in heaven."

Matthew 7:21

Matthew 7:21 is not a light warning. It also serves as an opportunity to check if we are living as true disciples. Do we only pay lip service to Jesus but at the same time ignore His preaching with our hearts and actions?

This passage's clear division is between verbal profession and obedient deeds. Professing Jesus as Lord involves more than words. Rather, it is a lifelong commitment shown through our actions. Christ is making it clear that the Kingdom of heaven is for more than just the talkers of words, but doers of the Father's will.

This tells us of the importance of obedience in the Christian life. It reminds us that genuine faith always accompanies a quick-acting and obedient heart. The Father's will embodies the commandments of love, justice, mercy, and humility guiding our daily decisions and actions.

Indeed, as followers of Christ, doing of the Father's will is essential to our true worship and love for our Savior. The gospel is a call to action – serving the least, loving unconditionally, forgiving abundantly, and walking righteously.

This is not about working to earn salvation. It is about showing the faith we claim to possess. Saving faith is the faith that works.

Prayer: You have led me, O Lord. Forgive me for the moments I have professed You with my lips and did not confess You in my acts and omissions. May You fill me with an obedient spirit so that everything I do becomes in harmony with Your divine will. Amen.

Embracing Shiloh:

December 4: The Unwavering Source of Good

Scripture for the Day
"Every good and perfect gift is from above, coming down from the Father of the heavenly lights, who does not change like shifting shadows."

James 1:17

Each day, the sun comes up in the morning, and its radiant beams inspire us with the stability of God's creation. However, it becomes quite difficult to focus on the unchangeable character of our Creator in the chaos of life. Today, let us draw near to the richness found in James 1:17

The metaphor of light is used by the brother of Jesus, James, to characterize the nature of God— a nature free of variation or shadow. Shadows, in olden times, represented untrustworthiness and change, while light was associated with truth and purity. This comparison recognizes that God is dependable, unlike our changeable situation. He is the fountain of all good, and His goodness does not change.

In this hectic world, it is indeed comforting to know that God pours down His good gifts, which are perfect in their design for our lives. His mercy, grace, and love are provided daily, though we often fail to see these treasures among the commotion of our lives.

Drawing attention to the perfection of the gifts of God prompts us to regard our life from Heaven's point of view. It asks us to refocus our thoughts from being shortsighted view of the mundane to see the eternal nature of spiritual gifts. It also requires us to think about using these heavenly blessings to bless others near us, a proof of our gratitude.

Prayer: Lord, You who are the provider of all good things. I thank You for Your faithfulness in a world of change. Thank You for Your unalterable personality, a guide of hope and truth. Guide me to see the presents You have given me—those that develop, support, and stimulate me. May I remember Your benevolence and become the conduit of Your goodness to the people around me. Amen.

December 5: Childlike Trust

Scripture for the Day

"Truly I tell you, anyone who will not receive the kingdom of God like a little child will never enter it."

Mark 10:15

The words of Jesus echo deeply and simply as He shares the mystery of the Kingdom of God. This Kingdom demands an attitude of openness and receptivity that differs from worldly instincts and into the world of children.

Children have a natural trust and can accept love without doubt. Their world is not complicated by the skepticism we have learned over years of frustrations and heartbreaks. Children throw themselves into the arms of their provider, confident of safety and love, whereas adults size life up, taking what they want with conditional acceptance.

As it relates to God, this brings us closer to the change in one's perspective. It does not call us to immaturity but to holy simplicity. It is a place where our complex doctrines, elaborate strategies, and magnificent structures of knowledge kneel to God's straightforward call to only trust Him.

To a child, a promise is a promise, hope is hope, and love is love. Such is the nature of attitude with which we are called to receive God—with a heart that does not doubt the goodness of its King, as one that relies upon Him without fear.

Today, let us ask for the wisdom of holy simplicity. We should take the Kingdom with the certainty of a child that runs into His loving arms.

Prayer: Lord God, with a child's heart, I come before You today. Bestow on me the humility to cast away my grown-up reservations and to accept Your kingdom with cheerfulness and enthusiasm. Assist me in confiding in Your goodness and love, simple and without doubt. Amen.

December 6: Offerings of Praise

Scripture for the Day
"Ascribe to the LORD, all you families of nations, ascribe to the LORD glory and strength."

Psalm 96:7

The psalmist's call echoes through nations and down the centuries, proclaiming worship as a deliberate exercise of attributing worth to our Creator. Worship is not idle but active, not a single act but a continuing exercise. This verse is beyond cultural, verbal, and geographical limits, joining us in a hymn of divine glory.

To give unto the Lord glory and strength is to recognize His sovereign power and majesty with fear and awe. It is to accept that every speck of beauty, every second of wonder, every bit of power in our surroundings is just evidence of His brilliance. We are from the "families of nations," a mosaic of humanity, woven together like a great quilt that bears His image and is designed to glorify His name.

Worship calls us to realize who God is and who we are in relation to Him. Our collective prayers help us see God's plan for unity in diversity, strength in unity, and universal recognition of His rule over all creation.

Today, as we stand before the Lord, let us consider the means through which we are to give glory to the Lord in everything. Let our lives mirror the song of adoration, and may our hearts vibrate with the eternal melody of worship, which all creation sings to the Lord.

Prayer: Dear Lord, I am in Your presence today as part of Your extensive family of nations. I would like to render unto You glory and strength that is Your due. My voice in humility, gratitude, and admiration join the chorus of Your praises in Heaven. Let me learn to praise You not only with my lips but also with my whole life, showing Your glory in all that I do. May my soul reverberate with the truth of Your strength and of Your holiness. Amen.

December 7: Eyes To See

Scripture for the Day

Jesus said to him, "Have I been with you so long, and you still do not know me, Philip? Whoever has seen me has seen the Father. How can you say, 'Show us the Father'?"

John 14:9 (ESV)

In Jesus, we are reminded that we have an immediate and close relationship with God's presence. At times, we miss His real presence, wanting to look at Him not just with the eyes of faith but with physical eyes or to hear His authentic voice. But in the human person of Jesus Christ, God became visible, accessible, and knowable. Jesus is the perfect and complete revelation of the heart and character of the Father. In Him, we see love, compassion, grace, and truth personified.

When He was among us, Jesus manifested heaven's reality on Earth. He offered to the sick healing, the broken forgiveness, and the despairing hope. By looking at His life, how He taught, and the miracles He performed, we see pieces of God's character and His yearning to interact with His creation in profound ways.

He who knows Jesus knows the Father. By means of Scriptural teaching and the Holy Spirit enlightening, we can have the same life-changing meeting with God as the disciples when they walked beside Jesus. As we receive Christ and give our lives to Him, we welcome the presence of God to live in us.

In times of uncertainty or confusion, may we recall that our Savior is willing to show us the heart of the Father. As we strive to become closer to God, let us concentrate our gaze on Jesus, who brings the path of divine truth before us and ushers us into the depth of our heavenly Father's love.

Prayer: Father, may You be praised for giving me Jesus so I can see You. As I meditate on the words of John 14:9 I am amazed at the profound truth that to know Jesus is to know You, our heavenly Father. Assist me, Lord, in growing my connection with You through Christ so that I will comprehend the fullness of Your glory. Amen.

Embracing Shiloh:

December 8: The Eternal Presence

Scripture for the Day

"God said to Moses, 'I AM who I AM. This is what you are to say to the Israelites: 'I AM has sent me to you.'"

Exodus 3:14

In the burning bush, Moses experienced the sacred experience that would revolutionize his life and free a nation. This moment in Exodus 3:14 did not merely become a historical marker; it splits the time, showing the unchanging nature of God and His association with people. "I AM who I AM," God says, His existence without any source while at the same time His independence and eternal constancy are openly confirmed. While humanity or the false gods of ancient religions change from time to time, the God of the Israelites is the same rock, the foundation of everything.

This passage establishes the identity of God in Himself, not in action, form, or function, but simply in His pure existence. This God is the One who is understood by His nature and nothing else. He is the Alpha and Omega, or as we would say A to Z. He is the One who always will be. Such an assurance is encouraging for His followers in situations where sudden change in social life, there's inner trouble, or personal struggle can seem very challenging. As change swallows us, God's constant and unchanging faithfulness is our grounds us.

Now is the time to contemplate this timeless truth: "I AM" does not cease to be and continues to interact with us – proving and showing us the way. We can be comforted that the God who led Moses and Israelites through the wilderness is the same God who guides us through our journeys of heartbreaking wilderness to where He wants us to be.

Prayer: Father, the One who is too extensive to be described by any word in our vocabulary, I have a calm in Your constant never changing character. In a world soaked in sentiments that fade fast and vanish with the lights, Your flame stands eternal as a persistent source of hope. Amen.

December 9: Embracing Divine Callings

Scripture for the Day

"In the sixth month of Elizabeth's pregnancy, God sent the angel Gabriel to Nazareth, a town in Galilee."

Luke 1:26

The Annunciation of Mary is a profound moment of the common touching the divine in God's epic story. In Luke 1:26, of God's complex design is revealed in the simplicity of everyday life. In the nothing-special town of Nazareth, Mary, a young woman, becomes the one that God uses to carry out His redemptive work.

God usually selects the most unlikely individuals in the most modest of conditions to accomplish purposes that are beyond human understanding. Mary was an individual—low in status but strong in faith.

The calling of Mary can impact the heart of every believer. God is always intentional; He knows what we can do and may achieve. Also, the initiation of the incarnation of Christ that took place in this very moment represents the fusion of the divine with humanity, God's personal participation in His creation.

In our lives we may not meet angels, or get news that can change the world, but still God is calling us. We are called every day to write a divine script of forgiveness, humility, and love. It is not necessarily the announcement of heavenly fanfare, but the call is important. We have the chance to carry Christ in our words, attitudes, and love towards other people.

Let us pause today to reflect upon how God is calling us. It might be in the hum of routine activities, in the company of those we love, or to a different goal. May we, like Mary, be willing to embrace the plan of God, whether it be extravagant or humble.

Prayer: O Lord, who sent Your angel Gabriel to tell an ordinary girl an extraordinary story, tune my heart to Your wonderful whispers. Prepare me to be responsive to Your voice in my life like Mary, ready to welcome Your purposes with courage and faith. Even if Your touch disturbs my dreams or brings me through unknown ways, I am confident that Your patterns sew within the threads of grace and kindness. In Jesus' name. Amen.

Embracing Shiloh:

December 10: Appointment with Eternity

Scripture for the Day
"Just as people are destined to die once, and after that to face judgment."

Hebrews 9:27

Life is an accumulation of moments, each one fleeting, leading to that inevitable appointment none can escape: death. Hebrews 9:27 reveals the ultimate fact of life: our journey on earth is limited and that the day of reckoning awaits. This can be a scary idea. However, in this truth there is an opportunity for profound spiritual reflection and change.

This text challenges us to act with the end in view. In the face of our mortality, we achieve purpose and order. Theological tradition teaches us that judgment is an instant of godly illumination when all our life is seen in the light of God's standards. This is a sobering truth that lifestyle is important, and the picture of our choices and our actions lasts forever.

Nonetheless, this verse is not about death *per se*; it is primarily about the life we lived before that. It demands us to live in a manner that shows our awareness of how temporary our existence is and the expectation of the eternal. In Jesus, the cross brings life, death, and judgment into a new light and offers grace that turns the final reckoning into anticipation for those who believe.

We are to be stewards of our days, aware that each one is a gift which should not be wasted. We are encouraged to pursue what is right, to love mercy, and to walk in humility with our God as we anticipate the day we will stand before our Maker.

Prayer: Eternal Judge and merciful Father, as I search the horizon of mortality and the nearness of judgment, endow me with a spirit of wisdom and humility. Let the reality of Hebrews 9:27 not bring fear but a life full of love, service, and the search for Your truth. May my days not be colored by the fear of death but brightened by the prospect of Your grace and the assurances of the deliverance of Christ Jesus. Amen.

December 11: The Tapestry of Thought

Scripture for the Day
"Finally, brothers and sisters, whatever is true, whatever is noble, whatever is right, whatever is pure, whatever is lovely, whatever is admirable—if anything is excellent or praiseworthy—think about such things."

Philippians 4:8

In the quiet hours of this day, as the light chases away the remnants of darkness, I am reminded of the power vested in our thoughts. The path to serenity and spiritual upliftment often begins within the silent chambers of our mind.

Philippians 4:8 serves as a divine tapestry given to us by the Apostle Paul to weave our daily thoughts. Each thread in this tapestry represents a choice, a directive to fill our minds with that which elevates and enriches. We are surrounded by noises, influences that vie for our attention, yet we are called to meditate on the elements of God's character—truth, nobility, righteousness, purity, love, and admiration.

What is true is God's unchanging nature and His reliable Word. What is noble, reminds us of the majestic grace that He extends towards us. To ponder what is right is to align our hearts with the just nature of God, and finding what is pure keeps our spirits untainted by the world. In seeking what is lovely, we appreciate God's artistic hand in creation and humanity, while to focus on the admirable is to celebrate the virtues that reflect His image.

As we contemplate these attributes, we find ourselves aligning with the divine. Our daily practices become a moving prayer; a living hymn sung in the quietness of our thoughts. God's presence is mirrored in the quality of our reflections.

Prayer: Heavenly Father, today I choose to weave my thoughts with the fibers of Your virtues. Guide me to fix my mind on what is true, noble, right, pure, lovely, and admirable. May my contemplation of these things draw me closer to You and transform the tapestry of my daily life. Let my thoughts bear the colors of Your love and grace so that others might see and be drawn to Your light. In Your holy name, Amen.

Embracing Shiloh:

December 12: The Heart of Worship

Scripture for the Day

"You are worthy, our Lord and God, to receive glory and honor and power, for you created all things, and by your will they were created and have their being."

Revelation 4:11

At the core of our existence, beneath the ebb and flow of our daily struggles and triumphs, lies a truth captured in the heavenly proclamation of Revelation 4:11. It infuses every breath with purpose and places our fleeting moments into an eternal frame: Only God is worthy.

When the sun dawns, bringing golden colors to the surrounding air, I am aware that every day is a portrait by the Creator's hand, an opportunity to be part of the cosmic symphony of adoration that echoes through the sky. Declaring God's worth is not just to sing a tune or say a prayer; it is to realize that creation itself, the perfect details of the universe, is evidence of His greatness and beauty.

All creatures, all stars, and whispered winds speak of His glory and are here by His will. We are here for a reason, and our lives have a purpose that speaks of God's sovereign plan and His desire for us to be His companion.

Worship is the continual presence of the heart and soul towards the One who is worthy of all the glory. In honoring our Creator's holiness, we orient our entire lives to the ultimate truth of His worthiness. Every act of goodness, pursuit of justice, and gesture of love echo the song heard around the throne: "Thou art worthy, O Lord."

Prayer: Lord of all, I arise to the symphony of the created order that proclaims Your glory. You are worthy of all glory, honor, and might. Unite my heart with the world's pulse, that my everyday life would be a prayer to You. Let me learn to see Your hand in all and dwell in the deep realization that I exist by Your will, created for Your pleasure and purpose. Amen.

December 13: My Strength and Song

Scripture for the Day
"The Lord is my strength and my defense; he has become my salvation."

Psalm 118:14

Let us center our hearts on a timeless declaration: "The Lord is my strength and my defense." This epitomizes the ever-living witness of the power of God in our lives.

At times when shadows appear to be all around us, and weights feel unbearable, this assurance lifts us above all that is temporal. To declare that the Lord is our strength is to seek the power overriding human weakness. He is the anchor that holds our shaking hands and strengthens our tired souls.

But what does it mean that He also is our protector? He not only protects but advocates. In the heavenly court, He stands as our defense in the accusations and trials. We find a fortress in His shelter that no foreign power can penetrate.

In our journey with God His power becomes our song, and His salvation is our story. We are the living epistles of His saving grace; every part of our lives is an open page of His loving-kindness and mercy.

Prayer: Lord, You are the unfading well of my power and the unbreakable wall of my existence. In my infirmity, You are my might; in my peril, You are my protection. My existence is coated in Your salvation. I breathe every breath in the exhilaration of Your redemption. My life resounds with the song of thanks because you grant me in salvation. My heartbeats repeat Your glory. Under Your wings, I am steadfast, immovable. Yours forever. Amen.

Embracing Shiloh:

December 14: In His Everlasting Arms

Scripture for the Day

"There you saw how the Lord your God carried you, as a father carries his son, all the way you went until you reached this place."

Deuteronomy 1:31

As we reflect upon the tender image found in Deuteronomy 1:31. The Lord our God, with deep love and tender care, takes us through the journey of life—as a father does his son.

This verse is a storehouse of comfort, saying that our Father in Heaven is always with us, who speaks from the sky, but as someone who holds us in His strong arms. As a child safely rests in the arms of a loving parent, we too can find comfort in God's sheltering embrace.

Our wanderings through the wilderness of this life are of the same nature as the Israelites' way to the Promised Land. It is a land beset with suffering, wealth, doubt, and supply. Even so, in each season, God always carries us to the place He guides for our lives. His steadfast love and truth form the basis of our being.

When the way is hard, and our strength fails, recall how we have been borne thus far. It is not us who sail the deep sea of life alone, but it is the sovereign hand of God that preserves and pushes us onward.

Prayer: Father, as I meditate on the way that brings me to this moment, I am amazed by the steadiness of Your concern. You took me through the valleys and over mountains, through the trials and victories, like a father does His child. Never let me take this divine promise for granted. I am in Your eternal embrace. I walk into the dark but confident because Your strength and love pull me on. Amen.

December 15: Conquest Over Adversity

Scripture for the Day
"And I will put enmity between you and the woman, and between your offspring and hers; he will crush your head, and you will strike his heel."

Genesis 3:15

In the cool of a once-perfect garden, humanity stood at the edge of an eternal cliff. Genesis 3 tells not only of the fall of man but introduces a promise, a ripple of hope in the aftermath of sin. Here, amid judgment and consequence, God gives a prophecy that tells of redemption and struggle that will span the ages.

Today's verse speaks of conflict but also of ultimate victory. God declares that the seed of the woman—a reference that theologians interpret as a foretelling of Christ—would one day come to crush the head of the serpent, the emblem of sin and Satan. The imagery is powerful; crushing the head is a symbol of decisive triumph; while the serpent's strike to the heel, though painful, is not fatal.

This spiritual conflict foreshadows the pivotal battle on Calvary, where Jesus, in His suffering and death, defeats the powers of darkness. His resurrection is the fulfillment of this promise, a sure sign that though we may overcome the serpent's sting in our lives. Christ's victory is assured.

As followers of Christ we too, participate in this struggle and the promise of conquest over the devil. While the "offspring of the serpent"—sin, temptation, the trials of this world—may assail us, the offspring of the woman, Christ within us, empowers us to overcome. Our trials become the backdrop against which God's sustaining grace is magnificently displayed.

Prayer: Heavenly Father, I am reminded of Your sovereign plan unfolded in the garden so long ago. I stand in awe of Your wisdom that ordained a Redeemer before I ever knew I needed one. Thank You for the promise in Genesis that points to the ultimate victory You achieved through Jesus Christ. Despite my struggles and the enemy's snares, I am comforted by the truth that He who is in me is greater than he who is in the world. Amen.

Embracing Shiloh:

December 16: The Promise of Immanuel

Scripture for the Day
"Therefore the Lord himself will give you a sign: The virgin will conceive and give birth to a son, and will call him Immanuel."

Isaiah 7:14

When darkness appears to dim the light of hope amid confusion, the Lord speaks into our situation with a word that changes history. Isaiah 7:14 is a heavenly proclamation that God would come to us. The name "Immanuel" means "God with us." Rather than a simple name, it is proof of God's constant presence with us in the middle of our woes.

This Immanuel's pledge was not only for the people of Isaiah's time but for every generation. It is a sign of the deep intimacy that God desires with each of us. He crosses every joy, test, and sadness with us. The prophecy that Jesus was to be born guarantees that we are never alone, and that divine fellowship is the eternal gift for us.

Whatever you are going through today, let the truth of "God with us" enter your soul. He is the fulfillment of any promise, the light in the darkness, the joy in any sorrow. Remember that you are always accompanied because God is with us as men to show us the way to Him.

Prayer: Everlasting Lord, Your name is a strong tower, a refuge for the weak, and a fortress in times of trouble. I humbly thank You for Your great promise—Immanuel, God with us. This promise is my unfaltering rock and my never-ending solace. Amen.

December 17: Prince of Peace

Scripture for the Day

"For to us a child is born, to us a son is given, and the government will be on his shoulders. And he will be called Wonderful Counselor, Mighty God, Everlasting Father, Prince of Peace."

Isaiah 9:6

The wear and tear of our daily lives makes us crave for comfort, for quietness the world cannot offer. Today's Scripture uplifts from the earthly struggles to the divine promise completed in Christ Jesus.

Isaiah predicted a Child who would bring hope and eternal rule—a Child who would bear the world's burdens and bring unending peace. In our struggle through life's difficulties, let us understand that the government on His shoulders is a significant guarantee that He is in full control.

This peace remains even amid the chaos. It is the peace Jesus spoke of when He said, "My peace I give you. I do not give to you as the world gives" (John 14:27). In adversity, His counsel is unfailing, His power is unbreakable, and His government is eternally good because He is our Mighty God.

The titles for Jesus in this passage are not simply names. They are qualities reflecting His relational closeness to us. He is our Mighty Counselor, illuminating the darkness that shadows our senses. He is our strong God, giving power when all our power is gone. Being our Everlasting Father, He loves us with a love that never passes and gives peace to our troubled hearts.

A Child was born for us—a Son given—in the small town of Bethlehem, wrapping divinity in humanity so that we could wrap our weary hearts in His peace.

Prayer: Father Eternal, I seek for peace in the activities of my days where peace is not to be found. Today, I look at You again, to Your promise of Your Son, Jesus, whose arrival Isaiah prophesied with such longing and grandeur. Thank You for sending the Prince of Peace into this broken world and into my broken heart. Amen.

Embracing Shiloh:

December 18: Brushstrokes

Scripture for the Day
"In the beginning was the word, and the word was with God and the word was God."

John 1:1

Today, we will approach the very beginning of everything. John 1:1 gives the starting point to an amazing journey that will actually make us laugh in amazement at how divine the world is that our Creator made.

In a world where painting is an art form, picture God as the greatest artist playfully turning the brush over the white canvas, poised to bring a masterpiece into existence. Like an expert painter, God chooses the perfect colors to create His masterpiece—the heavens and the earth. However, not using the usual paintbrushes, our divine artist chooses to immerse His fingers somewhat teasingly in pots of colors all over the universe.

At the beginning of the painting, God is enjoying the blue splashes, yellow ones, green ones, and red ones, which are intermingling beautifully on His canvas. With every brush, the Creator takes pleasure in the mixture of colors that whirl around Him, laughing as He fills nothing with life and beauty.

Like an artist paying attention to every stroke, our God takes care of every small detail. He carves the mountains with His fingertips, breathes life into the oceans, and shapes fragile petals on flowers with a gentle touch. With infinite love and a sparkle in His eye, God makes stars and planets, positioning them intricately in their celestial waltz.

Therefore, dearest friend, laugh today and let your mind soar. Discover the vivid colors of life, remembering that our heavenly Father—the Master Artist—rejoices in your walk. You are a masterpiece created with love and joy by the Divine Artist Himself. Embrace the grace and sense of humor in every little stroke of life!

Prayer: Father, Help me walk in the ways of stewardship and gratitude so that I may treasure and protect the beauty and harmony of the world You have placed in our care. May the realization that each particle is the result of a thought of God. Give me a sense of purpose and thankfulness every moment of my life. Amen.

December 19: The Invincible Light

Scripture for the Day
"The light shines in the darkness, and the darkness has not overcome it."

John 1:5

Amid a world that shrouded in shadow, John 1:5 becomes a lighthouse of hope. This line is not only poetic, but overflows with spiritual power. Light and darkness are common in the Scripture, signifying the opposition of good versus evil, enlightenment versus ignorance, and divine revelation versus human blindness.

The light in the Gospel of John symbolizes the life and truth in Jesus Christ, a light that breaks through the darkest night. This message resonates with the truth of the gospel: in His life, death, and resurrection, Jesus won a clear victory against darkness; all sins, death, despair, and alienation are defeated.

In addition, the statement that darkness "has not overcome it" is very emphatic. It is a declaration not only about a continuing war but also about the final victory of Christ. The darkness didn't and can't put out the light of Christ.

This truth gives hope and courage that the darkness we face cannot overshadow the light of Christ in our hearts. It calls on us to be children of light to confront darkness through our testimony to His truth and love.

The light of Christ is not a theoretical idea but rather a transforming energy, calling us to live lives in faith and under the guidance of the Spirit. In the light we find clarity, purpose, and a peace that passes understanding, because we are in line with the Invincible Light.

Prayer: Lord Jesus, Light of the World, I am in awe of the victory You declare – darkness never has nor will overcome Your light. At those times when shadows seem to close in on me, You assure me that Your light is never defeated. Assist me that I might hold on to this blessed assurance and walk in faith, knowing that no darkness is too deep for Your light to penetrate. Amen.

December 20: Witnesses of the Light

Scripture for the day
"He came as a witness to testify concerning that light, so that through him all might believe."

John 1:7

In the beginning, God spoke the words, "Let there be light," and there was light. The Gospel of John gives us another beginning that invites humanity to spiritual enlightenment in the personality of Jesus Christ. John the Baptist was not the light, but he was sent to witness to the Light so that all might believe. His life witnessed Christ's advent, a light marking the dawning of a new and brighter day.

Similarly, one's life is what reflects that light. To see Christ is to show His love, truth, and grace in the commonplace events of our lives and the fire of our tribulations. We are trusted with the holy task of leading others to the genuine Light, giving them direction to the faith by that Light manifested in our lives.

When you enter our world today, remember that everything you do, say, and even how you carry yourself can bear witness to the light of Christ. You have the divine potential to shine light into the darkness, so that others might believe.

Prayer: Sovereign and merciful God, thank You for being the True Light that shines upon the whole world. I am humbled by the commission to be a witness to Your glory, like John the Baptist in Your honor. Fill my life with Your light so that I can be the bright light to others, overcoming the darkness and leading them to hope and salvation in Christ. Amen.

December 21: Reflecting the True Light

Scripture for the Day

"He himself was not the light; he came only as a witness to the light."

John 1:8

The first chapter of John's Gospel presents a great doctrinal statement on the nature of Christ as the Light of the World. The role of John the Baptist is pointed out in verse 8, separating him as the witness from Jesus, the True Light. This distinction is essential: Even though John was a burning and shining lamp, he was not the light. He was reflecting the light of the One who is the source—Jesus Christ.

The identity and mission of John the Baptist was grounded in pointing beyond himself to Christ – the Word incarnate and the True Light that enlightens every person. The testimony of John the Baptist addresses every one of us as Christians in our calling. We also are called to testify to the light of Christ, who offers His truth, love, and grace to the world that otherwise would remain in the dark.

All believers are to be reflectors, not the sources of the divine light. We do not aim to attract people to ourselves. Rather, our goal is to point them to Jesus. In the way the moon has no light of its own but receives the sun's light and reflects it, so we shine with the light we get from Christ.

Enacting the life that is clear and that directs us to the origin of our righteousness, peace, and joy demands active participation. It is to live the life that, just as with John the Baptist, testifies to the changing influence of Christ.

Prayer: Holy Lord, You are the Light that shines in every darkness. Your brilliance humbles and honors me in its glory. Aid me in recollecting that I am not the light but the bright reflection of Your glory. Assist me to live in such a manner which makes others look not at me but at You. Amen.

Embracing Shiloh:

December 22: Dwelling Among Us

Scripture for the Day
"The Word became flesh and made his dwelling among us. We have seen his glory, the glory of the one and only Son, who came from the Father, full of grace and truth."

John 1:14

The Word, who is God Himself, decided to be flesh to connect divine and human. In Jesus, what could not be seen became visible, what could not be touched became touchable, and what was a distant roar of God's thunder became a gentle whisper of a baby's breath.

This verse teaches me a foundational Christian truth: God manifests Himself in Jesus Christ. However, this is more than just an ivory tower of ideas. This transforms the very center of my being. To consider that our Creator wanted to be near us so desperately that He took on the flesh of our world in the most intimate and fragile form is both humbling and exhilarating.

The Incarnation testifies that there is not a single aspect of human life that Jesus is not aware of. The One who made the stars knew what it was like to be accepted in warm human friendship and rebuffed by the coldness of betrayal. Graceful and truthful, He reveals the inconceivable kindness of God.

This knowledge forces me to look deeper—beyond the mundane tasks and the passing moments—to see the glory of God that is all around me. As I go through today, let me recall that God is not a far-off deity but a near Friend and Savior, full of grace to pardon and truth.

My prayer today is to dwell in the radiance of this incomprehensible gift—the Incarnation, which remains the spring of hope and root of faith to all who believe.

Prayer: God, my heart is amazed at the miracle of You who came as a human to Your world. You, Lord Jesus, have dwelled among us. May this truth become rooted in my soul today; may it change my perspective of myself and of others. I am grateful for Your mercy, which meets my weaknesses, and for Your reality, which releases me. May I be an example of Your love and Your light in all my ways to the glory of Your Name, Amen.

December 23: The Divine Encounter

Scripture for the Day

"The angel answered, 'The Holy Spirit will come on you, and the power of the Most High will overshadow you. So the Holy One to be born will be called the Son of God.'"

Luke 1:35

In the divine mystery of the Incarnation, we find the essence of God's redemptive plan for humanity gently unfolding. The angel's message to Mary in Luke 1:35 reveals the beautiful intersection of divine power and human humility.

As the Holy Spirit's overshadowing presence is observed in Mary's life, we, too, are recipients of a divine touch. No, not to bear the Christ Child—we celebrate that singular holy occurrence once for all time. Yet, we, too, are called to bear Christ in our lives. By the Spirit, the Most High does a work in us so that Christ may be seen through us.

We stand on holy ground here, witnessing the work of the Holy Spirit, a work that spans from the conception of Jesus to our own spiritual rebirth. This same Spirit that enabled Mary to carry the Son of God now dwells within us. We are emboldened by the power of the Most High, empowered to live out a calling that echoes with eternity. It's an embrace that calls us beyond the natural into the realms of the supernatural.

When we consider the humility and obedience of Mary, saying "Let it be to me according to your word," we are reminded of our own call to surrender. Mary's role was unique, yet her obedience is a model for us all. In the canvas of our own lives, we're invited to allow God to paint His masterpiece, just as He did with Mary. It's not without its cost, the path of surrender never is, but the outcome is nothing short of miraculous.

Prayer: Gracious Lord, I am in awe of the wondrous way You worked through Mary, bringing Your Son, our Savior, into the world. Holy Spirit, I invite You to work in my heart with that same power that overshadowed Mary. Grant me a willing spirit to echo her surrender, saying, "Here am I, Lord; use me as You will." Let my life bear witness to Your light and may Your power rest upon me that I might carry the presence of Jesus to those who have yet to know Him. In Jesus, I pray, Amen.

Embracing Shiloh:

December 24: The Journey of Faithfulness

Scripture for the Day

"He went there to register with Mary, who was pledged to be married to him and was expecting a child."

Luke 2:5

In the gentle murmur of a world asleep, there's a beautiful obedience and faithfulness that echoes through the passage in Luke 2:5. Joseph, a betrothed man to marry Mary, moves to Bethlehem not only to obey a decree for a census, but also to fulfill a divine assignment sent by God.

Imagine for a moment the tumult of thoughts Joseph must have wrestled with. The public humiliation, the bizarre awareness of Mary's divine impregnation, and the horrifying burden of being a guardian of the Messiah. However, in his obedience, Joseph becomes a faith hero. His silence is proof of his faith in God, even when the course was covered in fog.

In our everyday man-with-God-being, we are to imitate the model of Joseph. We all find our way to Bethlehem—a route where faith makes us place our bet on the promises of God despite the mountains of doubt and valleys of fear that stretch before us.

Our commitment to God is not a static posture but a dynamic, emboldened journey. It involves movement, growth, and sometimes, the traversing of difficult terrains. Let us, therefore, take solace in the assurance that when we tread the path of obedience, we are never alone. God's presence is our constant companion, His Word, a lamp unto our feet.

Prayer: Heavenly Father, In the quiet of my soul, I listen to Your invitation to walk along the tracks of loyalty and confidence. Just like Joseph, I want to find the courage to obey Your will even if the world may misinterpret and the road may be uncertain. Assist me in holding on to Your promises, empowering me to remain constant in faith in Your love and providence. May my life be the echo of obedience, and may my deeds be a silent hymn of praise to You. Amen.

December 25: Embracing Humility Amid Majesty

Scripture for the Day

"She gave birth to her firstborn, a son. She wrapped him in cloths and placed him in a manger, because there was no guest room available for them."

Luke 2:7

Through quiet talk by moonlight, the world's Savior became part of human history. Luke 2:7 freezes a moment of divine humility that would change the world forever. The King of kings, Son of God, was not laid in the luxury of a palace but among the humility of a stable, wrapped in some rough garment only. This picture calls us to stop and think about the deep meaning of God's love and His way to create.

The birth circumstances of Jesus are a powerful remembrance that the Kingdom of God does not come in pomp and worldly glitter but unveils itself in humility and lowliness. In this peaceful picture, the majesty of heaven is bound with the meekness of the earth—a picture that says a lot about God's nature and the redemption plan.

As God's beloved, we are called to embrace humility and to understand that in our own weakness, His power reigns. From the manger, we learn that our worth is not determined by our status or possessions but by the love and grace of our Lord Jesus Christ, who preferred our limitations to take us into His immeasurable love.

The manger story is a lesson in humility—to put away our pride and accept the gift of God's immeasurable grace. It urges us to live beyond grand expectations and humbly serve the world as Christ Himself did.

Prayer: Gracious Father, Lingering at the base of the manger, I am reminded of the humble character of Your love, the deep tenderness with which You came among us. Jesus, became a baby in hay to illustrate the extent to which You would bend to touch our lives. Teach me to accept the humility that You accepted, to treasure the lowly places as sites of Your greatest glory. Allow Your manager's spirit to reside within me so that I can live a life of reflecting Your love. Amen.

Embracing Shiloh:

December 26: Embracing the Joy of the Lord

Scripture for the Day
"Rejoice in the Lord always. I will say it again: Rejoice!"

Philippians 4:4

Philippians 4:4 is a call, not just for a moment of happiness, but for deep-seated joy that permeates our lives—rejoicing in the Lord always. This divine joy surpasses mere human happiness, for it is not dependent on the shifting sands of circumstance. It finds its root in the eternal unchanging God.

The Almighty is not an abstract concept nor a distant figure. He dwells within us, walks beside us, and surrounds us with His steadfast love. He is our constant in an ever-changing world, the faithful shepherd amid life's unpredictable wilderness. When Paul commands us to rejoice, he speaks from experience. Even in chains, his joy was unshackled for it was anchored in the grace and sovereignty of God.

Indeed, the joy Paul speaks of is one that looks beyond the horizon of present troubles and clings to the promises of God. It flows from a heart secured by Christ's redemptive work on the cross, a heart aware of the spiritual blessings that we possess in Him—forgiveness, purpose, and a hope that extends into eternity. No hardship, trial, or suffering can extinguish this flame; it is the true joy of our salvation.

So let us embrace joy as our strength, our comfort, and our anthem. Let it rise within us not only as an emotion but as a profound conviction that God is good, and His love endures forever. We rejoice not because life is perfect, but because our God is perfect.

Prayer: Heavenly Father, my heart sings to You, for You are my joy and my salvation. I praise You in all circumstances, for Your steadfast love is the melody of my life. Teach me, Lord, to rejoice always, to find the silver thread of Your grace woven through every experience. Help me to remember that my joy isn't based on what happens to me, but on Your presence in me. Amen.

December 27: Trust in the Divine Authority

Scripture for the Day

"If anyone asks you, 'Why are you doing this?' say, 'The Lord needs it and will send it back here shortly.'"

Mark 11:3

In this passage, Jesus shows His divine power over the whole creation, even over the things we value. The simple sentence "The Lord needs it," tells volumes of the relationship with God and His dominance over every aspect of our lives.

Jesus had a specific reason for wanting the colt – to accomplish the prophecy and to enter Jerusalem as the Messiah. His power was acknowledged by the owners, who let the colt go without any resistance to His followers. The grace of this interchange is in the silent confidence in the will of God. It was not about the youthful horse, but it was about a broader mission in God's divine narrative.

The Lord frequently calls us to surrender our grip on those things we hold dear in our lives, like comfort, possessions, and even plans, teaching us that He is the sovereign provider. We are custodians, not possessors. Like the Lord sure to give back the donkey, He encourages that our obedience is never wasted. In submission, we participate in the greater picture, a masterpiece shaped by the hands of the Almighty.

Prayer: Lord gracious and sovereign, in Your silent splendor, I am struck by the immensity of Your power and delicacy of Your care. Your trust in me as an administrator of Your many graces humbles me. Aid me in knowing when You are calling me to relinquish and surrender to Your divine intent. Make my heart firm to Your promises and open my eyes to Your plans. Amen.

December 28: Tears of Shiloh

Scripture for the Day
"Jesus wept"

John 11:35

Nestled within a powerful story of loss, love, and life, we encounter the shortest verse in the Bible, yet it carries profound weight—"Jesus wept" (John 11:35). These two words depict a Savior deeply moved by human sorrow, a God who is not indifferent to the anguish of His people.

As we reflect on these tears shed by Jesus, we are given a glimpse into the compassionate heart of God. We are reminded that our sufferings and burdens touch God's heart. Jesus' tears at the death of Lazarus are a mirror revealing God's empathy towards us in our moments of despair. This story is not only about the miracle of Lazarus being raised from the tomb but also about a God who is present in our trials and who weeps with us before He works through us.

By allowing Himself to be moved to tears, Jesus teaches us that our emotions are not to be shunned but embraced as part of our spiritual journey. God created us with the capacity to feel deeply. As we navigate the ebbs and flows of life, it is not beneath us to express our grief. Jesus' example validates our pain and dignifies our weeping.

Yet, as those who believe, we weep with hope. The same Jesus who wept at the grave declared Himself as the resurrection and the life. Our present tears are sown in the soil of a world marred by sin, but they will reap the joy of eternal life through Christ. As we take solace in Jesus' empathy today, let us also look forward to the day when God will wipe away every tear from our eyes.

Prayer: Lord Jesus, You wept at the death of Lazarus and know each pain I carry and every tear I shed. Thank You for showing me that I am not alone in my sorrow. Your tears remind me of Your love, which encompasses my deepest hurts. Teach me to find comfort in Your presence and to trust in Your sovereign power, which turns mourning into dancing. In Jesus name. Amen.

December 29: Of the World or Of God

Scripture for the Day
"They are from the world and therefore speak from the viewpoint of the world, and the world listens to them."

1 John 4:5

First John 4:5 calls upon us to know and identify the source of what we hear, see, and what we repeat. This verse speaks to the sharp contrast between the discourse of the world and the language of the Kingdom of God. "They" refers to the spirit of falsehood, which is at home in the world, where its voice is heard and eagerly received. They are expressions of this language – popular culture, dominant ideas, attractive philosophies – and once we speak its sayings, the world sees its own and listens closely.

But this is not the language of our blood. We, the born again in Christ, are encouraged to talk from the perspective of our heavenly citizenship. Our worldview is determined by the eternal, the holy, the true, and directed by the Spirit of Truth residing within us.

Reflect today on what dialect you operate in for all your decision-making, conversations, and thoughts. Are we fluent in the language of worldly wisdom, or do we speak the language of divine revelation? As Christians, cultivating a heavenly perspective is critical so that God's voice can determine our perception and reactions to the world.

Our calling is to live in this world but not to belong to it, to be representatives whose message is contrary to that of the world, a message that has the fragrance of Christ. This divine perspective may not be appreciated by most of the people; however, it will touch the hearts of the selected few who have ears to hear and eyes to see the Kingdom of God's reality.

Prayer: Father of all knowledge and truth, let me find my way in the deceptive narratives of the world with spiritually based discernment. May Your Holy Spirit direct my body, thoughts, and words. Teach me to know Your truth language so I might live a life of Your grace and love. Protect my mind from conforming to this world and renew it with Your living Word. Amen,

Embracing Shiloh:

December 30: True Reflections of Devotion

Scripture for the Day

"Religion that God our Father accepts as pure and faultless is this: to look after orphans and widows in their distress and to keep oneself from being polluted by the world."

James 1:27

In this one verse from James, we come to know a vital truth about the type of spiritual life we are asked to live. It is not enough to talk about our faith or to hold on to religious practices; our faith demands action.

Discipleship is more than following rules and practices. It is a journey to let the love of God pass through us to touch those that society usually forgets or rejects. The orphan, the widow, and the distressed are actual people among us looking for love and help. Caring for them is practicing the divine love we claim.

But James goes even further. He also pushes us to the holiness of self – "to preserve oneself from the world." This preservation is not only an issue of sin but is about not letting our hearts be turned to stone by cynicism and despair. Not to defile oneself is to remember that we are primarily citizens of the Kingdom of God, designed to live by a set of different values: love, mercy, and purity.

While meditating on this Scripture, it comes to me that my spirituality should be practical and hands-on. It must change the world around me, first my heart and then everything else into loving acts. This mirrors my soul, reflecting my daily life is the faith I embrace.

Today, let us rededicate ourselves to what our beliefs are. May our acts of kindness not just be tokens but the display of God's boundless love for the needy. And we shall keep our hearts tuned to the clarity of our commitment in a world constantly trying to spoil it.

Prayer: Father in heaven, I thank You for Your Word I follow daily. Enable me to adopt the pure and blameless religion that You desire, that serves those in need with an open heart and ensures that my soul remains unchanged by the world. May my deeds mirror Your love and my life be a never-ending worship unto You. In Jesus' Name, Amen.

December 31: Embraced in the Alpha and the Omega

Scripture for the Day
"I am the Alpha and the Omega, the First and the Last, the Beginning and the End."
Revelation 22:13

The echo of God's voice through the corridors of time resonates with the majesty and mystery of His nature in Revelation 22:13. In this final chapter of the holy text He declares Himself to be the Alpha and Omega, the Eternal.

In the chaos that often mark my daily existence, it is this eternal perspective that both humbles and uplifts my spirit. God is the beginning, before my problems took shape. His solutions were already in place. As the Omega, He stands at the end, where every tear will be wiped away and every brokenness made whole. This declaration by God is not merely a self-identification; it is an invitation into the timeless realm of His sovereignty, where all history and life find their purpose.

Look at Christ's complete and perfect nature as the beginning and the end of everything. Jesus embodies the entirety of the story that God is telling—beginning at creation and ending in redemption. Regardless of any clouds of uncertainty that may cover my path now, the One who controls time with His own hands is the One who holds me.

Maybe you are in the same place as me - standing in the middle of hard times, searching for a beacon to show you the way. Let the truth of this Scripture be your compass: The One who has written the beginning knows the ending. Our walk of faith moves one further step to the fulfillment of His promises, a step in the direction of the restoration of all things.

Naturally, dwelling on such a reality fills me with a weightless awe. For if He is the Alpha and the Omega, what have I to fear? What have I to expect of Him? My life revolves around His will, and through His mercy, I will endure.

Prayer: Lord, eternal, Alpha, and Omega, let my heart find peace in the truth that You are the first and the last of everything. Amid the complexity of life's challenges, direct me to believe in Your eternal design. Aid me in recalling that You are the author of my days and will complete the story of redemption that You have started in me. Embrace me today and give me the same confidence I will have at the end of eternity. May Your everlasting presence be my consolation, Your unalterable character my strength, and Your all-powerful hand my leader in the precious name of Jesus, my Redeemer, Amen.

www.ingramcontent.com/pod-product-compliance
Lightning Source LLC
Chambersburg PA
CBHW080432110426
42743CB00016B/3144